Norse Mythology
A to Z

THIRD EDITION

MYTHOLOGY A TO Z

MYTHOLOGY A TO Z

Norse Mythology

A to Z

THIRD EDITION

Kathleen N. Daly

Revised by Marian Rengel

CHELSEA HOUSE
PUBLISHERS
An imprint of Infobase Publishing

Norse Mythology A to Z, Third Edition

Chelsea House
An imprint of Infobase Publishing
132 West 31st Street
New York NY 10001

Library of Congress Cataloging-in-Publication Data
Daly, Kathleen N.
Norse mythology A to Z / Kathleen N. Daly ; revised by Marian Rengel. — 3rd ed.
p. cm.
Includes bibliographical references and index.
ISBN 978-1-60413-411-7 (hc : alk. paper)
1. Mythology, Norse—Dictionaries, Juvenile. I. Rengel, Marian. II. Title.
BL850.D34 2009
293'.1303—dc22   2009013338

Chelsea House books are available at special discounts when purchased in bulk quantities for businesses, associations, institutions, or sales promotions. Please call our Special Sales Department in New York at (212) 967-8800 or (800) 322-8755.

You can find Chelsea House on the World Wide Web at http://www.chelseahouse.com

Text design by Lina Farinella
Composition by Mary Susan Ryan-Flynn
Map by Patricia Meschino
Cover printed by Bang Printing, Brainerd, MN
Book printed and bound by Bang Printing, Brainerd, MN
Date printed: November, 2009
Printed in the United States of America

10 9 8 7 6 5 4 3 2 1

This book is printed on acid-free paper and contains 30 percent postconsumer recycled content.

CONTENTS

INTRODUCTION

WHAT IS A MYTH?

Myths are as ancient as humankind and have their origin in the efforts of primitive people to explain the mysteries of the world around them: thunder and lightning; floods and fire; rain and drought; earthquakes and volcanic eruptions; night and day; the Sun, Moon, and stars; the seasons; the existence of plants and animals, man and woman; and birth and death. Myths fulfill a need in people to believe in some higher being or beings who have power over the daily lives and fate of humankind. Many of the world's myth systems include a sky god or father of all and an Earth Mother. In many cases, including that of the Norse, people believed in a set of attendant gods and goddesses, as well as villains such as demons, dragons, and other monsters; giants and dwarfs; and supernatural forces.

Myths help people structure their lives. Myths reflect their codes of behavior, their cultural customs and rites, and their ways of worship. Myths are basically stories of the struggle between good and evil, between order and chaos. They predict the eventual breakdown of order, but also regeneration.

Ancient myths about the creation of the universe and the living creatures on Earth were passed orally from one generation to another, from family to family, and from one community to another. As people moved from one part of a continent to another, they adapted their stories to the changing landscape or climate. Stories that may have originated in India, the Middle East, or the south of Europe changed dramatically when people told them in the harsh, icy lands of the north, where summers were short and winters long and harsh.

Finally, myths are part of a moral and ethical, often spiritual, belief system. Many historians of myths and scholars of human social development see myths as part of a religious belief system and an attempt to explain human existence.

WHO WERE THE NORSE?

The Norse (people of the north) are known today as the Scandinavians—the people of Norway, Sweden, Denmark, Iceland, and the Faroe Islands.

Mistakenly, Norsemen are often thought of only as the fierce warriors of the Viking Age (A.D. 750–1070); however, Norse culture originated long before the dramatic explorations of the Vikings. It probably started to take root during the Bronze Age (1600–450 B.C.). No written sources describe early Norse culture, but surviving works in metal and stone depict gods and goddesses and provide glimpses of ancient myths and rituals. The Norse were superb shipbuilders and navigators, intrepid explorers, and people with a strong sense of family and clan loyalty. They also loved a good story, a quick wit, and fine craftsmanship, which we can see in the ancient carvings, weaponry, and utensils that have been discovered in a variety of archaeological sites across Scandinavia. The mythology of these strong, lively people was rich, vigorous, and clever.

Norse mythology originated in Asia, according to experts. It was modified in the European Mediterranean lands, and eventually was carried north and west by migrating Germanic tribes, in the third to sixth centuries A.D. during the breakup of the Roman Empire—a time known as the Migration Period. The roaming tribes included Angles and Saxons, Goths, Visigoths and Ostrogoths, Alemanni, Vandals, Franks, and others. As the migrating tribes settled, the stories they brought with them began to change with the local geography, climate, and temperament of the people. Later, during the Viking Age, the Norse began to explore and populate countries from the British Isles and the rest of Europe to Iceland, North America, the Near East, Byzantium, and Russia, settling in the lands they conquered and taking with them, too, their myths and their culture.

The Norse myths were not written down, however, until the 13th century, by which time Christianity was established in northern Europe and had displaced paganism, that is, the worship and the myths of the ancient gods. Thus much of the ancient lore is lost to modern audiences. What remains is fragmented, incomplete, and often distorted by the pious Christian monks who edited the pagan tales as they transcribed them onto vellum and parchment for the first time. Although the Norse myths as we know them today are often confusing and contradictory, they still present us with wonderful tales about these northern people. The more you learn of them, the less confusing they become.

The flat rock of Vitlycke in Sweden depicts a large ship, some smaller boats, and a man with long arms. *(Photo by Fred J./Used under a Creative Commons license)*

THE SOURCES OF THE NORSE MYTHS

The main sources of the Norse myths are

- poetry of the early skalds (poets) transmitted orally until the 13th century
- *Poetic Edda*, a collection of poems written by different poets at different times between the eighth and 13th centuries
- *Prose Edda*, a handbook written by the Icelandic poet, scholar, historian, and clan leader Snorri Sturluson, around 1220
- *Gesta Danorum*, written by Danish historian Saxo Grammaticus in about 1215
- historical observations by Roman author Tacitus, notably in *Germania* (end of the first century A.D.), the Arab traveler Ibn Fadlan (10th century A.D.), and the German historian Adam of Bremen (11th century A.D.)
- *Landnamabok* (*Book of Settlements*), a history of the settlement of Iceland from the 13th century A.D.
- the 13th-century Icelandic sagas (about 700 of them), many written by unknown authors, which are a valuable source of information about pre-Christian beliefs and practices, kings and bishops, Norse exploration and settlement, and legendary heroes such as Sigurd the Volsung

HOW TO USE THIS BOOK

The entries in this book are in alphabetical order and may be looked up as in a dictionary. Alternate spellings are given in parentheses after the entry headword, including spellings using Icelandic letters, which are found in the manuscripts but not found in English. Those include:

Uppercase	Lowercase	Pronunciation in English
Ð	ð	the "th" in "the"
Þ	þ	the "th" in "thing"
Æ	æ	"eye"
Ö	ö	rounded form of "ea" in "earth"

Spellings given in SMALL CAPITAL letters are variations of the names found in different original sources. Those appearing with standard capitalization are English translations. Within the main text, cross-references to other entries are also printed in SMALL CAPITAL letters.

In case you are not familiar with the Norse myths, here is a list of the chief characters and the stories in which they are most important.

First, the gods:

ODIN The one-eyed god, the All-Father, the god of wisdom, poetry, and magic, of war and death. Odin plays a principal role in many of the myths, including those of the CREATION, the AESIR/VANIR WAR, "The Death of Balder" (see BALDER), and RAGNAROK, the end of the world.

THOR God of thunder, son of ODIN and FRIGG. He was the strongest of the gods, of fiery temper but well loved. He had a hammer (MJOLLNIR), a magic belt (MEGINGJARDIR), and iron gauntlets and was forever at war with the GIANTS.

LOKI A mischievous god, Loki is involved in many of the myths. Loki often deceives the gods and creates dangerous situations and then comes to the rescue of the gods. He is admired yet distrusted by them.

The Karlevi runestone on the island of Öland, Sweden, is commonly dated to the late 10th century. The carving contains a full stanza of skaldic poetry that translators say describes Odin. *(Photo by Peter Rydén/ Used under a Creative Commons license)*

BALDER   Son of ODIN and FRIGG. He was the most beautiful and beloved of the gods. There is only one myth about him, but it is one of the best known.

NJORD   A VANIR god of the seas and seafarers. Njord has two major roles in the myths: as a peace token sent to ASGARD, the home of the AESIR gods, along with the twin deities FREY and FREYA, his children; and as the husband of the giantess SKADE.

FREY   A VANIR god, sent to ASGARD as a peace token along with his twin sister, FREYA, and his father, NJORD. Frey was a god of fertility, peace, and plenty and was much worshipped.

TYR   One of the most ancient gods and the most mysterious, he was also the bravest and most just of the gods when he undertook to put his hand into the jaws of the terrible wolf, FENRIR.

HEIMDALL   The watchman of the gods who guarded BILROST, the bridge that connected ASGARD (the domain of the gods) with MIDGARD (the Middle Earth). Heimdall had a trumpet, GJALLARHORN, with which he would summon the gods to battle at RAGNAROK.

The goddesses play a lesser role in the surviving Norse myths, according to extant manuscripts, but scholars believe they were important to the people who practiced Norse religion. They include:

FRIGG   The wife of ODIN. Her greatest role is in the myth of BALDER, her beloved son, whom she tries to protect from death.

FREYA   The goddess of fertility, the twin sister of FREY, and the daughter of NJORD. She is beautiful and has a fatal love of gold. She is loved by DWARFS and GIANTS alike. She may have been acquainted with magic and prophecy, but few facts are known about her.

IDUNN   The keeper of the apples of youth, she is known only through the myth "Idunn and the Golden Apples" (see IDUNN).

Other females in Norse mythology are the NORNS and the VALKYRIES. The Norns are the three Fates who represent the past, the present, and the future and who determine the destiny of all living creatures. The Norns are more powerful even than the gods.

The Valkyries are Odin's warrior maidens who select the fallen heroes and carry them to Odin's hall, VALHALLA.

The forces of evil are represented chiefly by the offspring of Loki: HEL, queen of death and the underworld; FENRIR, the monster wolf; and JORMUNGAND, the Midgard Serpent, who is so huge that he encircles the Earth and holds his tail in his mouth. Other wolves chase after the Sun and the Moon, and numerous JOTUNS try to outwit and outfight the gods.

Map of Scandinavia

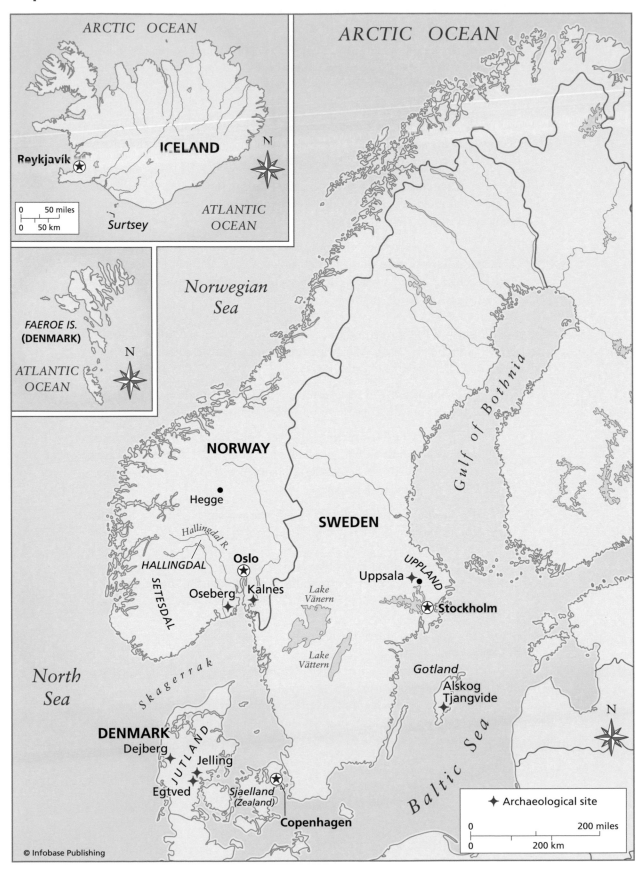

A-TO-Z ENTRIES

A

ADAM OF BREMEN   A German historian who lived and wrote his histories in the 11th century in Bremen, in northwestern Germany. In the fourth volume of his work, *Gesta Hammaburgensis Ecclesiae Pontificum* (*Deeds of Bishops of the Hammburg Church*), written in Latin, Adam of Bremen discusses the people and customs of SCANDINAVIA and includes a description of the temple to the NORSE gods in OLD UPPSALA, Sweden.

AEGIR (1) (ÆGIR)   A giant, the JOTUN lord of the sea. He was married to his sister, RAN, and was the father of nine daughters, the waves, who were said to be the mothers of the god HEIMDALL. Some stories say that Aegir was the brother of LOKI and Kari (Air). He belonged to a primeval order of gods, predating the AESIR, the VANIR, and the GIANTS, DWARFS, and ELVES. His dwelling is on the island of HLESEY, in coral caves beneath the land. His servants are ELDIR and FIMAFENG. Aegir often hosted the Aesir gods at banquets.

See also "Loki's Mocking," under LOKI, which takes place at a banquet in Aegir's hall; and "Thor and Hymir Go Fishing," under THOR, in which Thor and TYR bring back a cauldron that Aegir uses to brew ale for the feasting of the gods.

AEGIR (2) (ÆGIR; sea)   One of the two main characters in *SKALDSKAPARMAL*, the second portion of SNORRI STURLUSON'S *PROSE EDDA*, and his work of instruction to young SKALDS. Snorri says that Aegir, a magician, was also named Hler.

Aegir lived on Hler's Island and was very knowledgeable about black magic. One day he traveled to ASGARD and was a guest of the AESIR at a feast. He was seated next to the god BRAGI, who, when Aegir asked him to, recounted many of the stories of the gods. Later, Aegir questioned Bragi about many of the gods, people, animals, and objects of mythology, and Bragi provided long lists of answers.

AESIR   The race of gods who lived in ASGARD under the leadership of the chief god, ODIN. Other gods included BALDER, the beautiful; BRAGI, god of poetry; FORSETI, god of justice; FREY, god of fertility; HEIMDALL, the watchman of the gods; NJORD, the sea god; THOR, god of thunder; TYR, a brave sky god; ULL, a winter god; VALI (2), the avenger; and VIDAR, the silent god.

Not many myths survive about the ASYNJUR goddesses except for those concerning FREYA, the fertility goddess; FRIGG, wife of Odin; IDUNN, keeper of the apples of youth; and SIF, the golden-haired wife of Thor.

AESIR/VANIR WAR   The AESIR were the warrior gods who lived in ASGARD. The VANIR gods existed long before the first Aesir gods appeared. They were beautiful beings of light and wisdom who lived in their realm called VANAHEIM, sending forth gentle sunshine and rain and fertility. They never set foot in Asgard, nor did they seem to know of the existence of the Aesir.

One day, according to some tellings of this story, a beautiful witch named GULLWEIG or HEID appeared in Asgard, and the seeds were sown for a battle between the Aesir and the Vanir, the very first war. Gullweig had a great hunger for gold. She could never have enough. She talked about it constantly, disturbing the gods. Wickedness had come to Asgard. The great god ODIN was very angry and decided that the witch must die.

Three times the Aesir cast Gullweig into the fire, and three times she rose up, more beautiful than ever. She went into every hall in Asgard, casting spells and teaching magic.

Then Gullweig went to the Vanir and told them how cruelly she had been treated by the Aesir. Soon an army of Vanir, perhaps led by brave NJORD, appeared at the walls of Asgard, ready to avenge Gullweig. Odin cast his spear, GUNGNIR, and the battle raged until both armies grew tired of the slaughter. It seemed that neither side could win—or lose.

The leaders of the Aesir and the Vanir got together to discuss terms. In the end, they agreed that there should be eternal peace between them and that together they would stand fast against the common enemy, the GIANTS.

To seal the peace treaty, the Aesir and the Vanir spat into a jar, as was the custom of the Northmen when making treaties. From the spittle formed KVASIR, the wisest of the wise (see "The Mead of Poetry," under ODIN).

As a sign of good faith, the sides exchanged gods. Odin sent his brother HOENIR and the wise god MIMIR (2) to live among the Vanir. And Njord and his son and daughter, FREY and FREYA, settled in Asgard.

At first the Vanir were delighted with the handsome Hoenir. They made him one of their leaders, but they soon noticed that Hoenir could make no decisions unless he consulted Mimir. They felt that the Aesir had cheated them. They did not dare harm Odin's brother, however, so they cut off Mimir's head and sent it back to Odin. Odin immediately used his magic to restore the head to life. He placed it in a spring, known as MIMIR'S WELL, at the foot of the sacred tree, YGGDRASIL, and he regularly went to seek wisdom from Mimir.

According to some scholars, this myth may represent folk memory of the conflict between the adherents of two different cults, which were then brought together. After the conflict, the Aesir win control of the embodiment of wisdom and inspiration—Kvasir—in one myth, and the head of Mimir in another, they learn the magic of the Vanir, and all the gods are now referred to as Aesir.

AGNAR Son of HRAUDING and brother of GEIRROD (2). When he and his brother were shipwrecked, they were befriended by an old couple who were ODIN and FRIGG in disguise. Frigg took special care of Agnar, who was eventually betrayed by his brother, Odin's protegé.

In later years, another Agnar (probably the son of Geirrod) took pity on Odin, who had been captured and slung between two fires. After Agnar had given Odin ale to quench his thirst, Odin chanted a song that was known as the GRIMNISMAL.

ALFABLOT A sacrifice made by humans to the *alfa*, or ELVES. Traditionally, the alfablot took place in the worshipper's home at the beginning of winter and was performed by women. A skaldic poet who traveled through ICELAND in the early 11th century recounts this ritual in his work. Information from SWEDEN suggests that in some parts of SCANDINAVIA the alfablot was an outdoor ritual during which people sought help from the elves.

ALFHEIM The home of the LIGHT-ELVES and one of the NINE WORLDS of NORSE mythology, according to SNORRI STURLUSON in his *GYLFAGINNING*. Alfheim was located at the top of the world tree, YGGDRASIL, with ASGARD, the home of the AESIR, and VANAHEIM, home of the VANIR.

According to the poem *GRIMNISMAL*, part of the *POETIC EDDA*, in very ancient times the gods gave Alfheim to the god FREY, who was sometimes connected with elves, as a gift when he cut his first tooth.

ALFODR (All-Father) A name for ODIN used frequently in the *POETIC EDDA*, SKALDIC POETRY, and SNORRI STURLUSON's work. Odin is recognized as the father of all the AESIR gods and goddesses, but he has this role in name only. He is also known as the father of all dead warriors. In addition Odin can be considered the father of all human beings, for when Odin and his brothers, VILI and VE, found the shapes of the first man and woman, ASK and EMBLA, on a beach, they gave them the spirit, mental powers, and warmth they needed to become fully human.

ALFRIGG One of the four DWARF brothers who made the marvelous BRISINGA MEN necklace for the goddess FREYA. The brothers were talented at the smith crafts and were discovered one day by Freya as they worked on the golden necklace. They drove a hard bargain for the necklace.

The brothers of Alfrigg—BERLING, DVALIN (1), and GRERR—are named only in the *SORLA THATTR*, a tale found in the manuscript *FLATEYJARBOK*.

ALSVID (ALSVITH; ALSVIN; All-Swift or All-Strong) One of the two horses that drew the SUN's chariot through the sky. The other horse was Arvakr. The fair maiden Sol drove the pair of horses. Although they pulled the heat of the Sun, according to the poem *GRIMINSMAL*, the gods placed a cool iron under their yokes to keep them comfortable.

SNORRI STURLUSON references Alsvid and Arvakr in *GYLFAGINNING* when he tells the story of how the gods punished MUNDALFARI for naming his children MOON and Sun. Snorri says that it is a bellows that keeps the horses cool.

ALVIS (All-Wise) A DWARF, tricked by THOR, who was turned to stone. Alvis had come to ASGARD to claim the bride (perhaps THRUD, daughter of the god THOR) whom the gods had promised him. Thor, knowing that Alvis, like many dwarfs, liked to show off his considerable knowledge, lured the dwarf into a lengthy question-and-answer game. Thor asked Alvis for alternative names for the 13 words that were most important in the lives of VIKING-AGE Scandinavians. These names the dwarf gave according to the main groups of beings that inhabited the worlds of NORSE mythology. Alvis talked as the night wore on. At dawn, the Sun, which the dwarf had called "DVALIN's DELIGHT," came up and turned Alvis to stone, as was the fate of all dwarfs caught in the sunlight.

The 13 words for which Alvis gave alternative names are given in the *ALVISSMAL* (*The Lay of Alvis*) in the *POETIC EDDA*. They are as follows:

Alvis's Answers

Thor	men	Aesir	Vanir	giants	dwarves	elves
men	Earth	Field	The Ways	Ever Green		The Grower
heaven	Heaven	The Height	The Weaver of Winds	The Up-World	The Dripping Hall	The Fair-Root
moon	Moon	Flame		The Goer	The Gleamer	The Teller of Time
sun	Sun	Orb of the Sun		The Ever Bright	The Deceiver of Dvalin	Fair Wheel
clouds	Clouds	Rain Hope	Kites of the Wind	Water-Hope	Weather Might	
wind	Wind	The Waverer		The Wailer		Roaring Wender
calm	Calm	The Quiet	The Hush of the Winds	The Sultry	The Shelter of the Day	Day's Stillness
sea	Sea	The Smooth Lying	The Wave	Eel Home	The Deep	Drink Stuff
fire	Fire	Flame	Wildfire	The Biter	The Burner	
woods	The Wood	The Mane of the Field	The Wand	Flame Food		Fair Limbed
night	Night	Darkness		The Lightless	The Weaver of Dreams	Sleep's Joy
seed	Grain	Corn	Growth	The Eaten		Drink Stuff
ale	Ale	Beer	The Foaming	Bright Draught		

ALVISSMAL (*The Lay of Alvis; The Words of the All-Wise*) A skaldic poem from ICELAND, probably written in the late 1100s and most likely written by a trained and talented poet. *Alvissmal* tells of the contests of words between THOR and the dwarf ALVIS, who is seeking the god's daughter's hand in marriage.

Alvissmal provides a significant amount of mythological information, presenting poetic names for common aspects of life, such as the SUN and MOON, HEAVEN and EARTH, and even ale and grain. Some scholars suggest that it was a learning poem for young skalds. Others argue that it is an unreliable source in some aspects—in particular the comparison of names Alvis gives the god THOR in answer to his questions.

The poem is included in the *CODEX REGIUS* of the *POETIC EDDA*.

AMSVARTNIR (AMSVARTNER; Red-black) The lake that surrounded the island of LYNGVI, the place where the AESIR bound the wolf FENRIR with the silken ribbon that held him captive until RAGNAROK. The lake and the island are named by SNORRI STURLUSON in *GYLFAGINNING*.

ANDHRIMNIR (Sooty Faced; Sooty in Front) The gods' chef at VALHALLA. Each day Andhrimnir roasted the magical boar SAEHRIMNIR in the magical kettle ELDHRIMNIR, and each night he fed the meat to the EINHERJAR, the eternally fighting human warriors. Andhrimnir, along with the boar and the kettle, are named in *GRIMNISMAL*. SNORRI STURLUSON quotes this poem in *GYLFAGINNING* but adds no further details about the chef.

ANDLANG One of the heavens that is located directly above and slightly south of the highest level to which the world tree, YGGDRASIL, reaches. It is above ASGARD, the realm of the gods, and below a higher HEAVEN, VIDBLAIN.

SNORRI STURLUSON describes this realm in *GYLFAGINNING* when he explains what protects the ASGARD from the destruction of RAGNAROK to GYLFI.

ANDVARANAUT (Andvari's Gem) A magical ring. The god LOKI stole Andvaranaut from the dwarf ANDVARI. Loki, ODIN, and HOENIR used the ring to cover the final whisker of the otter they had killed, who was actually the dwarf OTR in disguise.

The ring had the power to both create more golden rings and to attract gold as a magnet attracts iron.

The story of Andvaranaut and Andvari's gold are part of the poem *REGINSMAL*, which is in the *POETIC EDDA*, and part of the story of the *VOLSUNGA SAGA*. The *Drap Niflunga* (*The Slaying of the Niflungs*), a short narrative section found in the *CODEX REGIUS*, tells of the fate of the ring. (See "Otr's Ransom" under OTR.)

ANDVARI The DWARF whom LOKI, the trickster god, robs of his hoard of gold. Andvari had put a curse upon his treasure, including the ring, which

Depiction of Andvari the dwarf (upper right) on a runestone *(Photo by Berig/Used under a Creative Commons license)*

was called ANDVARANAUT. Loki gave the treasure to the magician HREIDMAR in compensation for killing his son OTR. Eventually, Andvari's gold became the hoard guarded by the dragon FAFNIR.

ANGANTYR (1)

A BERSERKER. According to the poem *HYNDLULJODH* and the Icelandic *HERVARAR SAGA*, Angantyr was one of the 12 sons of Arngrim and Eyfura and became a warrior with the strength of two men. In this HEROIC LEGEND, Angantyr inherited the cursed SWORD Tyrfing from his father, who received the sword as a wedding gift when he married Eyfura. Tyrfing had been crafted by the DWARFS, Dvalin and Durinn.

Angantyr died after he and his 11 brothers fought a furious battle, before which they all entered a trance and became wild and ferocious beings. Angantyr's daughter retrieved the sword from her father's grave and passed it down through the family until it became the weapon of the legendary hero ANGANTYR (2), a distant descendent.

ANGANTYR (2)

A human hero of the Icelandic legend of the cursed SWORD Tyrfing and the sword's final owner. Angantyr was the son of King Heidrek and a distant descendent of Angantyr (1), the Berserker.

Angantyr appears primarily in the final portion of the HEROIC LEGEND *HERVARAR SAGA*, which tells the story of several generations of owners of the sword. In the end of the tale, Angantyr, who has become the king of the Goths, kills his half-brother Hlod, who is king of the Huns, with the sword Tyrfing. This is the final act of the DWARFS' curse.

ANGRBODA

(Bringer of Sorrow) The GIANTESS wife of LOKI, the trickster god. According to 13th-century poet SNORRI STURLUSON, Angrboda was the mother of three monsters by Loki: the wolf FENRIR; the goddess of death HEL (1); and the MIDGARD SERPENT known as JORMUNGAND.

Her name is invoked in the poem *HYNDLULJOD* as the mother of the wolf.

ARNAMAGNAEAN CODEX

The first part of a manuscript apparently written in ICELAND in the late 1100s or early in the 1200s, now located in the Árni Magnússon Institute in Copenhagen, Denmark. The *Arnamagnaean Codex*, formally known as AM 748 Ia 4to, is a source of many of the poems that tell the stories of NORSE mythology.

The six pages of this handwritten vellum manuscript contain the only known source of the poem *BALDRS DRAUMAR*. In addition, the *Codex* features all or parts of five of the poems from the *POETIC EDDA*. *GRIMNISMAL* and *HYMISKVITHA* are complete. Most of *SKIRNISMAL*, *HARBARTHSLJOTH*, and *VAFTHRUDNISMAL* are also in this manuscript. However, only the beginning of *Volundarkvitha*, a HEROIC LEGEND that tells the story of the life of VOLUND, has been preserved.

ARVAK

(ARVAKR; Early Waker) One of the two horses that pulled the SUN's chariot, driven by the fair maiden SOL, across the sky. The other horse was ALSVID. They are named in *GRIMNISMAL*, part of the *POETIC EDDA*, and by SNORRI STURLUSON in *GYLFAGINNING*.

The horses' names are often used in descriptions of the Sun. In the poem *Sigrdrifumal*, part of the *Poetic Edda*, ODIN writes runes on Arvak's ear and Alsvid's hoof.

AS, ASA

Prefixes in Old NORSE that mean "god." Occasionally, some gods are known by two versions of their names in the Old Norse Icelandic manuscripts. One example is THOR, who is also called Asa-Thor. The word ASGARD means "realm of or enclosure of the gods." The name As-Bru, an alternative name for the bridge BILROST, means "Aesir-bridge" or bridge to the gods.

ASGARD

The realm of the AESIR gods. ODIN presides over Asgard, the topmost level of the NINE WORLDS. Here the gods and goddesses had their palaces and mansions, called halls.

Asgard was surrounded and protected by a mighty wall constructed by the GIANT MASTER BUILDER. In the center of Asgard was the green field IDAVOLL, around which stood the 13 halls of the gods. Among them were: GLADSHEIM, the main hall of the gods; BILSKIRNIR, the hall of THOR; FENSALIR, which belonged to FRIGG; BREIDABLIK, where BALDER and his wife, NANNA, lived; HIMINBJORG, the abode of HEIMDALL; GLITNIR, where FORSETI presided; SESSRUMNIR, Freya's hall; and VALHALLA, where Odin entertained the slain heroes of the world. BILROST, the Rainbow Bridge, connected Asgard to MIDGARD (Middle Earth). At RAGNAROK, the end of the world, all the beautiful mansions would be destroyed, but the golden playthings of the gods—chess pieces—would remain, and a new world would arise.

Asgard's Wall and the Giant Master Builder

The Aesir gods wanted to build a new wall around

their stronghold, Asgard, to protect them from the GIANTS. The VANIR had destroyed the original wall in the first and last battle between the two races of gods (AESIR/VANIR WAR).

The gods were good at building fine halls and glittering palaces, but to build a fortresslike wall seemed an enormous task.

One day a large man trotted his horse over Bilrost, the Rainbow Bridge, and told Heimdall, the watch-man god, that he had a plan to put before the gods. Heimdall reported the news to the chief god, Odin, who assembled all the gods and goddesses together to meet the stranger.

The tall man, who was a giant in disguise, said he would rebuild the wall around Asgard in three seasons. For his fee, Giant Master Builder would take the goddess Freya to be his wife. He would also take the SUN AND MOON.

The gods roared with anger. Odin said he would never part with beautiful Freya nor with the Sun and the Moon, which gave warmth and light to the world. He ordered the mason to leave.

LOKI, the sly god, begged the other gods not to be hasty and asked the mason for some time to consider his plan. The mason left the hall, and the gods and goddesses clustered around Loki while Freya began to weep tears of gold.

Loki suggested that if they could get the mason to promise to build the wall in six months—before springtime—they would have nothing to fear, for obviously it was impossible for anyone to complete the wall so quickly. But at least the mason could dig the foundation and get a good start on the wall, thus saving the gods a lot of work. And, said Loki, they would not have to pay him a thing.

Odin called the builder back into the hall and told him their decision. At first the mason seemed dismayed by how little time he would have to finish the work, but at last he agreed to try, provided that he could have his great stallion, SVADILFARI, to help him. They struck a bargain.

As the giant began to build the wall, the gods looked on in amazement. Never had they seen a man cut such huge blocks of stone, nor a horse pull such heavy loads. The wall began to take shape, getting higher and higher and stronger and stronger. Though the winter was cruel, the tall man labored on undaunted.

At last the cold and the snow and the ice abated. The last day of winter was near, and the wall was almost finished.

The gods met again. If the mason finished the wall in time, they would lose their treasured Freya and the Sun and the Moon. Suddenly they wondered how they had arrived at this terrible predicament. Then they remembered. They threw dark looks at Loki.

Odin commanded Loki to use his cunning once again, this time to save the goddess Freya and the Sun and the Moon. Terrified of Odin's anger, Loki promised to find a way to outwit the builder.

That evening, as the mason led Svadilfari toward the pile of stones to be hauled, the stallion pranced gaily. He could smell spring in the air. Suddenly he spied a beautiful young mare. She danced up to him and swished her tail. It was more than Svadilfari could stand. With a mighty bound he broke free of his harness and bolted after the mare.

The mason shouted with rage and set off in pursuit, but it was useless. Svadilfari had worked through a long, lonely winter, and now he wanted some lighthearted fun with the pretty mare.

Dawn came and with it the end of winter.

The wall stood unfinished. The mason lost the bargain and was slain by the thunder god, Thor.

When Loki returned to Asgard several months later, he led a handsome young colt. It had eight legs and obviously would grow up to be a magnificent horse. Indeed, its father was the mighty Svadilfari, and its mother was none other than Loki himself, who had shape-shifted into the pretty mare. Odin claimed the colt for his own and named it SLEIPNIR, the glider.

This myth, told by SNORRI STURLUSON in GYL-FAGINNING, shows the enmity between the gods and the giants—a theme that occurs in most NORSE myths and does not end until Ragnarok. When the giant demands the Sun and the Moon and also Freya, he intends to deprive the gods not only of the four seasons but also of the possibility of regeneration, for Freya was the goddess of love and fertility.

ASH   A tree of the olive family (genus *Fraxinus*). In NORSE mythology the ash YGGDRASIL is considered sacred and is called the World Tree as it plays a dominant part in the makeup of the NINE WORLDS.

The AESIR gods created the first man, ASK, by breathing life into the trunk of an ash tree. (See also "The First Humans," under CREATION).

ASK   The first man, created from the trunk of an ASH tree by the first three AESIR gods, ODIN, VILI, and VE. All human beings, it is said in Norse mythology, are descended from Ask and EMBLA, the first woman. (See "The First Humans," under CREATION.)

ASS   In Old NORSE, the singular form of "god." The plural is aesir.

ASYNJUR (ASYNJER)   The AESIR goddesses, the female form of the word *Aesir*. The most prominent Asynjur was FRIGG, wife of ODIN, who was goddess of love, marriage, and motherhood. The 13th-century chronicler of NORSE myths, SNORRI STURLUSON, named 20 Asynjur in two separate lists. They are BIL, EIR, FREYA, Frigg, FULLA, GEFJON, GERDA, GNA, HLIN, IDDUN, LOFN, NANNA, SAGA (2), SIGYN, SJOFN, SNOTRA, SOL, SYN, VAR, and VOR. Many of these goddesses are considered by scholars to be handmaidens of Frigg.

Snorri does not include among the Asynjur the more dominant goddesses, SIF, wife of THOR, or SKADE, wife of NJORD.

AUD (Wealth)   The son of NOTT and her first husband, NAGLFARI. Aud's brother is DAG (day) and his sister is JORD (earth). Very little is known of Aud. He is referred to only in the works of SNORRI STURLUSON.

AUDHUMLA (AUÐHUMLA)   The first cow, formed at the CREATION of the world. Audhumla appeared at the same time as YMIR, the first giant, and fed him with her milk. She herself derived nourishment by licking the salty stones around GINNUNGAGAP, the primeval void. As she licked, she uncovered a handsome, manlike creature from the ice. He was BURI, the first ancestor of the gods.

In many mythologies the cow is a symbol of the Great Mother and of creation. Audhumla appears in the *PROSE EDDA* and in the *POETIC EDDA*.

AURGELMIR   According to the *VAFTHRUDNISMAL*, a poem in the *POETIC EDDA*, Aurgelmir was the first and oldest among the GIANTS and the grandfather of BERGELMIR. The poem *Vafthrudnismal* tells of the creation of the race of giants.

Audhumla licking Buri as four rivers of milk pour from her udders. From the 18th-century Icelandic manuscript SÁM 66, care of the Árni Magnússon Institute in Iceland

According to SNORRI STURLUSON, however, Aurgelmir was the name the RIME-GIANTS gave to YMIR, the first giant from whose body the gods of the AESIR created the world. Some scholars suggest that Snorri, as a writer, was attempting to bring some order to the giants' lineage as presented in the poems he used as sources.

AURORA BOREALIS   Shimmering lights or luminescence that sometimes appears in night skies in the Northern Hemisphere. Also called the northern lights. In NORSE mythology this beautiful sight was said to be the radiance emitted by GERDA, the JOTUN maiden who became the wife of the god FREY.

AURVANDIL   Known as "The Brave," he was the husband of the seer GROA. Not much is known about Aurvandil except that the god THOR rescued him from the giants and carried him across the poisonous rivers of ELIVAGAR in a basket. One of Aurvandil's toes froze. Thor plucked it off and threw it into the sky, where it shone forevermore as the bright star

Aurora borealis in Norway *(Photo by Rafal Konieczny/Used under a Creative Commons license)*

Aurvandil's Toe. The story is in Snorri Sturluson's *Skaldskaparmal*.

Austri (East) One of the four dwarfs named after the cardinal compass directions. The others are Vestri (West), Nordi (North), and Sudri (South). Though these four dwarfs are mentioned in early Norse poetry, it was Icelandic poet Snorri Sturluson who gave Austri and his three companions the job of holding up the four corners of the sky.

Austri is a name used often in Norse poetry. In some cases the name refers to a person involved in a conflict who is smaller and weaker than his opponent. In another use, Austri refers to the dwarf who steered a ship filled with dwarfs.

B

BALDER (BALDR) The beloved son of the great god ODIN and his wife, FRIGG. The story of the god Balder is one of the most famous and one of the most complete in NORSE mythology. It has been retold many times over the centuries, from SNORRI STURLUSON's account in the *PROSE EDDA* to the story by the Danish scholar SAXO GRAMMATICUS and the poem by the English poet Matthew Arnold ("Balder Dead").

Balder's Dreams When Balder became a young man, he began to have fearful dreams that seemed to foretell his death. None of the gods could understand the meaning of these dreams. His unhappiness cast sadness over all who lived in ASGARD, the home of the AESIR gods.

Odin, determined to solve the mystery of his son's dreams, mounted his horse, SLEIPNIR, and made the long journey to the underworld, NIFLHEIM. There he called up a seeress, one of the VOLVA. When she arose from her tomb, Odin introduced himself as VEGTAM, the Wanderer, son of Valtam.

Odin asked the Volva why the halls of HEL were decked with gold and the tables set for a grisly feast. The seeress replied that it was for Balder.

Odin asked who would slay Balder. The seeress answered that the blind HODUR would cast a fatal branch at his brother.

Odin then asked who would avenge Balder's death. The seeress answered that Odin would take RINDA as a wife, and their son would be VALI (2), who would take vengeance when he was only one night old.

Odin asked who would refuse to weep for Balder. At this question, which revealed that Vegtam knew or guessed more of the future than an ordinary mortal could, the Volva realized that Vegtam was in fact Odin, or ALFODR.

She refused to answer any more questions and sank into her tomb, vowing to speak no more until Loki's chains were unbound—that is, until the end of the world. This story is found in *BALDRS DRAUMAR* (*Balder's Dreams*) in the *POETIC EDDA*.

Frigg and the Mistletoe When Frigg realized that her son Balder's life was in danger, she sent her messengers to every corner of the world to extract promises not to harm her beloved son. Stones and metals, water and wind, fish and birds, reptiles and mammals, trees and flowers, insects, spiders, and scorpions, all creatures alive and all objects large and small swore that they would not harm Balder. Only one small green plant, the MISTLETOE, which grew on the mighty OAK tree, was not asked to make the promise, for it was so frail that no one paid attention to it.

The Gods at Play Word soon spread through Asgard that Balder was absolutely invulnerable: Nothing could harm him. The young gods, always ready for fun, made a game of throwing things at Balder: stones, knives, sticks. Whatever they threw glanced off Balder's body, leaving him totally unharmed, to the merriment of all.

Only Loki did not join in the fun. Instead he disguised himself as a woman and paid a visit to Frigg. Pretending to be astonished and disgusted at the sport the gods were making of Balder, Loki tricked Frigg into revealing the information he sought: that there was indeed one object in the world that had not taken the vow to be harmless to Balder. That object was the mistletoe that grew on the branches of the oak tree outside VALHALLA.

Loki hurried away, plucked a sprig of mistletoe, and hastened to the field of IDAVOLL, where the merry young gods were still at play. Only the blind god, Hodur, hung back, for he could not see.

Loki approached Hodur, put the mistletoe branch into his hands, and offered to guide his aim. Hodur gladly accepted.

The Death of Balder Hodur threw the fatal weapon and killed Balder. When Balder fell dead, a terrible silence fell upon the gods, and then they cried out in a fearful wail. Balder, the good, the beautiful, the god of light, had been snuffed out like a bright candle. The gods would willingly have killed Hodur there and then, but ancient laws forbade that blood should be shed in Idavoll.

Balder's Funeral Pyre The gods built a huge funeral pyre on *HRINGHORNI*, Balder's dragon ship. On it they laid the body, surrounding it with rich tapestries, heaps of flowers, vessels of food, clothes, weapons, and precious jewels, as was the custom of the Norse.

NANNA, Balder's loving wife, fell grief-stricken over the body and died, so the gods placed her tenderly on the pyre beside her husband. Then they killed Balder's horse and hounds and placed them beside their master so he should lack for nothing.

One by one all the gods drew near to say farewell to their beloved companion. Last of all came Odin, who took off his magic arm ring, DRAUPNIR, and placed it on his son's body. Then he stooped and put his mouth to Balder's ear, but nobody knew what he had whispered.

When the gods tried to launch the ship, it was so heavy that not even THOR's phenomenal strength could move it. The gods accepted the help of HYROKKIN, a giantess who galloped onto the scene riding a huge wolf and holding reins of writhing snakes. Hyrokkin gave the vessel a mighty shove and launched it into the sea.

The funeral pyre burst into flames, and Thor went on board to consecrate the fire with his magic hammer, MJOLLNIR. As he was performing the rite, the dwarf LIT got under his feet, and Thor kicked him into the flames, where he burned to ashes along with Balder and Nanna.

The ship drifted out to sea, burning brightly, and the gods watched it in mourning until it disappeared and the world became dark.

Hermod's Journey When she had recovered sufficiently to speak, Frigg asked that one of the gods visit HEL (1) in Niflheim and beg her to send Balder back from the land of the dead. Gallant HERMOD, another of Odin's sons, immediately volunteered to make the dreaded journey. Odin lent him Sleipnir, and for the second time the brave horse made the journey to the underworld. After traveling for nine days and nine nights and crossing many rivers, Hermod came to a stream, GJOLL. Sleipnir's hooves made the bridge over Gjoll shudder, and the sentry, MODGUD, challenged the rider. Upon learning that Balder was indeed in Niflheim,

Hermod and Sleipnir made a great leap over the gate, Helgrind, and landed safely on the other side. Balder could not leave the land of the dead without Hel's permission, and Hel refused to let him go unless all the world should shed tears for him. Hermod spent many hours with Balder and his wife, Nanna. They gave him gifts, including Odin's magic arm ring, Draupnir, to take back to Asgard.

Then Hermod left to tell the gods his news. Surely the whole world would willingly weep to set Balder free.

Thokk When Hermod returned from the underworld with the news about Hel's condition for the return of Balder, messengers at once set out for every corner of the Earth. Soon every god and goddess, every man and woman, every plant and every animal on land and sea and air, and every stone and metal was shedding tears for Balder.

In a dark cave sat an old woman, the giantess THOKK. She alone remained dry-eyed and hard of heart. "Balder never did anything for me," she said grimly. "Let Hel keep what is her due, for I have no tears for Balder." She was, many think, the trickster Loki in disguise. The messengers returned to Odin and Frigg with heavy hearts, and the gods mourned once more, for they knew now that Balder would never return to them.

Vali Kills Hodur Vali, Odin's youngest son, appeared in Asgard on the day of his birth, miraculously grown to full stature and carrying a quiver of arrows. He shot one of these at Hodur, who died. Thus the Norseman's code of a death for a death was satisfied, and the Volva's prophecy was fulfilled.

Ragnarok At RAGNAROK, the time of the Regeneration, Balder came back from the dead, leading his blind brother, Hodur. All the survivors returned to Idavoll, where they created a new world.

Pieces of the stories of Balder are found in many poems in the *POETIC EDDA* and retold by Snorri Sturluson in GYLFAGINNING.

BALDRS DRAUMAR (Balder's Dreams) A 14-stanza poem of the *POETIC EDDA* found only in the Icelandic manuscript known as the *ARNAMAGNAEAN CODEX*. BAULDRS DRAUMAR tells the story of ODIN's ride to HEL (2) and his conversation with a seer about why his son, BALDER, is having horrible dreams. The seer tells Odin that HODUR will kill Balder and that VALI, a yet unborn son of Odin, will avenge his brother's death by killing Hodur.

The story in the poem is similar to a portion of the *VOLUSPA*, the first poem found in the *CODEX REGIUS* manuscript of the *Poetic Edda*. SNORRI STURLUSON retells the story of Balder's Dreams with varying detail in *GYLFAGINNING*.

BALEYG AND BILEYG Names used by ODIN to refer to himself as he recounts his travels and the many names he has used during them in the poem *GRIMNISMAL*. These two names in particular are special, according to mythologists, as they refer to Odin's single eye and to his ability to see into the future. Baleyg means "flaming eye" and Bileyg means "shifty-eyed." Both are also used in SKALDIC POETRY in a variety of KENNINGS.

BARLEY One of the oldest cultivated cereal grasses, barley is widely distributed throughout the world. In northern lands it was used to make a beer and was a symbol of spring growth. FREY and GERDA are married in the barley patch named BARRI.

BARRI (BARREY; the Leaty) The name of a forest, or a grove within a forest, in which the GIANTESS GERDA finally chose to meet the VANIR god FREY. Frey's servant, SKIRNIR, had been attempting to persuade Gerda to meet with the lovesick god for quite some time. At last she consented and chose Barri for the rendezvous. The story of Gerda and Frey is told in full in the poem *SKIRNISMAL* and in an abbreviated version by SNORRI STURLUSON in *GYLFAGINNING*.

BAUGI (Ring-Shaped) A giant, the brother of SUTTUNG. Baugi employed ODIN, who was disguised as a worker, BOLVERK. Bolverk worked so well that Baugi agreed to lead him to the mountain, named HNITBJORG, where the MEAD of poetry was hidden, guarded by GUNLOD, Suttung's daughter. Baugi drilled a hole in the mountain with his augur, RATI, and Odin changed into a serpent and slithered through the hole to find Gunlod and the mead. The story is in SNORRI STURLUSON's *SKALDSKAPARMA*.

BELI A member of the JOTUN killed by the VANIR god FREY. Beli was a son of the giant GYMIR (1) and the brother of the giantess GERDA, whom Frey loved. After winning Gerda as his wife, Frey killed Beli with a deer horn in a fight. Frey did not use his magical SWORD in the struggle for he had given it to Gymir as a BRIDE PRICE for Gerda.

Much of the story of Beli has been lost. What remains is hinted at in the surviving poetry and briefly sketched by SNORRI STURLUSON in *GYLFAGINNING*.

BERGELMIR Son of the HRIMTHURSSAR (frost giant) Thrudgelmir and grandson of AURGELMIR, who was also YMIR, the primeval giant who appeared at the CREATION. Bergelmir and his wife were the only GIANTS to survive Ymir's death and the flood that followed. They rode the flood on a hollowed-out tree trunk, the first boat. Because of them, the races of frost giants and ogres were able to survive in JOTUNHEIM.

BERLING One of the four DWARFS who made the golden necklace or collar known as the BRISINGA MEN. The goddess FREYA found the dwarfs making the piece of jewelry and bargained with them for it. Berling's brothers were ALFRIGG, DVALIN (1), and GRERR. They are named only in the *SORLA THATTR*, which is found in the manuscript *FLATEYJARBOK*.

BERSERKERS Savage, reckless, furious warriors of an elite corps who fought for ODIN wearing only bear or wolf skins and no armor. In the sagas, they were named after Berserk, a NORSE hero of the eighth century who went into battle with his 12 sons.

In modern English, to *go berserk* means to "go into a frenzy."

BESTLA A RIME-GIANT, or proto-giant, one of the first creatures to exist, according to NORSE mythology. According to SNORRI STURLUSON in *GYLFAGINNING*, Bestla was the daughter of the giant BOLTHUR. She was also the mother of three gods by BOR: ODIN, VILLI, and VE. Bestla is named in the *POETIC EDDA*, but little is known of her other than this relationship to Odin. Scholars find it significant that the greatest of the Norse gods, Odin, was the son of GIANTS, whose JOTUN offspring were the greatest enemies of the AESIR gods.

BEYLA A servant to the VANIR god FREY and the wife of BYGGVIR, also a servant to Frey. With their master they attended the feast given for the gods by the SEA god AEGIR. This story is told in *LOKASENNA*, part of the *POETIC EDDA*. In the poem, LOKI, who continually insults the gods during the dinner, yells at Beyla, telling her to be silent and accusing her of being full of sin and filth. (See "Loki's Mocking" under Loki.)

BIL AND HJUKI (BILL AND YUKI) The two human children stolen by MANI, the man of the MOON, to help him drive his chariot across the skies. They were the children of VIDFINN, who had sent them to fetch water from the spring, BYRGIR, in the pail, SAEGR, on the pole, SIMUL.

While the story and names of Bil and Hjuki seemed to early scholars of NORSE mythology to be a creation of 13th-century poet and historian SNORRI STURLUSON, recent scholars have suggested that Snorri knew of a very old riddle poem in which Bil was the waning (shrinking) Moon and Hjuki was the waxing (growing) Moon.

In his book *Curious Myths of the Middle Ages*, the 19th-century British scholar Sabine Baring-Gould claimed that the popular nursery rhyme about Jack and Jill, who "went up the hill to fetch a pail of water," had its origin in the tale of Bil and Hjuki.

See also "Sun and Moon" under CREATION.

BILLING'S DAUGHTER OR BILLING'S GIRL

The maiden featured in a section of the poem *HAVA-MAL* that tells of ODIN's lust for a young woman and her cunning rejection of him.

When Odin encounters a beautiful human maiden, whom he refers to as "Billing's daughter," asleep in a camp, he immediately falls in love with her and pursues an intimate union with her. The girl tells Odin to wait and come back at night when she will give herself to him. However, when the god returns, he finds the camp lit up brightly and all of the warriors who guard the maiden up and about. He quickly leaves, not wanting to be seen, and returns in the morning only to find a dog in the maiden's place. His advances scorned, Odin abandons his quest for the girl.

Little else is known of Billing's daughter. Scholars speculate on her connection to Billing, the king of the Ruthians, or Billing, the dwarf mentioned in the *VOLUSPA*. This section of the *Havamal* appears to have been inserted at a later date than much of the rest of the work was composed.

BILROST (BIFROST; Trembling Path)

The flaming, three-strand bridge between ASGARD and MIDGARD, also called the RAINBOW BRIDGE. HUMANS see the bridge as a rainbow spanning the distance between HEAVEN and Earth.

The AESIR gods built Bilrost out of fire, air, and water, the three materials that can be seen as the colors of the rainbow: red (fire), blue (air), and green (water). Though it looked fragile, Bilrost was immensely strong.

The gods appointed HEIMDALL to be the watchman of the bridge, for his senses were keen and he had a marvelous horn, GIALLARHORN, whose blast would ring throughout the NINE WORLDS if the HRIMTHURSSAR set foot on Bilfrost.

The Aesir gods crossed Bilrost regularly to go to council meetings at URDARBRUNN, a sacred well. Only THOR, the thunder god, could not walk or ride across Bilrost, lest the heat of his lightning harm the bridge.

At RAGNAROK, the end of the world, Bilrost would shatter under the terrible weight of the MUSPELL and GIANTS who came to fight the gods on VIGRID, the vast battlefield.

BILSKIRNIR

The great hall of THOR. The word Bilskirnir means "flashing light," or "illuminated suddenly" (as if by lightning), an appropriate name for the thunder god's home. Bilskirnir stands within Thor's kingdom of THRUDHEIM, which, along with the other homes of the gods, is in ASGARD.

According to the Eddic poem *GRIMNISMAL*, Bilskirnir had 540 rooms, offering plenty of space for all of the huge banquets Thor held for the gods. However, some scholars argue that the surviving manuscripts of *Grimnismal* do not actually describe Thor's hall but rather VALHALLA, ODIN's great hall, which precedes mention of Bilskirnir. Little else is known of Thor's hall.

BOAR

A male swine or pig. People have admired the boar since ancient times for its courage. It has been hunted and killed for its succulent flesh, tough bristles, sturdy hide, and sharp tusks. In fact, no part of this creature goes unused by humankind.

In NORSE mythology, FREY's golden boar was named GULLINBURSTI (Golden Bristles). Gullinbursti's image is found on helmets and shields worn by Viking warriors as a symbol of good luck in battle.

Also mentioned in Norse mythology is the golden boar HILDISVINI, belonging to Frey's sister, FREYA, and the boar SAEHRIMNIR, who was nightly sacrificed at Odin's VALHALLA for the feasting of the heroes. In winter, a sacrificial boar was offered up to the god Frey. The pagan custom is still remembered in many countries at Yuletide or Christmas (see also "The Mead of Poetry," under ODIN), where roast pig, pork, or ham may be the festive dish. In SWEDEN, Yuletide cakes are baked in the shape of a boar.

BODN (BOÐN; Vessel, Pot)

A vat or keg used by the DWARFS FJALAR (2) and GALAR for making and storing the MEAD of poetry, a brew that bestows the art of poetry on anyone who drinks of it. Bodn was one of two containers used to hold the mead;

the other was SON. The dwarfs also used the kettle, ODRERIR, when they killed the wise poet, KVASIR (1), and used his blood to make the mead.

SNORRI STURLUSON uses the names Bodn and Son in *SKALDSAPARMAL*, his work of advice to young poets. Odrerir, the kettle, is named in early works of NORSE mythology. (See "The Mead of Poetry" under ODIN.)

BOLTHUR (BOLÞORN; BOLTHORN; Thorn of Evil) The HRIMTHURGGAR father of BESTLA and a son whose name is unknown but is probably the god mimer. Bestla married BOR and bore him three sons, ODIN, VILI, and VE. Thus Bolthur was Odin's grandfather.

When Odin hanged himself from the World Tree, YGGDRASIL, to gain wisdom, he learned nine songs from the son of Bolthor, Odin's uncle (see "Lord of the Gallows," under Odin). In NORSE mythology, and folklore, there was often a close bond between a man and his maternal uncle, who sometimes acted as godfather or surrogate father. Bolthur is identified in the poem *HAVAMAL* and in *GYLFAGINNING*.

BOLVERK (Evil-Doer) The name ODIN used when he went to JOTUNHEIM to steal back the MEAD of poetry. Odin took the form of a tall, strong man. When he found nine slaves working wearily in a field, he offered to sharpen their scythes with his WHETSTONE.

The slaves were so impressed with the sharpness of their blades after Bolverk had honed them that they asked for the whetstone. Odin-Bolverk threw it up in the air. As they scrambled to catch it, the nine workers managed to kill one another with their scythes. Thus Odin-Bolverk was able to ingratiate himself with their master, BAUGI, who now had no workers and was glad to employ the stranger.

As a reward for his work, Baugi eventually led Odin to the cave where the MEAD of poetry was hidden. The story is told in the poem *HAVAMAL* and in SNORRI STURLUSON's *GYLFAGINNING*.

BOR (BUR) Son of BURI, who was known as the father of the gods. According to early NORSE poetry, Bor married BESTLA, the daughter of a RIME-GIANT. Bor's sons killed the first giant, YMIR, and created the world from his body parts. According to SNORRI STURLUSON, Bor's sons were ODIN, VILI, and VE.

BRACTEATES (bractates) Small stamped pendants or amulets of metal, usually gold, similar to hand-

made coins from around 400–550 A.D. Bracteates are found across most of SCANDINAVIA, usually in graves or sites of ship burials.

Many have depictions of scenes or objects that scholars connect to NORSE mythology. For example, one shows a man's hand being bitten off by a wolf, part of the story of TYR and FENRIR. Some bracteates even depict RUNES; several contain the complete runic alphabet.

Some scholars suggest that bracteates were magical charms worn to bring the blessings of the gods or to ward off evil.

BRAGI The god of poetry, eloquence, and music. Bragi was the son of ODIN and GUNLOD and husband of IDUNN. Bragi does not play a major role in NORSE myths. He played a harp and sang so sweetly that even the trees and flowers were charmed by him. Norsemen called their poets or skalds *bragamen* or *bragawomen*. Because Odin had a great knowledge of poetry, some scholars see Bragi as another facet of Odin's personality.

BREIDABLIK (Broad Splendor; Wide View) The shining hall of the god BALDER, located in ASGARD. Breidablik is the seventh of the gods' homes described in the poem *GRIMNISMAL*. It is located in a land free from evil, where only fair things dwell, including

Bracteate from Funen, Denmark, featuring an inscription that includes the term "The High One," a name for Odin *(Photo by Bloodofox/Used under a Creative Commons license)*

Balder, who was known as the fairest and best of the gods.

The author of the *PROSE EDDA*, SNORRI STUR-LUSON, uses most of the details from *Grimnismal* to portray Breidablik in his own work but adds that Balder's hall is located in HEAVEN and that nothing harmful dwells there, not even harmful RUNES.

BRIDE PRICE In the VIKING AGE, the money or goods (dowry) given to the family of the bride by the bridegroom or his family. In the story "Frey and Gerda," FREY's magic sword was the bride price for GERDA. In another NORSE story, the giant THRYM offers THOR's stolen hammer in return for FREYA as his bride.

BRISINGA MEN (Brising's Necklace) The golden necklace made by the DWARFS ALFRIGG, BERLING, DVALIN (1), and GRERR and coveted by the goddess FREYA. Freya was the VANIR goddess of fertility, and a necklace is often a fertility symbol. When she saw the dwarfs making the necklace under their stone, she bargained with them for it. This part of the necklace's story is told in the *SORLA THATTR*.

Freya lent the Brisinga men to THOR to help him retrieve his hammer, MJOLLNIR, from the RIME-GIANT THRYM. This story is told in the poem *THRYM-SKIVITHA*, which is part of the *CODEX REGIUS* of the *POETIC EDDA*.

A golden necklace, ca. 300–700, found in Torslunda, Färjestaden, Sweden *(Photo by Thuresson/ Used under a Creative Commons license)*

It is not made clear in the mythology who the Brisings were, but some experts believe the name refers to the dwarfs themselves.

BROKK A dwarf who was the son of Ivaldi and brother of EITRI. All three were well-known crafts-men among the dwarfs.

In the *PROSE EDDA*, SNORRI STURLUSON tells the story of how the trickster god LOKI persuaded Brokk and Eitri to make SIF's golden hair, the ship SKID-BLADNIR, and ODIN's spear GUNGNIR. After this, Loki bet Brokk that his brother could not make gifts for the gods as wonderful as those the two had already made together. Brokk accepted the bet and set out to help Eitri make a BOAR with bristles and a mane of gold, the golden ring DRAUPNIR, and THOR's great hammer, MJOLLNIR.

Brokk worked the bellows to blow air on the fire to keep it hot while Eitri crafted the objects. Meanwhile, Loki turned himself into a fly to pester Brokk. As Eitri worked on the final gift, Thor's ham-mer, Loki bit Brokk hard on the eyelid. When Brokk swiped at the blood that dripped into his eye, he took one hand off the bellows handle and caused the fire to cool just enough to halt the complete formation of the hammer's handle. This is why Thor's hammer has a short handle. Despite Loki's interference, Brokk won the bet. (See "Treasure of the Dwarfs" under Loki.)

BURI Ancestor of the gods. Buri appeared at the time of the CREATION, when the cosmic cow AUD-HUMLA brought him to life from under the primeval ice. In time, Buri had a son named BOR who married the giantess BESTLA and became the father of the gods ODIN, VILI, and VE.

BYGGVIR A servant to the VANIR god FREY. Byggvir is married to BEYLA, also a servant of Frey. With their master they attend the feast given for the gods by the SEA god AEGIR. The story is told in *LOKASENNA*, a part of the *POETIC EDDA*. During the feast, Byggvir dares to speak out against LOKI as he taunts the gods and goddesses at the feast. Byggvir threatens to crush Loki, but the trickster god accuses the servant of cowardice. (See "Loki's Mocking" under Loki.)

BYLEIST (BYLEISTR) Little-known brother of the trickster god LOKI. Byleist is a giant (as opposed to a god) as his and Loki's parents, FARBAUTI and LAUFEY, were GIANTS. "Brother of Byleist" occurs as a KENNING, or another name, for Loki in the *VOLUSPA* and *HYNDLULJOTH*, both of which are in the *POETIC EDDA*. SNORRI STURLUSON uses this reference when he describes Loki's family, along with HELBINDI, another brother of Loki. No more information about Byleist survives.

BYRGIR   The well to which the Earth children, BIL AND HJUKI, had gone to fetch water before being stolen away by MANI, the man of the Moon.

C

CAT In world mythology, the domestic cat is often venerated or feared as a witch in disguise or as a witch's "creature." In NORSE mythology, the goddess FREYA, who had magical powers, had a chariot drawn by two gray or black cats.

CAULDRON A large pot or kettle used for boiling. In "Thor and Hymir Go Fishing," THOR goes in search of HYMIR's huge cauldron because the gods need it for brewing ale. Later, in "Loki's Mocking," (see under LOKI), the sea god AEGIR gives a banquet for the gods. He brews the ale in the cauldron that Thor and TYR took from Hymir. The cauldron features in many medieval tales, especially those in which witches brew magic broths.

COCK A rooster; a male chicken. Also, a beacon or a warning device of evil things to come.

According to a myth, when the three cocks crow, they announce the coming of RAGNAROK, the final struggle between the gods and the GIANTS at the end of the world. FJALAR (1), the red cock, crows to wake up the giants in JOTUNHEIM. GULLINKAMBI, the golden cock, awakens the gods and dead heroes in ASGARD. An unnamed rust-red bird crows at the doors of HEL (2) to awaken the spirits of the underworld. They are named only in *VOLUSPA*, generally considered to be the first poem in the *POETIC EDDA*.

Svipdagsmal, a poem often included in the *Poetic Edda* but which appears to have been written down in the 17th century, names Vithofnir as the cock that awakens the giants or perhaps the gods. Either way, according to the poem, the giants fear this cock and attempt to kill him before he can crow and bring about the end time.

Cocks were used as sacrificial animals to accompany the dead on their journeys to the afterlife.

CODEX REGIUS A 13th-century manuscript found in the 17th century in a farmhouse in ICELAND. Bishop Brynjolfur Sveinsson presented it to the king of DENMARK, and it became part of the royal collection for several centuries.

Roughly half of the manuscript is composed of the poems that make up the *POETIC EDDA*, a principal source of stories and information on NORSE mythology. This portion is formally known as the *Codex Regius* of the *Poetic Edda* and scholars refer to the manuscript as GKS 2365 4to.

The other half of the document contains the *PROSE EDDA* by SNORRI STURLUSON and some of his other works, such as the *Nafnathulur* and his poem *Hattatal*; this portion is known as the *Codex Regius* of *Snorra Edda*. It also contains two 13th-century works of SKALDIC POETRY. The manuscript number for this portion is GKS 2367 4to.

Until 1971, the manuscript was preserved in the Royal Library of Copenhagen, Denmark. In that year, it was returned ICELAND and is now in the Árni Magnússon Institute in Reykjavik.

COW This female mammal is noted for the nurturing properties of her milk. In many world mythologies, she is the symbol of the Great Mother and of CREATION. In the *PROSE EDDA* and the *POETIC EDDA* of the NORSE, the cow is named AUDHUMLA.

CREATION The mythology of each people has its own story of how the world was created. In NORSE mythology, at the beginning there was a swirling chaos of mists and fog, freezing cold, howling winds, and terrifying fire.

The following story of the creation is from SNORRI STURLUSON's *PROSE EDDA*; his major sources were the poems *VOLUSPA*, *GRIMNISMAL*, and *VAFTHRUDNISMAL*.

The Chasm There were no Sun, no Moon, no stars, no land or sea. There was only a great yawning void called GINNUNGAGAP.

To the north of Ginnungagap was NIFLHEIM, land of cold mists; to the south was MUSPELL-HEIM, the land of fire. From Niflheim's spring, HVERGELMIR, flowed the 11 poisonous rivers of the ELIVAGAR. They emptied into the chasm, froze, and filled it with venomous ice. From Muspellheim came sheets of fire that turned the ice into mists and dense fog.

For millions of years fire and ice interacted with each other until at last there came sparks of life. The first life took the form of a huge, proto-giant, YMIR, and a gigantic cow, AUDHUMLA, that nourished Ymir with her milk. She in turn licked the salty stones around Ginnungagap for nourishment.

As Audhumla licked at the icy, salty stones, she uncovered the hairs of a man's head. Soon she uncovered the entire head and finally the whole body of a handsome, manlike creature. He was BURI, the ancestor of the gods.

Buri produced a son named BOR, who married a giantess, BESTLA, who gave him three sons, ODIN, VILI, and VE, the first gods.

Meanwhile, as Ymir slept, hordes of hideous giant children sprouted from his body. They were the HRIMTHURSSAR, also known as the RIME-GIANTS or frost giants.

Odin and his brothers, the sons of Bor, quarreled with the unruly gang of giants. Finally, they attacked and killed Ymir, the father of them all. Immense floods of blood spurted from the fallen giant and drowned all the rime-giants except BERGELMIR and his wife, who rode out the flood on a hollowed tree trunk.

Odin, Vili, and Ve dragged Ymir's huge body to Ginnungagap, and there they set about creating the worlds. They made the earth from his flesh, mountains and hills from his bones, and rocks and boulders from his teeth. His curly hair became leafy trees and all vegetation. The lakes and seas and oceans were made from his blood.

Sky Then they made the sky's dome from Ymir's skull and flung his brains aloft to make the clouds. Snorri says the four DWARFS NORDI, SUDRI, AUSTRI, and VESTRI held up the four corners of the sky. The four points of the compass—north, south, east, and west—are named after these dwarfs. The gods took sparks and embers from Muspellheim's fires and made the Sun, Moon, and stars.

Jotunheim The new gods, the sons of Bor, gave to the new generation of giants, known as the JOTUN—the race founded by Bergelmir—the land named JOTUNHEIM. They asked that the giants stay there.

Midgard Then they put Ymir's eyebrows around a green piece of land, forming a pleasant enclosure they called MIDGARD, or Middle Earth.

Night and Day Once the gods had created the world and placed the Sun and Moon in the sky, they made night and day.

NOTT (Night) was a beautiful GIANTESS with a dark complexion and hair of midnight black. She was the daughter of NARFI, one of the first giants. She married three times. Her first husband was NAGLFARI, father of AUD. Her second was ANNAR, father of JORD. With her third husband, DELLING, she had a son named DAG (Day).

The gods sent Nott and Dag into the heavens in horse-drawn chariots to ride around the world. They created darkness and light, as one followed the other through the skies.

Nott drove first, with her lead horse, HRIMFAXI. The froth from his bit fell to Earth as dewdrops. After Nott came Dag with his horse, SKINFAXI. His golden glow lit up the heavens and the Earth.

Sun and Moon The gods placed the Sun and the Moon in chariots, also drawn by splendid horses. The horses were driven by SOL and MANI, the daughter and the son of a man from Midgard whose name was MUNDILFARI.

Sol's horses were ARVAKR and ALSVID. A shield, SVALIN, in front of Sol's chariot protected her from the Sun, whose brilliant rays would have burned her to a cinder. Mani's horse was ALDSVIDER.

Mani, the man of the Moon, stole two Earth children to help him drive his chariot. Their names were BIL AND HJUKI.

Sun and Moon could never pause in their journeys across the heavens, for they were forever pursued by the terrible wolves SKOLL and HATI HRODUITTNIS-SON. Each month Hati, it was said, took a bite out of the Moon and tried to gobble it up. But the Moon escaped and grew whole again. In the end the wolves devour both Sun and Moon and cast the world into darkness at RAGNAROK.

The First Humans The first man was ASK (Ash) and the first woman, EMBLA (Elm). The first three AESIR gods, Odin, Vili, and Ve, created them.

The gods were walking along the seashore when they saw two tree trunks lying at the edge of the water. The forms of the trees were beautiful. Odin breathed life into them. Vili gave them the ability to speak and think. Ve gave them warmth and color and movement.

The gods gave them Midgard in which to live. All human beings were descended from Ask and Embla. HEIMDALL later created the three social classes of men and women.

The Dwarfs   The gods made gnomes and dwarfs from the grubs in Ymir's rotting corpse. They gave them human form and endowed them with brains, but they were ugly, misshapen creatures, greedy and selfish. The gods gave them SVARTALFHEIM, the dark realm underground, and put them in charge of the Earth's treasures of gold, other precious metals, and gems. The dwarfs were master smiths.

See also "Treasures of the Dwarfs" under LOKI.

Asgard   The gods created for themselves the beautiful realm of ASGARD, home of the Aesir gods. It was linked to Midgard by BILROST, the RAINBOW BRIDGE, and it was sheltered by the great World Tree, YGGDRASIL, which touched all of the worlds.

DAG (Day)   The son of Nott and her third husband, Delling. Odin set Nott and Dag in the sky to ride around the world, bringing darkness and light at regular intervals. Dag's horse was Skinfaxi (Shining Mane) whose golden glow lit up the Earth.

See also "Night and Day" under creation.

DAIN (1)   A dwarf mentioned only in *Hyndlul-joth*, a part of the *Poetic Edda*, as one of the creators of the gold-bristled boar Hildisvini. According to this poem, Dain and his brother, Nabbi, made the magical boar.

Peter Nicolai Arbo's painting of Dag riding Skinfaxi (1874)

DAIN (2)   One of four full-grown male deer, or stags, that lived among the branches of Yggdrasil, the World Tree. Dain ate Yggdrasil's leaves, even the highest ones, by standing on his back legs and stretching his neck. The other three stags were Duneyr, Durathror, and Dvalin (3). The deer are named in the poem *Grimnismal*, by Snorri Sturluson in *Gylfaginning*.

DAINSLEIF (Dain's Heirloom)   A sword made by the dwarf Dain (1), according to Snorri Sturluson. This sword was cursed: Once drawn, it must kill a man before it can returned to the sheath. A blow from this magical sword never failed to kill or cause a wound that never healed. To rescue his daughter Hild, the legendary warrior and king Hogni drew Dainsleif to kill her abductor, Hedin Hjarrandason.

DEER   The male deer, which is also called a hart or stag, appears in several descriptions of the worlds of the Norse gods. For instance, four stags eat the highest twigs of the World Tree, Yggdrasil, while the great hart Eikthyrnir nibbles at the branches of Laerad, the tree that stands next to Valhalla, the great hall of Odin.

Scholars suggest that the male deer, with his impressive antlers, was a sign of nobility and strength. The red deer and the reindeer, both common species in Scandinavia, were often portrayed in the mythology, folklore, and art of northern Europe.

DELLING (The Dayspring)   The father of Dag, who is the day, and whose mother was Nott, the night. Delling was the third husband of the giantess Nott and was a little-known member of the Aesir. He was shining and fair, for Dag took after him. The details are known from *Vafthrudnismal*,

This rock carving of a deer is one of the major features of the Bolareinen (*Bola reindeer*) rock carvings site in Steinkjer, Norway. *(Photo by Orland/Used under a Creative Commons license)*

which is found in the *POETIC EDDA*, and in SNORRI STURLUSON's *GYLFAGINNING*.

In the Eddic poem *HAVAMAL*, ODIN says he knows a charm that is supposed to be chanted in front of the doors of Delling. Scholars suggest that Delling's doors represent the sunrise.

See also "Night and Day" under CREATION.

DENMARK A nation in northwestern Europe consisting of the Jutland peninsula and many nearby islands in the Baltic Sea. Denmark is part of SCANDINAVIA and shares a common history with NORWAY, SWEDEN, and ICELAND. The VIKINGS are the ancestors of the people in these modern-day nations.

According to a story by SNORRI STURLUSON, the goddess GEFJION plowed the island for Zealand (Sjaelland in Danish) from the mainland of Sweden, using the strength of her four sons, who were giant

oxen. Important archaeological finds concerning NORSE myths have come from this country. Zealand, for example, has an important collection of rock carvings—runestones, from the late Bronze Age, which began around 1000 B.C., that portray religious scenes. Two elaborately carved little wagons, which would have carried the gods, came from a site near Dejbjerg on the Jutland peninsula. Also a tree coffin, in which the trunk was carved out to make room for the body, was found near Egtved. The National Museum of Denmark houses many Norse artifacts.

DISABLOT A sacrifice made to the DISIR, the female nature spirits who watched over families and were the household guardians of death.

Several *disablot* ceremonies are mentioned in the historical works of SNORRI STURLUSON. They are also known from the SKALDS and from the SAGAS from ICELAND. Studies of place names have also helped scholars piece together the importance of the Disir and *disablot* ceremonies in SCANDINAVIA during the MIGRATION PERIOD and the VIKING AGE.

Experts suggest that these ceremonies were conducted in private households in the western regions of Scandinavia, such as ICELAND, and in public places in the eastern regions. A large public *disablot* was held in OLD UPPSALA, in SWEDEN, according to Snorri. The more private ceremonies were most likely healing rituals, whereas the public rituals were held in community spaces at the beginning of winter to honor the spirits. The rituals were reported by historians of the time to include human and animal sacrifices.

DISIR Female guardian spirits associated with death. The Disir (singular, Dis) watched over individuals, families, and perhaps entire neighborhoods. Some experts believe the Disir were malicious, harmful spirits who sought bad things for the people they watched over; however, other experts suggest that the NORSE people also believed in a positive influence of the Disir in a person's life and that a Dis brought good to a home and its family. People honored these spirits in private and public ceremonies known as DISABLOT. The goddess FREYA was referred to as Vanadis, which means the "Dis of the VANIR."

This type of spirit is mentioned in the Eddic poem *GRIMNISMAL*, and the Disir play an important role in the *Saga of Tryggvason*. More information about them survives in place names in SCANDINAVIA and in histories written in later centuries.

DIVINATION The act or practice of predicting the future, particularly through a ritual or ceremony. The ancient NORSE people held strong beliefs in the ability of some people, animals, and objects to foretell the future. They sought omens and warnings from sacred horses, performed ceremonies full of chants (known as GALDRAR) and singing and led by a seeress to learn what would happen in battle, and studied the arrangement of twigs to learn of their fates. Divination was closely connected with the magical art form known as SEID.

DRAGON A mythical beast, usually represented as a large, winged, fire-breathing reptile similar to a crocodile or a SERPENT. In NORSE mythology the dragon NITHOG feeds on the root of the World Tree, YGGDRASIL. In Norse and GERMANIC legend, from which Norse mythology evolved, the dragon FAFNIR guards his ill-gotten treasure and is eventually slain by the hero SIGURD.

DRAUPNIR (Dropper) The golden ring or arm ring made for the great god ODIN by the dwarfs EITRI and BROKK. Every ninth night, eight other rings dropped from Draupnir, each as heavy and bright as the first.

In the story "Frey and Gerda" (see under FREY), GERDA was not tempted by the ring. In "Balder's Funeral" (see BALDER), Odin placed Draupnir on the funeral pyre; it was then returned to him by HERMOD, the messenger god who had gone to the underworld to try to bring Balder back to the living.

See "Treasures of the Dwarfs" under LOKI.

DROMI The second of three chains with which the gods tried to bind the dangerous wolf FENRIR. Though stronger than the first chain (LAEDING), this ordinary metal chain could not hold tight the powerful and evil wolf. Only the magical third rope, GLEIPNER, successfully secured Fenrir until the time of RAGNAROK, the conflict that brought an end to the world of the gods.

DUNEYR One of the four DEER that live within the limbs of the World Tree, YGGDRASIL, gnawing at its leaves and branches and reaching the highest leaves by stretching their necks. The other three are DAIN (3), DVALIN (3), and DURATHROR. They are found in the story of Yggdrasil told in GRIMNISMAL, part of the

POETIC EDDA, and retold by SNORRI STURLUSON in GYLFAGINNING.

DURATHROR One of the four DEER that live within the limbs of the World Tree, YGGDRASIL, gnawing at its leaves and branches and reaching the highest leaves by stretching their necks. The other three are DUNEYER, DAIN (3), and DVALIN (3). They are found in the story of Yggdrasil told in GRIMNISMAL, part of the POETIC EDDA, and retold by SNORRI STURLUSON in GYLFAGINNING.

DURINN (1) The second of the DWARFS created by the AESIR from the maggots that oozed from the body of the first giant, YMIR, at CREATION. The first dwarf created was MOTSOGNIR. One day, after they had created their individual worlds from the proto-giant's body, the gods were at work creating objects and creatures to place in their realms. They paused in the process, sat and thought, and then decided to make dwarfs and make them resemble humans. So the gods transformed a maggot into Motsognir, and after that they made Durinn.

Together, these two dwarfs themselves created many more dwarfs, all in the likeness of man. The story is told in the VOLUSPA, part of the POETIC EDDA. In GYLFAGINNING, SNORRI STURLUSON gives Durinn credit for telling this story.

DURINN (2) One of the two DWARFS who crafted the great SWORD Tyrfing. The other was DVALIN (2). The dwarfs were forced to make the sword for a powerful king and, in revenge, they put a curse upon it. The story of that curse in the lives of the sword's owners forms the center of an Icelandic HEROIC LEGEND. It is told most completely in the manuscripts of the HERVARAR SAGA.

DVALIN (1) (DWALIN) A DWARF who, with his brothers ALFRIGG, BERLING, and GRERR, fashioned the golden BRISINGA MEN necklace coveted by the goddess FREYA. They are part of the story that begins *The Tale of Hogni and Hedinn*, which is also known as the *SORLA THATTR*. When the goddess Freya discovers the brothers making the beautiful Brisinga men, she desperately wants the necklace and bargains with the dwarfs in order to own it.

The other three dwarfs are not mentioned in other works of NORSE mythology, but Dvalin is a common dwarf name. However, scholars don't know how many references to Dvalin the dwarf refer to the same character.

DVALIN (2) One of the two DWARFS who crafted the great SWORD Tyrfing. The other was DURINN (2). The dwarfs were forced to make the sword for a powerful king and, in revenge, they put a curse upon it. The story of that curse in the lives of the sword's owners forms the center of an Icelandic HEROIC LEGEND. It is told most completely in the manuscripts of the *HERVARAR SAGA.*

DVALIN (3) One of the four DEER that live within the limbs of the World Tree, YGGDRASIL, gnawing at its leaves and branches, reaching the highest leaves by stretching their necks. The other three deer are DUNEYR, DURATHROR, and DAIN (3). They are found in the story of Yggdrasil told in *GRIMINISMAL*, part of the *POETIC EDDA*, and retold by SNORRI STURLUSON in *GYLFAGINNING.*

DVALIN'S DELIGHT The ironic name given by the DWARFS to the SUN. Dwarfs, gnomes, trolls, and other denizens of underground caves are terrified of the Sun, for it turns them to stone. They must never be caught aboveground in daylight.

See also ALVIS.

DWARFS The small, ugly, misshapen creatures made at the CREATION from the grubs in the giant YMIR's dead body. They were given the realm of SVARTALFHEIM (land of the dark ELVES) in which to live. The gods put them in charge of Earth's underground treasures: precious metals and gems. They were master craftsmen and fashioned many treasures for the gods (see "Treasure of the Dwarfs under LOKI).

The poem *VOLUSPA* lists many dwarfs' names, most repeated by SNORRI STURLUSON in *GYLFAGINNING*, but few of them are ever heard of again in the surviving records of NORSE myths. Among the more memorable ones are

- ALVIS, who, like many of the dwarfs, had a vast store of knowledge and poetically listed the various names for the 13 most important words in the medieval SCANDINAVIAN vocabulary
- BROKK and EITRI, who fashioned various gifts for the gods
- DVALIN, one of the dwarfs who made the BRISINGA MEN coveted by the goddess FREYA and who was turned into stone at sunrise
- ANDVARI, the dwarf who was tricked by LOKI into giving up his gold hoard, upon which he then placed a curse
- LIT, the dwarf who was inadvertently cremated on BALDER's funeral pyre
- NORDI, SUDRI, AUSTRI, and VESTRI, the four dwarfs who were bidden to hold up the four corners of the sky

Here is the list of dwarfs named in *Voluspa*:

Ai, Alf, Althjof (Mighty Thief), An, Anar, Andvari, Aurvang, Austri, Bifur, Bild, Billing, Bofur, Bombur, Bruni, Buri, DAIN, Dolgthrasir, Dori, Draupnir, Duf, DURINN, Dvalin, Eikinskjaldi (Oak Shield), Fili, Fith, FJALAR, Fraeg, Frar Hornbori, Frosti, Fundin, Gandalf (Magic Elf), Ginnar, Gloi, Hannar, Har, Haugspori, Hepti, Heri, Hlaevang, Hliodolf, Hoggstari, Jari, Kili, Lit, Loni, Mjodvitnir (Mead-wolf), Moin, MOTSOGNIR (the Mightiest), Nain, Nali, Nar, Nidi, Niping, Nordri, Nori, Ny, Nyr, Nyrad, Ori, Radsvid (Swift in Counsel), REGIN, Skafid, Skirfir, Sudri, Svior, Thekk, Thorin, Thrain, Thror, Vestri, Vigg, Vindalf (Wind Elf), Virvir, Vit, Yngvi

EAGLE   A symbol of strength and death in Norse mythology. The eagle was also an image of the battlefield, for it often ate at the dead bodies.

An eagle was one of the three birds of Odin—the other two were ravens—who was the god of death, among other things. Odin is often pictured with an eagle. He occasionally took on the form of an eagle, as did other gods and giants. An eagle also sat on the topmost branches of Yggdrasil, the World Tree, where it flapped its wings and created the winds in Midgard, the world of humans.

Many images of the eagle appear in stone carvings dating from the era of the Norse gods and found in Scandinavia. They also appear frequently on helmets and small brooches. The eagle's curved beak distinguishes this bird from ravens, which have straight beaks.

EARTH   In Old Norse, both Jord and Fjorgyn (i) mean "Earth." Both are names of mythological beings and are used at times to refer to the land or the soil. Jord is the most frequent name used for the giantess who was the mother of Thor, son of Odin; in this role she is sometimes known as Fjorgyn. Jord is also found in skaldic poetry as a name for the celestial body Earth.

EARTH MOTHER (Earth Goddess)   A general name for a female spirit or deity worshipped by peoples all over the world. Believers prayed to her for fine weather and good crops, for food and shelter, and for numerous sons and daughters. In Norse mythology, the first Earth goddesses had no distinct form but later were identified with Jord, Fjorgyn (i), Frigg, and Freya.

EDDAS, THE   Two distinct works: the *Poetic Edda*, also called the *Elder Edda*, and the *Prose Edda*, sometimes known as the *Snorra Edda* or *Younger Edda*. The *Eddas* are the main sources of knowledge about Norse mythology.

The *Poetic Edda* is a collection of poems on mythological and legendary themes, written down at different times and by different poets between the eighth and 13th centuries. They were discovered in 1643 by the Icelandic bishop Brynjólfur Sveinsson. The *Poetic Edda* was sometimes called *Saemund's Edda* in the mistaken belief that it had been written by the medieval bishop Saemund Sigfusson.

The *Prose Edda*, "younger" because it was not put to paper until around 1220, was written by Icelandic poet, historian, and diplomat Snorri Sturluson. It is a handbook of Norse mythology, designed as a guide for poets to encourage them to write in the style of the ancient poets of the Viking age.

These two great books helped keep alive the memory of the ancient gods and their exploits, which otherwise might have been lost forever with the coming of Christianity to the northern lands.

EGGTHER   A giant. Eggther was the watchman of the giants who announces the beginning of Ragnarok, the great conflict that ends the world of the Norse gods. He is mentioned and named only in the *Voluspa*, a poem in the *Poetic Edda*. In that poem, Eggther, called "the joyous," sat upon a hill and played his harp while the cock Fjalar crowed to awaken the giants for this final battle.

EGIL   Two characters with this name appear in Norse mythology. The existing documents leave it unclear whether each use of the name referred to one figure or to different people. Egil, apparently, was a common name in the folklore of Scandinavia.

One person named Egil was a servant of Thor, according to Snorri Sturluson. He guarded Thor's goats while the god was visiting the giant HYMIR. This Egil may have been the father of Thor's human servants THIALFI and ROSKVA.

Another Egil is the subject of a popular Icelandic SAGA, or epic story, known today as *Egil's Saga*. He was a very skilled and talented archer and the brother of Weland, the blacksmith best known from GERMANIC mythology.

EIKTHYRNIR (EIKÞYRNIR) (Oak Thorny) The fully grown male deer, or stag, that stood on the roof of VALHALLA, ODIN's famous palace, and nibbled at the leaves of the great OAK tree LAERAD, around which the hall had been built. Drops of an unnamed fluid dripped from Eikthyrnir's antlers, and from it came all of the great rivers of the world. Besides being named in Norse manuscripts, Eikthyrnir is portrayed on the 10th-century carved stone cross from Gosforth, Cumbria, England.

EINHERJAR (Lone Fighters) The fallen HUMAN warriors chosen by ODIN to live and revel with him in VALHALLA until the end of time, known as RAGNAROK. These special warriors are described in many written sources from ICELAND. Older poems and stories describe them as special warriors of Odin who are served by the VALKYRIES. In other works, including the *PROSE EDDA* written by SNORRI STURLUSON, the Einherjar are dead warriors who go to live in Valhalla with Odin. There they feast each day on the meat of the magical boar SAEHRIMNIR and practice their warfare in preparation for Ragnarok, the final conflict between the gods and the giants.

Scholars suggest that the image of the Einherjar is based on a very ancient cult that worshiped Odin, the god of the dead and of battle. Many kings and princes of SCANDINAVIA were followers of this cult and dedicated themselves and the people they killed in battle to Odin.

EIR A goddess and healer or physician. Little is now known of Eir. She appears in the works of SNORRI STURLUSON and is mentioned once in the older *POETIC EDDA*. Eir is one of the 12 or 13 highest-ranking goddesses, according to Snorri's list of deities. She is also one of the handmaids of the beautiful giantess MENGLOD.

Eir means "peace," "mercy," or "clemency," traits some see as important to her role as a physician. That Snorri and others even named this goddess suggests to scholars that Eir once played an important role in Norse religion.

EITRI A dwarf who was the son of Ivaldi and brother of BROKK. The three were well-known craftsmen among the dwarfs.

In the *PROSE EDDA*, SNORRI STURLUSON tells the story of how the trickster god LOKI persuaded Brokk and Eitri to make SIF's golden hair, the ship SKIDBLADNIR, and Odin's spear GUNGNIR. After this, Loki bet Brokk that his brother could not make gifts for the gods as wonderful as those the two had already made together. Brokk accepted the bet and set out to help Eitri make a BOAR with bristles and a mane of gold, the golden ring DRAUPNIR, and THOR's great hammer, MJOLLNIR.

Brokk worked the bellows to blow air on the fire to keep it hot while Eitri crafted the objects. Meanwhile, Loki turned himself into a fly to pester Brokk. As Eitri worked on the final gift, Thor's hammer, Loki bit Brokk hard on the eyelid. When Brokk swiped at the blood that dripped into his eye, he took one hand off the bellows handle and caused the fire to cool just enough to halt the complete formation of the hammer's handle. This is why Thor's hammer has a short handle. But despite Loki's interference, Brokk won the bet. (See "Treasure of the Dwarfs" under Loki.)

ELDHRIMNIR (Sooty with Fire) The great kettle in the kitchen at VALHALLA in which the chef, ANDHRIMNIR, boils the magical boar, SAEHRIMNIR, each day. The boiled meat feeds the hordes of the EINHERJAR, the fallen human heroes who dwell in ODIN's great hall, every night.

This kitchen scene is depicted in the poem *GRIMNISMAL* and repeated by SNORRI STURLUSON in *GYLFAGINNING*. The three NAMES for kettle, cook, and boar refer to the sooty conditions of the kitchen or of the pot itself from hanging over the fire every day.

ELDIR (Man of Fire) One of the two servants of the ancient sea god AEGIR. Eldir was on duty as the gatekeeper, or outer guard, to Aegir's castle when LOKI tried to return to the banquet where he had killed Aegir's other servant, FIMAFENG. Eldir challenged Loki, the trickster god, by making him feel guilty for his acts, but Loki convinced Eldir to allow him back into the castle.

ELIVAGAR The collective name for 11 venomous rivers that surged from the spring HVERGELMIR in the underworld, NIFLHEIM. The rivers had fearsome NAMES that related to howling and boiling and storming: Fimbulthul, Fjorm, GJOLL, Gunnthra, Hrid,

Thor Wrestling with Age. Sculpture by Einar Jónsson (1873–1954), Reykjavik, Iceland *(Photo by Fingalo/Used under a Creative Commons license)*

Leipt, Slid, Syol, Sylg, Vid, and Ylg. The rivers froze and roared into GINNUNGAGAP, the abyss, as glaciers. The first giant, YMIR, was formed from the frozen poison of the Elivagar (see CREATION).

In the story "Thor's Duel with Hrungnir," THOR tells of carrying AURVANDIL in a basket across the Elivagar. In the story "Thor and Hymir Go Fishing," Thor and TYR journey to the east of the Elivagar in Thor's GOAT-drawn chariot.

ELJUDNIR (ELVIÐNIR; Damp with Sleet) The hall of the goddess HEL (1) in her realm, NIFLHEIM, also known as HEL (2), the underworld. Eljudnir was a great home with very high walls, high banisters, and huge gates. Her maidservant in this palace was GANGLOT, and GANGLATI was her manservant. Some sources say that it was in Eljudnir that Hel met with the god HERMOD when he traveled to the underworld to rescue the spirit of the god BALDER.

ELLI (ELLE; Old Age) An old woman. Elli was the nurse of the giant UTGARD-LOKI. To test THOR's strength when the thunder god visited, Utgard-Loki

challenged him to wrestle the old woman Elli rather than the strong men of Utgard-Loki's bodyguard. Thor accepted the challenge. Elli stood fast as Thor struggled long and hard to defeat her. Finally, Elli put a hold on him to drive him to the ground, but Thor only fell to one knee before Utgard-Loki ended the match. The next day Utgard-Loki explained to the god that the woman he wrestled was Old Age herself and none could wrestle with her better than Thor had.

SNORRI STURLUSON tells this story in GYLFAGINNING.

ELVES Mythological and folkloric beings with magical abilities. One of the NINE WORLDS at the top of YGGDRASIL was ALFHEIM, the realm of the LIGHT-ELVES. In Old NORSE, the word for elf was *alfar*.

Elves are mentioned frequently in Norse mythology, often in phrases that associate them with the AESIR. However, they do not play an active part in the stories.

The DWARF ALVIS included the words elves use for the things THOR quizzes him about in the Eddic poem *ALVISSMAL*. This inclusion gives elves a prominence in the mythology that the surviving stories do not explain.

Snorri Sturluson, the 13th-century Icelandic poet and historian, categorized the elves, distinguishing the light-elves who lived in Alfheim (elf-world), a kingdom high in Heaven, from the dark-elves who lived in Svartelfheim, a land deep below the earth. While the light-elves were fairer than the sun, the dark-elves were pitch black. Some translators and scholars see similarities between the dark-elves and the dwarfs, as both types of beings lived underground.

People offered sacrifices to elves in a ceremony known as an alfablot, which was usually held in the privacy of the home, though at the beginning of winter some communities held the ceremony as a public event.

Elves are also important to the skaldic poetry and to the sagas of Iceland and Scandinavia, works that are more closely tied to folklore than to the gods and their stories.

EMBLA   The first woman, who was created from an alder or elm tree by the first three Aesir gods, Odin, Vili, and Ve (see "The First Humans," under creation). In Norse mythology, all humans were descended from Embla and Ask, the first man.

FAFNIR Son of the magician HREIDMAR and brother of REGIN and OTR. Fafnir was a DWARF and SHAPE-SHIFTER who turned himself into a DRAGON to guard the hoard of gold he had stolen from Regin after the brothers had killed their father.

The story of how Fafnir came by his gold was recounted early in the 13th century by Icelandic poet SNORRI STURLUSON in *SKALDSKAPARMAL*. Regin's hunt for Fafnir is found in the Eddic poem *REGINSMAL* and forms a part of the *VOLSUNGA SAGA*, a late 13th-century prose epic that contains the HEROIC LEGEND of the Volsung family and the hero SIGURD. In this work, Regin persuades Sigurd to hunt Fafnir, who is still hiding as a dragon guarding his treasure. The poem *FAFNISMAL*, also part of the *POETIC EDDA*, as well as the Volsunga Saga, completes the tale of Sigurd, Fafnir, and Regin. The story is depicted in a famous RUNESTONE, or rock carving, found in Sodermanland, SWEDEN.

FALCON A bird of prey that hunts during the day. Like its relatives the hawk and the EAGLE, the falcon has extraordinary eyesight and powers of flight. In Norse mythology, the goddess FREYA possessed a suit of falcon feathers that enabled her to travel wherever she wanted.

Freya lent her suit of feathers to LOKI so he might rescue IDUNN and again so he might find MJOLLNIR, the hammer (see "The Theft of Thor's Hammer," under THOR). On another occasion, in "Thor and the Giant Geirrod," Loki borrowed a falcon suit from FRIGG, the wife of ODIN.

FARBAUTI (Cruel Striker) A giant, or JOTUN, the father of the trickster god LOKI. Loki's mother was the giantess LAUFEY, according to SNORRI STURLUSON. Some say Farbauti struck Laufey with a bolt of lightning, after which she gave birth to Loki.

FAROE ISLANDS (FAEROE ISLANDS) An island chain north of Scotland and about halfway between NORWAY and ICELAND.

Norwegians settled the Faroe Islands in the middle of the ninth century, at the same time as they settled Iceland. The Faroe Islands are considered part of SCANDINAVIA and their inhabitants share cultural traits with the people of Iceland. Since the VIKING AGE, they have been a stop on the regular shipping route between Norway and Iceland. Archaeological research in the Faroe Islands has revealed farms and settlements similar to those found in Iceland and Greenland.

A medieval history of the Faroe Islands written between 1200 and 1215 by an Icelandic author is known as *Faereyinga Saga* and is part of the manuscript *FLATEYJARBOK*. The Faroe Islands also have a few runestones similar to those found in Norway and SWEDEN, which help tell the story of the islands' connection with the NORSE myths.

FENJA AND MENJA Two very strong GIANTESSES, who were the daughters of the giant HRUGNIR, the strongest of GIANTS, and granddaughters of THJAZZI, a powerful storm giant. The two sisters had the gift of being able to see into the future. The legendary King Frodi of DENMARK, who was said to be the great-grandson of ODIN, mistakenly bought them as slaves.

Fenja and Menja turned the great millstone, named Grotti, at the command of Frodi and produced gold, peace, and goodwill for the nation. However, the king never let the giantesses stop to rest. In revenge, they used a magical chant on the mill and ground out an army to defeat Frodi.

A sea king led the army and, after destroying Frodi, kept Fenja and Menja at work on the mill grinding salt. He, too, would not let them rest, and so they ground the mill until the sea filled with salt.

The story of Fenja and Menja is part of the *SKALDSKAPARMAL* by Snorri Sturluson. The Icelandic historian and poet retold the *GROTTASONG* (*The Lay of Grotti*) and then quoted the entire poem in his work.

FENRIR (Fenris) The wolf who was the offspring of the trickster god Loki and the giantess Angrboda. He was the brother of Hel (1) and of Jormungand, the Midgard Serpent. Fenrir was so huge that when he opened his mouth, his jaws stretched from Earth to Heaven. He was eventually bound by the gods and doomed to remain in chains until Ragnarok (the end of the world), when he would kill the great god Odin. Fenrir in turn would die at the hands of Vidar, one of Odin's sons.

Snorri Sturluson's vivid version of this myth in the *PROSE EDDA* is the only surviving source.

Fenrir and the Gods Fenrir was so huge and hairy that the Aesir, the gods of Asgard, were frightened of him. Only Tyr was brave enough to befriend the monster wolf and feed him. As Fenrir grew bigger, the gods decided to protect themselves and chain him. The first chain they tried was called Laeding, the second, Dromi. Fenrir easily broke these chains. Then the gods sent Skirnir, the servant of the god Frey, to seek the help of the dwarfs, who lived in the Earth.

The dwarfs fashioned a silken bond, called Gleipnir, from

- the sound of a cat's paws
- the hairs of a maiden's beard
- the roots of a mountain
- the sinews of a bear
- the breath of a fish
- the spittle of a bird

Because none of these things seems to exist on Earth, no person or thing could break this bond.

The gods persuaded Fenrir to go with them to a lonely island, Lyngvi, in the middle of Lake Amsvartnir. They asked Fenrir if he would allow himself to be tied up once more and use his mighty strength to break the bond. He agreed to be bound if one of the gods would put a hand into Fenrir's mouth and guarantee that the wolf would be set free. After no one else spoke up Tyr, the most fair-minded of the gods, agreed to put his hand into Fenrir's mouth.

Once secured in Gleipner, Fenrir could not break the bond. He clamped down on Tyr's hand and bit it off. The gods attached Gleipnir to a heavy chain, Gelgja, and passed the chain through a hole into a large rock named Gjoll (1). Then the gods thrust a sword into the wolf's mouth so it would remain wide open. There Fenrir remained bound and gagged until the fatal day of Ragnarok, when Fenrir got his revenge and killed Odin.

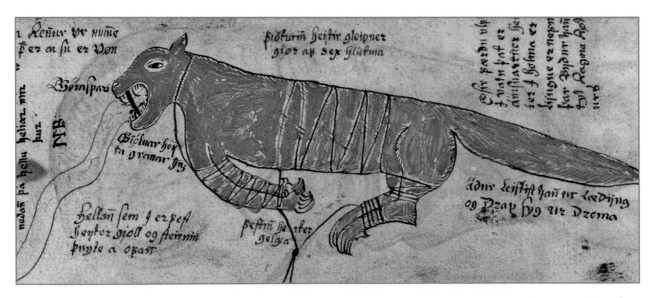

Depiction of Fenrir the wolf from the 17th-century Icelandic manuscript AM 738 4to, in the care of the Árni Magnússon Institute in Iceland

For the Norsemen of SCANDINAVIA, the wolf was an ever-present danger.

FENSALIR (Water, Sea, or Bog Hall) The palace or home of the goddess FRIGG, wife of ODIN and mother of BALDER. In this hall, the god LOKI tricked Frigg into revealing that her son's one vulnerability was MISTLETOE. Some experts suggest that Fensalir was located in a swamp or bog because followers of Frigg worshipped near a spring.

FIMAFENG (Swift Handler) An unfortunate servant of the SEA god, AEGIR. Fimafeng and the other servant, ELDIR, received much praise from the AESIR guests at a banquet Aegir held one night. It was Fimafeng's misfortune to be nearest the trickster god LOKI, who stabbed him to death in a jealous fit.

Fimafeng is part of the prose introduction to the 10th-century poem *LOKASENNA*, a part of the *CODEX REGIUS* of the *POETIC EDDA*.

FIMBULVETR (Mighty Winter) The winter of winters, the worst of all possible winters. The Fimbulvetr lasted for three years without respite and took place just before RAGNAROK, the end of the world. It brought terrible hardships, with driving snowstorms, vicious winds, bitter cold, and unyielding ice. People starved and lost all hope and goodness as they fought for their lives. They committed terrible crimes and started many wars. Fimbulvetr is described in the *POETIC EDDA*.

FJALAR (1) (All Knowing) The beautiful red rooster, or COCK, that crowed to call the GIANTS to fight at RAGNAROK, the conflict that ends the world of the Norse gods. Fjalar's counterpart, GULLINKAMBI, called the gods and fallen human heroes to the battle. An unnamed rust-red rooster summoned those who lived in HEL (2).

Fjalar is named in the *VOLUSPA*, an Eddic poem in the *CODEX REGIUS*.

FJALAR (2) (Deceiver) One of the two deceitful DWARFS who killed the wise man KVASIR (1) and made the MEAD of poetry from his blood. The other dwarf was Fjalar's brother, GALAR.

After making the mead, the two also killed the giant GILLING and his wife. Their son, SUTTUNG, avenged his parents' deaths by stranding Fjalar and Galar on a rock that would be flooded at high tide.

To save their lives, the brothers gave the mead to Suttung.

Their story is told by SNORRI STURLUSON in *SKALSKAPARMAL*. (See also "The Mead of Poetry" under ODIN.)

FJALAR (3) A common name in NORSE mythology. It means "deceiver." In addition to the COCK that awakened the GIANTS at RAGNAROK (1) and the DWARF that helped kill the poet KVASIR (2), Fjalar is found in the lists of dwarfs in the THULUR. It also appears in the *POETIC EDDA* as the name for the giant SKYRMIR. Some linguists suggest the word was a common noun in certain instances, rather than a name or proper noun.

FJOLSVID (FJOLSVITH) The GIANT who guarded the gates behind which lived the fair GIANTESS MENGLOD. Fjolsvid maintains the ring of fire that surrounds the house. He challenges and tests the human hero, SVIPDAG, who seeks Menglod, his true love.

The story is a part of the Eddic poem *SVIPDAGSMAL*, which is itself a combined work consisting of two parts known as *Grogald* (*Groa's Spell*) and *Fjolsvinnsmal* (*The Lay of Fjolsvid*).

FJORGYN (1) (FJORGVIN; Earth) One of two names (the other being JORD) for the GIANTESS who was the mother of THOR, the thunder god and son of ODIN, the most powerful god. The word *fjorgyn* is also used in NORSE mythology to refer to the "land" or "earth."

FJORGYN (2) (FJORGYNN) The father of the goddess FRIGG, according to the works of Icelandic poet SNORRI STURLUSON. According to modern experts in the Old NORSE language, the similarity between the feminine form of this word, which was the name of a GIANTESS (see FJORGYN [1]), and the masculine form is a result of transliteration, the methods of using the alphabet of one language to replicate the sounds of another language. In Old Norse spelling, there are distinctions between the names for the mother of THOR and the father of Frigg that are not evident in modern English.

FLATEYJARBOK (Book of the Flat Island) An Icelandic manuscript compiled in the late 1380s and early 1390s by two priests. It is written on parchment, a form of paper. Some pages were added to the manuscript in the 1500s. The manuscript was found in 1651 in the possession of a man living in ICELAND when the King of DENMARK gathered up many manuscripts from the people of that island. After being kept in Copenhagen for centuries, *Flateyjarbok* is now in the Árni Magnússon Institute in Iceland.

Most of that institute's enormous collection is made up of the semihistorical stories of the kings of Norway. *Flateyjarbok* does, however, contain poems that are important to NORSE mythology. *HYNDLUL-JOTH* tells of the goddess FREYA, the AESIR, and THOR. It also includes, by way of the genealogy of Freya's human lover OTTAR, the NAMES of many of the rulers of SCANDINAVIA.

The *SORLA THATTR*, a poem found in the *Flatey-jarbok*, tells the story of LOKI's transformation into a fly in order to enter FREYA's bedroom and steal her famous necklace, BRISINGA MEN. From a fly, Loki turns himself into a flea, bites Freya, undoes the clasp of the necklace, and takes the necklace to ODIN.

Flateyjarbok contains many *thaettir* (*þættir*), which are short stories, or small narrative pieces, found in many medieval Icelandic manuscripts. Some of *Flateyjarbok's thaettir* combine elements of the HEROIC LEGEND with mythical features, including battles with monsters and heroes with extra-human strength. Scholars attribute the addition of these short stories to the works of the scribes who copied the manuscripts. The *Sorla Thattr*, for example, retells the story of the Aesir gods as humans, which is part of SNORRI STURLUSON's *Heimskringla*.

FLOOD   At the time of CREATION in NORSE mythology, the giant YMIR was killed by the gods. His spurting blood created a flood. All the giants were drowned except BERGELMIR and his wife, who created a new race of giants.

Oceans, seas, and lakes were formed from Ymir's blood. Stories of floods occur in many mythologies around the world, from India and Russia to New Guinea and North and South America.

FOLKVANG   (FOLKVANGR; People Field; Field of the Folk)   The part of ASGARD that belonged to the goddess FREYA. The meaning of the word *Folkvangr* suggests a battlefield. To this great section of Asgard, Freya welcomed her half of the slain human heroes who died each day. The other half went to ODIN's VALHALLA.

In Folkvangr, Freya built her hall, SESSRUMNIR. Freya's portion of Asgard is first named in *GRIMNIS-MAL*, a poem in the *POETIC EDDA*, and described by SNORRI STURLUSON in *GYLFAGINNING*.

FORNJOT   (Destroyer)   A giant. Thirteenth-century Icelandic author SNORRI STURLUSON identified Fornjot as the father of the wind. Modern scholars believe him to be a very old giant, perhaps one of the oldest figures in NORSE mythology. Fornjot may also have been father of the HRIMTHURSSAR, or RIME-GIANTS.

FORSETI   God of justice and conciliation. Forseti was the son of BALDER and NANNA. His hall was GLITNIR.

Not much is known about Forseti, but place-names such as Forsetlund, near Oslo Fjord in Norway, suggest that he once may have been an important god.

FREKI   (Ravenous)   One of the wolf companions of the god ODIN. The other was GERI, whose name also means "ravenous." Odin fed the wolves all the meat that was given to him, for he needed only to drink the divine MEAD to survive. The wolves attended him at HLIDSKJALF, his high seat, and also at VALHALLA.

FREY   (FREYR; Lord)   One of the great gods of NORSE mythology. His name means "lord," as his sister FREYA's means "lady." Frey was the lord of the Sun, rain, and harvests. He was a shining god, bringing fertility and prosperity to all. Son of the VANIR god NJORD, Frey was one of the hostages asked to live in ASGARD after the AESIR/VANIR WAR. His home was ALFHEIM (elf-world), and he was sometimes known as Lord of the ELVES.

Among the treasures of the dwarfs that belonged to Frey were the ship SKIDBLADNIR, which could carry all the gods and their horses and armor and yet be folded small enough to fit in a pouch; the golden boar GULLINBURSTI, which plowed the earth and made it green; and a magic sword that struck out at JOTUNS and trolls of its own accord. Frey gave this sword as a BRIDE PRICE to GERDA's father, GYMIR. He would regret its loss at RAGNAROK, when he battled with the fire demon SURT and lost his life.

Frey wed Gerda after his servant SKIRNIR had wooed her for him. Many scholars interpret the story "Frey and Gerda" as a legend about the wooing of the frozen Earth (Gerda) by the warm Sun (Frey).

Gotland, Sweden, runestone depicting Thor, Odin, and Frey *(Photo by Berig/Used under a Creative Commons license)*

Historically, the worship of Frey was widespread and persistent, especially among the people of SWEDEN. Around the year 1200, there was a magnificent statue of Frey (called there Fricco, the Lover) alongside the two other great gods ODIN and THOR in Uppsala, Sweden.

Frey and Gerda One myth has it that Frey dared to climb onto Odin's high seat, HLIDSKJALF, where no one but the great god and sometimes his wife, FRIGG, were allowed to sit. From this vantage point Odin could see all the NINE WORLDS.

Frey looked about him, and his gaze was transfixed by a dazzling vision. He saw GERDA, the fair daughter of the giant Gymir. As she opened the gates to her palace, her shapely arms shone with such radiance that the Earth and the sky around her shimmered.

Frey left Odin's palace feeling sad and desolate. He knew that because Gerda was a Jotun, a daughter of one of the hated enemy, and he, Frey, was Lord of the Elves, he could never win her. Besides, it was said that her heart was as frozen as a seed in the hard winter earth.

Frey was so unhappy that he could not eat, sleep, or speak. Everyone was troubled for him. Trees lost their leaves, and flowers faded. All nature mourned for Frey. At last Frey's father, Njord, sent Skirnir to speak to his son.

Skirnir was Frey's friend and trusted servant. It did not take him long to find out what troubled Frey. Skirnir said he would woo the maiden for Frey if Frey would lend him BLODIGHOFI, the wondrous horse that could leap through fire unharmed, and Frey's magic sword.

Frey agreed, and Skirnir set off to JOTUNHEIM, the land of the giants. When he came to a wall of fire, Blodighofi leaped with Skirnir through the flames. They both came out unscathed.

Outside Gymir's hall, huge hounds set up a fearsome barking, howling like the winds of winter.

Skirnir asked an old shepherd for advice, but the man offered no help. Instead he told Skirnir that he had no hope of winning Gerda, for her heart was made of ice. He said that Frey was doomed to failure and death.

Skirnir knew that the NORNS had decided his fate and when he should die. There was nothing he could do except to go about his duty with hope and courage.

Inside her hall, Gerda looked coldly at Skirnir. First he offered her golden APPLES if she would give her love to Frey, but Gerda had plenty of gold. Then he offered her Odin's magic ring, DRAUPNIR, but Gerda had plenty of jewels.

Next Skirnir tried threats: He would cut off her head with the magic sword. Gerda replied that her father would kill Skirnir first and keep the magic sword for himself. Skirnir followed by drawing from his belt a wand and a knife. He said he would carve the most terrifying magic RUNES upon the wand and strike her with it. The runes would be curses that doomed her to be forever lonely and filled with longing. She would have no friends, no husband, no children. Only the horrible frost giant HRIMGRIMNIR would pursue her with foul corpses for companions. Food and drink would taste loathsome to her. She would always be cold and miserable and would slowly dry up like a dying thistle, trampled underfoot and forgotten by all.

At this dreadful threat, Gerda at last promised to marry Frey. Skirnir left Frey's magic sword behind as a bride price for Gymir and rode back to Frey with the happy news that Gerda would wed him in nine days at the sacred BARLEY patch, BARRI. (In Norse mythology, nine days symbolize the nine months of a northern winter.) The long delay dismayed Frey.

It is said that after they were married, Frey and Gerda were the happiest couple in the world, for the warmth of Frey's love had melted Gerda's icy heart, just as the Sun of spring thaws the frozen earth and brings forth the plants from seeds hidden inside it.

The story of Frey and Gerda is told in *SKIRN-ISMAL*, a 10th-century poem in the *POETIC EDDA*, and by SNORRI STURLUSON in his 13th-century *GYLFAGINNING*.

FREYA (Lady) The goddess of love and fertility. Freya was the daughter of the VANIR god NJORD and the sister of FREY. Freya came to ASGARD with her brother and father after the AESIR/VANIR WAR ended in an eternal peace treaty. Freya's home in Asgard was in the region known as FOLKVANGR in a hall named SESSRUMNIR.

Freya was married to OD, but this mysterious character (whose name means "roamer") disappeared. Freya was said to roam the Earth looking for him and shedding tears that turned to pure gold. Freya and Od had a daughter named HNOSSA, which means "jewel." Freya was exceedingly beautiful, and many fell in love with her, including GIANTS, DWARFS, and HUMANS.

Like most of the Vanir, Freya had a talent for witchcraft. It is said that when she came to Asgard, she instructed the gods in the magical arts of SEID.

Freya also had a warlike side and shared Odin's love of battle. It is said that she and ODIN divided the slain human heroes between them so that some went to Odin's VALHALLA while others went to Sessrumnir. Freya's boar, the gold-bristled HILDISVINI, was a symbol of war. Its name means "Battle Boar."

Freya possessed a boar chariot and a chariot pulled by two gray or black CATS. She also had a FALCON skin that she sometimes donned to fly away. She lent the falcon skin to LOKI, the trickster god, in the stories "Idunn's Apples" (see under IDUNN) and "The Theft of Thor's Hammer" (see under THOR). Her most precious possession was the BRISINGA MEN.

Freya, Ottar, and the Giantess Hyndla Freya, goddess of love and fertility, was loved by many, including the human male OTTAR. In the *Lay of Hyndla* (see *HYNDLULJOTH*) from the *POETIC EDDA*, Freya transforms Ottar into the shape of her boar, Hildisvini, and visits the GIANTESS HYNDLA in her cave. Hyndla is a powerful seeress. Freya cajoles and bullies Hyndla into telling Ottar all about his ancestors from far back so he may win a wager with another mortal. In VIKING times, it was very important to know one's lineage; proof of it was often used to settle disputes over land and other property. One of Ottar's ancestors turned out to be SIGURD, the hero of the *VOLSUNGA SAGA*, so he was sure to win his bet.

Once Hyndla had finished reciting the list of Ottar's ancestors, she wanted to leave Freya and her "boar." Freya used witchcraft to persuade Hyndla to brew some "memory beer" for Ottar, so he would remember every detail of what Hyndla had told him. Freya caused flames to dance around the giantess until she gave Ottar the brew.

Freya and the Golden Necklace Freya had an enormous greed for gold and jewelry of all kinds. One day she went to the cave of the black DWARFS ALFRIGG, BERLING, DVALIN, and GRERR. These master craftsmen had made a golden necklace of outstanding beauty. Freya knew at once that she would do anything to get the necklace that the dwarfs called the Brisinga men.

She offered the dwarfs gold and silver, but as Dvalin pointed out, they already had all the precious metals and gems of the underworld for the taking. Freya began to weep golden tears. At last Dvalin said they would give her the necklace if she would agree to spend a day and a night with each of the dwarfs. Freya was so overcome with greed that she gave herself to the company of the four ugly little creatures for four days and four nights. When she went back to her palace at Folkvangr, she was wearing the Brisinga men around her neck.

Now Loki, the mischief maker, had followed Freya to SVARTALFHEIM, the home of the dwarfs, and had seen everything that had happened. He ran to tell ODIN. Odin was furious when he heard the story. He asked Loki to take the necklace from Freya and bring it to him.

Loki had a hard time getting into Freya's sleeping chamber at Sessrumnir, her palace, for all the doors and windows were tightly shut. At last the SHAPE-SHIFTER turned himself into a small fly and entered the room through a hole as small as a needle's eye. Loki saw that Freya was wearing the necklace around her neck, with the clasp underneath her so he could not reach it. Never at a loss, Loki turned himself into a flea and bit the goddess on her cheek. She turned restlessly in her sleep and exposed the clasp. Quickly Loki turned back into his own shape, removed the necklace, unlocked the door, and crept out.

When Freya discovered her loss, she ran to Odin and told her story, weeping bitterly. Cold with anger at Freya's tale of greed and lust, Odin said he would retrieve the jewel for her only if she would agree to stir up a terrible war between two powerful chieftains on Earth. He demanded killing and bloodshed. Afterward Freya should bring the slain heroes back to life. Freya willingly agreed to the terms, for like Odin, she had the gift of sorcery and a lust for battle and heroes. Then Odin sent for HEIMDALL, the WATCHMAN OF THE GODS, and told him to go after Loki and bring back Freya's trinket.

Loki turned himself into a seal and swam to a rock near Singastein, but a moment later Heimdall, too, had become a seal. The two fought a fierce battle. In the end Heimdall, with the necklace in his hand, led the dripping Loki out of the water and back to Odin.

The story of the Brisinga men is from the 10th-century skaldic poem *Husdrapa* and the *SORLA THATTR*, found in the 14th-century manuscript *FLATEYJARBOK* (*Book of the Flat Island*).

FRIDAY In modern English, the sixth day of the week, or the fifth working day. Friday takes its name from FRIGG, the AESIR goddess of love and marriage and wife of ODIN. In some GERMANIC languages, the name for this day of the week comes from FREYA, principal VANIR goddess, also of love and fertility.

Both goddesses serve similar functions in NORSE mythology, and scholars propose that it is not surprising that their names are similar and that they influence place names, and even the name of the day, in a similar manner.

FRIGG (FRIGGA, FRIJA) The chief AESIR goddess; wife of ODIN; her father is FJORGYN (2). Frigg herself is called EARTH MOTHER. She is associated with love, marriage, and motherhood. Frigg is frequently pictured as being very beautiful, wearing a girdle hung with household keys, and weaving clouds on her spinning wheel. Eleven handmaidens attended her in her hall, FENSALIR. Frigg was the mother of BALDER, and, according to some sources, she was also the mother of THOR, the thunder god, and of HODUR, the blind god who unwittingly killed Balder.

Because of the fragmentary nature of the NORSE EDDAS and SAGAS, there are conflicting views of Frigg. Besides her portrayal as a devoted wife and mother, Frigg also appears as a sorceress who wears a FALCON skin and sees into the future and as a wanton woman who covets gold and jewelry and the love of men. She and the goddess FREYA have a lot in common. Some believe they are various facets of the same deity.

FULLA (FYLLR, FYLLA; Bountiful) One of the female goddesses, or ASYNJUR, named by 13th-century Icelandic writer SNORRI STURLUSON in his work GYLFAGINNING. Fulla wore her hair loose, with a golden band around her head. A virgin, Fulla served the goddess FRIGG by carrying her basket, tending her shoes, and keeping her secrets. Fulla was one of the three GODDESSES to whom the dead god BALDER sent gifts from HEL (2). She received a gold ring.

Some scholars believe Fulla was an ancient goddess of fertility modified over time into the smaller role of Frigg's servant.

FYLGIE (Follower) As well as the NORNS, or Fates, the NORSE ascribed to each human being a guardian spirit or double, which accompanied a person throughout his or her life. The fylgie had a human or animal shape but was invisible except in dreams or at the moment of death. When the fylgie appeared to a person who was awake, it was a sign of that person's death. When a person died, the fylgie passed on to another member of the family.

G

GALAR (Yeller) One of the two deceitful DWARFS who killed the wise man KVASIR (1) in order to make the MEAD of poetry from his blood. The other dwarf was his brother, FJALAR (2).

The brothers also killed the giant GILLING and his wife. Their son, SUTTUNG, avenged his parents' deaths by stranding Fjalar and Galar on a rock that would become flooded at high tide. To save their lives, the brothers gave the mead to Suttung.

Their story is told by SNORRI STURLUSON in *SKALSKAPARMAL*. (See also "The Mead of Poetry" under ODIN.)

GALDRAR Magic charms or spells. In NORSE mythology, *galdrar* involved RUNES, magic numbers, chants, and specialized uses of words to bring about a variety of magical events, such as healing, reviving the dead, defending against storms, and seeing into the future. The use of *galdrar* and magic was originally seen as a woman's craft. In the poem *Oddrunargratr* (*Oddrun's Lament*), a part of the *POETIC EDDA*, Oddrun chants a magical charm to help Borgny deliver twins, a boy and a girl.

The strongest form of *galdrar* was the SEID, a powerful magical chant associated with women, which allowed the user to go into a deep trance so she could see into the future and talk with spirits.

Although magic was seen as a typically female craft, ODIN was known as the father of *galdrar*. The poem *HAVAMAL* lists 17 chants that Odin knew and gave to men, not women, so that they would possess the skills they needed in life: chants for things like breaking chains, shooting arrows, starting fires, strengthening shields, and winning a fair maiden's love.

GANG One of the RIME-GIANTS, brother of THJAZZI and IDI and son of OLVALDI, who left piles of gold to be divided among his sons. The brothers, in choosing how to divide the treasure, decided that each should take as much as his mouth would hold.

Gang is mentioned in *SKALDSKAPARMAL* by poet and historian SNORRI STURLUSON. (See also "Skade and Njord" under SKADE.)

GARM The fearsome, howling hound that stood at the gates of HEL's realm, guarding the kingdom of the dead. In some stories, Garm could be quieted only by a piece of cake given to him by those who had already given bread to the poor. In *The Lay of Grimnir* (see GRIMNISMAL), Garm is described as the fiercest of all hounds. In *Balder's Dreams* (see BALDRS DRAUMAR), when ODIN went to the underworld to consult a seeress, the blood-caked hound of Hel howled at him, but Odin went on, undeterred by the hideous noise. At RAGNAROK, Garm fought with one-handed TYR, and they killed each other. Garm is sometimes thought to be another name for the WOLF FENRIR.

GEFJON (GEFION; Giver) A GODDESS of fertility, associated with the plow. In one myth told by SNORRI STURLUSON in *GYLFAGINNING*, Gefjon disguised herself as a beggar. She asked GYLFI, the king of SWEDEN, to give her some land. The king told her that she could have as much land as she could plow in a day and a night. The old woman went off to find her four sons, who were huge oxen that had been fathered by a giant. Gefjon hitched the oxen to a plow and proceeded to cut deeply into the land of Sweden. Then she and the oxen towed the land into the sea, where it is now known as the island of Zealand, part of DENMARK.

GEIRROD (1) The giant who, with the help of the trickster god LOKI, persuaded the god THOR to visit him without his famous weapons. It was a trap, but thanks to the friendly GIANTESS GRID, Thor was

The Gefjon Fountain by Anders Bundgaard (1864–1937), in Langelinie, Copenhagen *(Photo by Hans Andersen/Used under a Creative Commons license)*

able to kill Geirrod and his two ogress daughters, GIALP and GREIP.

GEIRROD (2)   Son of King HRAUDING and brother of AGNAR. Geirrod betrayed his brother and took his throne. Later he killed himself by falling upon his own sword, as ODIN, his benefactor, had prophesied in GRIMNISMAL (*Lay of Grimnir*).

Geirrod and Agnar   The two brothers, Geirrod and Agnar were the sons of King Hrauding of the Goths. When the children were eight and 10 years old, respectively, their little fishing boat was wrecked in a storm. The boys landed on an island and were taken care of by an old couple who were Odin and FRIGG in disguise. Frigg took special care of Agnar and Odin took care of Geirrod, giving them many words of advice before sending them back to their own land. As their boat approached shore, Geirrod leaped out, taking the oars with him, and shoved the boat back out to sea. Geirrod was welcomed home,

and because his father had died, he became king in place of Agnar, who was presumed dead.

Many years went by before Odin and Frigg thought about the two boys they had rescued from the sea. Then Odin boasted that his foster son, Geirrod, was king of a great country, while Frigg's Agnar was a nobody who lived in a cave. Frigg retorted that Geirrod was mean and treacherous. When Odin decided to go to MIDGARD to test Geirrod, Frigg sent her maidservant, FULLA, to warn Geirrod that he was not to trust the visitor who was coming to him, wearing a sky-blue cape.

Geirrod heeded the warning. Odin arrived wearing a sky-blue cape. He called himself GRIMNIR, but more than that he would not say. In a fit of rage at what he considered insolence, Geirrod had Grimnir slung between two fires. There he stayed for eight days and nights, without food or drink. Then Agnar, the son of Geirrod, named after his lost uncle, took pity on Odin-Grimnir and quenched his thirst with ale.

Grimnir began to chant a song that was known as *GRIMNISMAL* (*The Lay of Grimnir*). The song contained a great deal of knowledge about ASGARD, the home of the gods, and about the gods themselves and their possessions, especially about Odin and his many names. When Geirrod finally realized that his captive was Odin, he leapt up to release him, but he fell on his own sword and killed himself. Then Odin disappeared, and Geirrod's son, Agnar, became king and ruled for many peaceable years.

GELGJA   The name that 13th-century Icelandic writer SNORRI STURLUSON gave to a very strong chain used to help secure FENRIR, the giant, monstrous WOLF. After learning that Fenrir, a son of the god LOKI, would eventually help destroy them, the gods decided to chain the wolf to a huge rock and keep him captive forever. Finally, through magic, they managed to get the rope GLEIPNIR around the wolf's neck. They fastened Gleipnir to Gelgja, a shackle or chain. Some experts believe Gelgja, too, was made of magical materials. Finally, the gods fastened Gelgja to the rock GJOLL. (1).

GERDA   (GERD; Enclosed Field)   The daughter of the JOTUN GYMIR and AURBODA; the sister of BELI; the wife of FREY, whose servant SKIRNIR, wooed and won her for his master. Gerda spurned APPLES and gold but finally gave in at the terrible threat of eternal cold and loneliness, thus personifying winter giving in at last to the warm sunshine of spring. The nine nights of waiting between her consent to become Frey's bride and the actual union is symbolic of the long nine months of hard winter in northern countries before spring arrives. In some mythologies the radiance of Gerda personifies the AURORA BOREALIS (northern lights).

GERI   (Ravenous)   One of the WOLF companions of the god ODIN. The other was FREKI, whose name also means "ravenous." Odin fed the wolves all the meat that was served to him, for he needed only to drink divine MEAD for sustenance. The wolves attended him at HLIDSKJALF, his high seat, and also at VALHALLA.

GERMANIC   A term for the family of languages spoken by the peoples of northern Europe or for the peoples themselves. Historians and archaeologists point out that when referring to the people or the languages, the term Germanic does not necessarily apply to the same geography over the millennia.

The Germanic family of languages is a branch of the Indo-European languages. They likely developed in northern Europe during the first millennium B.C., though linguists and historians suggest that the original proto-German language developed in parts of Eastern Europe and western Asia before the peoples moved into northern Europe.

The languages of SCANDINAVIA, including ICELAND, developed into a group of related languages known as Northern Germanic. All of these people used a similar alphabet of RUNES in the earliest surviving writings created in the earliest centuries of the first millennium A.D.

The people of the Germanic tribes that shared a common or related language settled in northern Europe and then spread into Scandinavia and westward into the islands of the north Atlantic during the last millennium B.C. and during the rise and fall of the Roman Empire in the Mediterranean. By the MIGRATION PERIOD, which began about 400 A.D., they had developed into distinct cultures in the lands surrounding the Baltic and North seas. They shared a history but were, by the beginning of the VIKING AGE in the late 700s A.D., separate peoples.

GESTA DANORUM   A 16-volume history of the Danish people from prehistoric days to the 13th century written by SAXO GRAMMATICUS, a Danish scholar and historian. Books 10 through 16 are strictly historical, and scholars believe Saxo wrote these before writing Books 1 through 9, which record the oral myths and legends of the NORSE people, including those living in DENMARK. Saxo apparently learned these stories from well-educated and well-traveled men from ICELAND. The *Gesta Danorum* is considered a very important source of information on the legends, myths, and religions of the Scandinavians.

GIALP   (GJALP; Howler)   The daughter of the giant GEIRROD (1). Her sister was GREIP.

Gialp tried to drown the god THOR by straddling the river VIMUR and letting her bodily fluids add to the flow of the river. Thor threw a huge bolder at her in order to plug the sources of the flood. He hit her and Gialp ran off screaming.

Thor killed Gialp and Greip by breaking their backs after they tried to kill him by hiding under his chair and lifting him hard against the ceiling when he was in Geirrod's house.

These stories are told by SNORRI STURLUSON in *SKALDSAPARMAL.*

GIANT MASTER BUILDER The giant who tricked the gods into hiring him to build a new wall around ASGARD that was intended to protect the gods from the GIANTS. SNORRI STURLUSON tells the story in *GYLFAGINNING*.

The old wall had been destroyed in the war with the VANIR. This unnamed giant took the form of an ordinary builder and traveled to Asgard, his great stallion SVADILFARI pulling a wagon. He told the gods he could complete the job for them in three seasons if they paid him by giving him the SUN AND MOON and the fertility goddess, FREYA. Mischief-maker LOKI persuaded the gods to accept the offer under the condition that the builder complete the task in less than half a year. The giant accepted the new terms.

Once the builder started working, the gods discovered that he was a giant, aided by a giant stallion. They grew dismayed and fearful that they might indeed lose their goddess and the Sun and Moon in a very bad arrangement. Three days before the wall was completed, Loki, the SHAPE-SHIFTER, turned himself into a mare and lured the stallion away from the construction site, thereby spoiling the giant's plan.

GIANTS Giants play a central role in NORSE mythology, mainly as the enemy of the gods but also as the race from which the gods most likely were offspring. The different roles that giants play in the surviving stories are so confusing that some experts suggest that in Norse religious beliefs, the giants were gods themselves or perhaps the gods were giants.

The proto-giant YMIR was the first being in the cosmos, according to 13th-century writer SNORRI STURLUSON's version of the Norse CREATION myth. Details from Snorri's *PROSE EDDA* tell how Ymir evolved from the heat and cold in the beginning times, and from the parts of his body were born the HRIMTHURSSAR (RIME-GIANTS). At the same time that Ymir came into being, the first cow, AUDHUMLA, formed out of the chaos. She licked at a salt block and uncovered BURI, whose son BOR mated with BESTLA, one of the first giantesses. From these latter two, one a giant, came the first gods: ODIN, VILI, and VE. When these brothers killed Ymir, his blood caused a flood that killed all of the rime-giants but BERGILMIR, and his wife, who survived to become the ancestors of all the giants.

This shared ancestry of gods and giants has caused much curiosity among modern scholars, though no answers to the puzzle exist in surviving records. Most commonly, the giants are interpreted as representing the wild forces of nature that threatened people living in northern climates more so than those in southern lands. The giants lived in mountains and often hurled huge boulders at one another. They loved darkness and often confronted the gods at night.

GIANTESS A female giant in NORSE mythology. Defeating a giantess brings extra power and stature to the gods of the myths. Giantesses are often the love interests of the AESIR. Thor frequently does battle with giantesses, worthy foes of even this mightiest of the gods. LOKI assumes the shape of the giantess THOKK to deceive the AESIR when they seek his help in restoring BALDER to life. FREY falls in love with and woos the giantess GERDA.

HEIMDALL, the WATCHMAN OF THE GODS, has nine giantess mothers, which are the source of the strength he requires to sit by the gates of HEL (2) and protect the land of the Aesir. According to the poem *HYNDLULJOTH*, these women sat at the edge of the world and gave their son the ice of the sea for his blood. They are GIALP, GREIP, Eistla, Eyrgjafa, Ulfrum, Angeyja, Imth, Atla, and JARNSAXA.

The NAMES of giantesses occur frequently in the works in the *POETIC EDDA* as kennings, or metaphors, as mothers of the gods, and for locations and objects in nature.

GILLING A giant killed along with his wife by the DWARFS FJALAR and GALAR. After Fjalar and Galar kill the wise man KVASIR (1) and use his blood to make the MEAD of poetry, the two dwarfs invite Gilling and his wife to visit. They ambush the pair, drowning Gilling and crushing his wife's head with a millstone.

Gilling and his wife were the parents of SUTTUNG, who sought revenge for their death by threatening the dwarfs and taking the mead in exchange for their lives.

The story of the mead is told by SNORRI STURLUSON in *SKALDSAPARMAL*. (See also "The Mead of Poetry" under ODIN.)

GIMLE A mountain, or a great hall, where the next generation of NORSE gods will dwell after the destruction of the pantheon at the time of RAGNAROK.

In the *VOLUSPA*, the first poem in the *CODEX REGIUS* of the *POETIC EDDA*, Gimle is described as a mountain on which stands a hall roofed in gold where the righteous will dwell in the new world that rises out of the destruction of the old world.

In *GYLFAGINNING*, SNORRI STURLUSON adds to the story, naming Gimle as the hall itself and telling poets that it lies at the southern end of HEAVEN. Gimle is the most prominent of the halls in this world. Other new halls include NIDAFJOLL, which is made of red gold and stands in SINDRI, and Brimer, which is in Okolnir. (See "Regeneration" under Ragnarok.)

GINNUNGAGAP (Yawning Void) A great void; the nothingness at the beginning of time. In his depiction of Ginnungagap, the 13th-century poet and historian SNORRI STURLUSON draws on sources still known to scholars today, such as the *POETIC EDDA*, and contemporary sources that have not survived the passage of time in order to give a vivid picture of this aspect of the CREATION myth.

In Snorri's portrayal, Ginnungagap lies between NIFLHEIM, a place of misty ice, and MUSPELLHEIM, a place of raging fire; both are as timeless as the great void. Ginnungagap had mild, calm air, even as the rising heat of Muspellheim met the falling ice of Niflheim. Into this emptiness the VENOM from the rivers of ELIVAGAR dripped to form YMIR, the oldest of the RIME-GIANTS. From him came other GIANTS.

The gods ODIN and his brothers came from the blocks of salt licked by the cow AUDHUMLA, who also resided in Ginnungagap. They, in turn, destroyed Ymir, throwing his body parts into Ginnungagap to form the heavens and Earth and the seas and mountains. They took embers from Muspellheim and threw them into the great void to make the stars.

Linguists who study the Old Icelandic language of Snorri's writings suggest that the meaning of Ginnungagap suggests a realm of great magical power.

GJALLARHORN (Ringing Horn) The trumpet horn of the god HEIMDALL that sounded throughout the NINE WORLDS. Heimdall found the horn hidden under YGGDRASIL. He sometimes left Gjallarhorn beside MIMIR'S WELL. At RAGNAROK, the end of the world, the sound of Gjallarhorn would summon gods and men to battle.

Gjallarhorn is usually pictured as a *lur*, the ancient bronze trumpet of SCANDINAVIA, dating back to about 1000 B.C. *Lurs* were made in pairs, twisting in opposite directions so that the two held side by side looked like the horns of a large animal. Some *lurs* have been excavated from the peat bogs of DENMARK and can still be played.

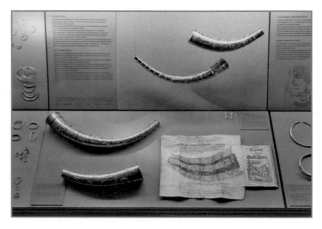

Golden horns of Gallehus in the National Museum in Copenhagen *(Photo by Jan Mehlich/Used under a Creative Commons license)*

GJALLARBRU (GIALLARBRU) The bridge that crosses the river GJOLL (2) and connects the worlds of the living with the worlds of the dead. The god HERMOD must cross the Gjallarbru to rescue the spirit of the recently deceased BALDER, son of ODIN and FRIGG.

GJOLL (1) (GJÖLL; GIOLL) The great rock that the gods found deep in the earth and to which they fastened the chain GELGJA. Gelgja was then attached to the silken strand GLEIPNER, which would eventually hold the wolf FENRIR. SNORRI STURLUSON in *GYLFAGINNING* provides the proper names for these magical binding objects.

GJOLL (2) (GIOLL) The river that divides the worlds of the living from the worlds of the afterlife. The bridge GJALLARBRU crosses this river. The god HERMOD crossed the Gjoll over Gjallarbru as he hurried to rescue the spirit of BALDER, ODIN's son, shortly after Balder's death.

GLADSHEIM Either the land in which ODIN's great hall VALHALLA was built or the most beautiful hall in the world and one of Odin's homes.

According to the poem *GRIMNISMAL*, Gladsheim is a region in ASGARD, as are THRUDHEIM, THOR's kingdom, and THRYMHEIM, THJAZZI's home.

In SNORRI STURLUSON's *GYLFAGINNING*, however, Gladsheim is a great hall built by Odin on the plains of IDAVOLL. Here Odin established the thrones, or high seats, of all the AESIR gods. Gladsheim was made from one solid piece of gold.

Scholars tend to disagree on which is more likely the correct version of Gladsheim.

GLASIR (GLASER)   A grove of trees with red-gold leaves that stood in front of VALHALLA, ODIN's hall.

While Glasir is mentioned in the *POETIC EDDA*, in *Helgakvida Hjorvardssonar* (*The Lay of Helgi the Son of Hjorvarth*), that poem does not explain its meaning. In his work *SKALDSKAPARMAL*, SNORRI STURLUSON instructs SKALDS to use the phrase "the needles of Gladsir" as a poetic substitute, or KENNING, for gold. According to him, Glasir was the fairest forest in existence and the tree with the red-gold leaves was the best among trees.

GLEIPNER   The magical rope, as smooth as a silken ribbon, made by the DWARFS to bind FENRIR, the great WOLF.

According to SNORRI STURLUSON in *GYLFAGIN-NING*, the dwarfs made Gleipnir from the noise of a cat's footfall, a woman's beard, the roots of a mountain, the sinews of a bear, the breath of a fish, and a bird's spit. Though these items add up to nothing, for none of these things exist, with their magic the dwarfs made the rope strong enough to hold the mighty wolf, son of LOKI.

Gleipner was the third and final fetter the gods used to try to bind the wolf, which they knew would finally help to destroy them. The first and second chains were LAEDING and DROMI, respectively, but Fenrir easily broke those. So the gods resorted to magic, the only force strong enough to hold the wolf.

Once Fenrir was ensnared in Gleipner, the gods fastened the silken strand to a chain called GELGJA, which they then fastened to the rock GJOLL (1). There Fenrir remained until freed at the time of RAGNAROK, the final battle between the gods and GIANTS. (See also TYR.)

GLEN   The obscure husband of SOL, a servant to the SUN and daughter of MUNDILFARI. Glen is mentioned only in SNORRI STURLUSON's *GYLFAGINNING*. According to some scholars and a careful reading of *Gylfaginning*, the marriage of Sol to Glen may have been the act that angered the gods and caused them to send Sol up to the heavens, where she drove the horses that pulled the chariot of the SUN.

GLITNIR (Glittering, Shining)   In ASGARD, the hall of FORSETI, about whom little is known. The hall had pillars of gold and a roof of silver. According to *GRIMNISMAL*, a poem in the *POETIC EDDA*, and SNORRI STURLUSON in *GYLFAGINNING*, Forseti sat in judgment in his hall, settling the disputes of all who came to Glitner.

GNA   One of the minor goddesses of the AESIR, according to 13th-century writer SNORRI STURLUSON. Gna ran errands for the goddess FRIGG, ODIN's wife. When she needed to deliver a message in a hurry, Gna rode her horse, Hofvarpnir (Hoof-Thrasher), through the air. Her Old NORSE name came to refer to very high things or something that soars high.

GNIPAHELLIR (GNIPA; Cliff Cave)   The cave that stands at the entrance to HEL (2), the land of the dead. GARM, the fierce hound that guarded the gates to Hel lived in Gnipahellir. The cave is featured in a refrain in the *VOLUSPA*, a part of the *POETIC EDDA*.

GOAT   A mammal related to the sheep family. In NORSE mythology the god THOR had a cart drawn by two billy goats, TANNGNIOST and TANNGRISNIR. These goats could be killed and eaten and then revived again the next day.

GOTHS   A GERMANIC tribe that in the third and fifth centuries invaded and settled in parts of the Roman Empire.

In the story "Geirrod and Agnar" (see under GEIRROD [2]), HRAUDING was king of the Goths. His son Geirrod succeeded him.

GOTLAND   An island in the Baltic Sea, part of SWEDEN and southeast of that nation's coast. Many archaeological finds that are important to the study of NORSE mythology are located on this large island. Most prominent are the rock carvings, runestones, that appear to portray scenes from Norse myths. They are similar to the rock carvings found throughout much of SCANDINAVIA and in GREAT BRITAIN and the FAROE ISLANDS.

In some rocks on Gotland, the background was carved away, leaving the images raised above the surface. Archaeologists believe the images were carved in the sixth century A.D. and were originally painted. One famous raised picture stone from Alskog Tjangvide shows what appears to be SLEIPNIR, ODIN's eight-legged horse. The carving has been dated to the eighth century A.D.

Gotland, Sweden, runestone depicting various mythological figures *(Photo by Mats Halldin/Used under a Creative Commons license)*

GREAT BRITAIN

Geographically, Great Britain is the largest of the islands in the British Isles, which arc to the northwest of the main European continent. Politically, Great Britain is formed by the countries of England, Scotland, and Wales and forms a part of the United Kingdom of Great Britain and Northern Ireland.

The stories of NORSE mythology came to Great Britain after 787 A.D., when VIKINGS from DENMARK and NORWAY began attacking Scotland and the northern region of England. These Viking raids would continue over the next 200 years. Following successful attacks and conquests, settlers from Norway and Denmark began to resettle portions of Great Britain, bringing their culture and religion with them, including their pagan worship of the Norse gods.

Icelandic histories written in the 11th and 12th centuries tell of Norse settlements located in the northern British Isles, including the Orkney and Shetland islands, which lie to the northeast of Great Britain. Geographical names in northern England also reveal the influence of VIKING AGE culture.

RUNESTONES found on the Isle of Man in the Irish Sea and in Gosforth, Cumbria, in northwest England, tell stories of Norse mythology and demonstrate the influence of the settlers from SCANDINAVIA. Scholars suggest that Viking culture directly influenced early English literature, particularly as seen in *Beowulf*, an Old English heroic poem set in Scandinavia that was composed sometime before the 11th century. Over time, many of the stories and beliefs of the Viking peoples came to be incorporated into the history of Great Britain and the British Isles.

GREIP (GRIP)

A GIANTESS. Greip was the daughter of the giant GEIRROD (1) and the sister of GIALP. When he visited the house of their father, the thunder god THOR killed Greip and Gialp by breaking their backs after they tried to kill him by hiding under his chair and lifting him hard against the ceiling.

This story is told by SNORRI STURLUSON in *SKALDSAPARMAL*.

GRERR

One of the four DWARFS who made the golden necklace BRISINGA MEN, which they traded in a bargain with the goddess FREYA. The dwarfs lived beneath a rock and were experts in working with all kinds of metals. Grerr's brothers were ALFRIGG, BERLING, and DVALIN (1). Their story is told in the *SORLA THATTR*, which is found in the manuscript known as *FLATEYJARBOK*.

GRID

The GIANTESS who was one of the wives of the god ODIN and the mother of their son, VIDAR. Friendly to the gods, she helped THOR by lending him her magic gloves, girdle, and staff when Thor visited the giant GEIRROD (1). Some legends say that she also made the shoe that Vidar wore at RAGNAROK to kill the wolf FENRIR.

GRIMNIR (Hooded One)

One of the god ODIN's many names. When he went to MIDGARD to visit his foster son, GEIRROD (2), Odin wore a sky-blue hooded cape. Odin chanted the *GRIMNISMAL* (*The Lay of Grimnir*), while he was held captive at the hall of Geirrod.

GRIMNISMAL (*The Lay of Grimnir*)

GRIMNIR, who was the god ODIN in disguise, was captured by GEIRROD (2) and tied between two fires. Geirrod's son, AGNAR, quenched Grimnir's thirst with horns of ale, and Odin rewarded him by singing this lay.

Grimnir's song told of the halls of the gods in their realm, ASGARD, including YDALIR, GLADSHEIM, and especially VALHALLA, with details about the hall itself and the cook, BOAR, and sooty CAULDRON in which the boar was cooked to feed the slain heroes of Valhalla. It also told of Odin's animal companions, the WOLF and the RAVEN, and of VALGRIND, Valhalla's outer gate, through which 800 warriors could march side by side.

The song continues about Valhalla and then names all the rivers of the HVERGELMIR. The song explains how the gods gallop over BILROST, the RAINBOW BRIDGE, to meet the council at the well URDARBRUNN. It also tells of the World Tree, YGG-DRASIL, and of those who prey upon it. It mentions the names of the VALKYRIES who wait upon the dead heroes of Valhalla.

Other features of the song include the names of the horses that draw the chariots of the SUN AND MOON, the terrible wolves that chased the chariots, the giant YMIR and how his flesh and bones and hair created EARTH (see CREATION), and TREASURES OF THE DWARFS. And finally the captive Grimnir tells of the many names of Odin. It is then that Geirrod realizes that his prisoner is the great god Odin himself. Geir-rod rises up to release his prisoner but falls upon his own sword and kills himself.

Grimnismal was a mnemonic poem (a sort of memory bank) for storytellers, poets, and minstrels who passed on information about myths, legends, and folktales to people from one generation to another and in different communities all over SCANDINAVIA. *Grimnismal* is part of the *CODEX REGIUS* of the *POETIC EDDA*, a 13th-century manuscript, and the *ARNAMAH-NAEAN CODEX*. It was an important source for SNORRI STURLUSON in his *PROSE EDDA*.

GRJOTUNAGARD (GRIOTUNAGARD; Place of Stones, Stone Fence)

The location in JOTUNHEIM where the duel between the god THOR and the giant HRUNGNIR took place.

Fearing the might of Thor, before the duel Hrungnir had his servants build a decoy of himself, a clay monster they named MOKKURKALFI. But Thor's servant THJALFI easily defeated the decoy. Thor then killed Hrungnir but received a great injury when a piece of the WHETSTONE the giant had hurled at the god lodged in Thor's head.

SNORRI STURLUSON tells the full story of Hrungnir in *SKALDSAPARMAL*, wherein he quotes at length the work of skaldic poet Thjodolfr (þjoðolfr) of Hvin, creator of the poem *Haustlong.*

GROA

The wife of AURVANDIL the Brave and mother of SVIPDAG, who visited her for advice in NIFLHEIM after her death in the poem *SVIPDAGSMAL*, part of the *POETIC EDDA*. In another story, Groa uses her magic spells to cure THOR's headache but fails to remove the WHETSTONE fragments from his skull.

GROTTASONG (*The Lay of Grotti*)

An Icelandic poem that blends mythology and HEROIC LEGEND to tell a parable about greed. *Grottasong* survives as a poem in SNORRI STURLUSON's *SKALDSAPARMAL*.

The poem tells of FENJA AND MENJA, two very strong women bought as slaves by Frodi, the king of DENMARK. Frodi made the mistake of judging the women only by their strength and appearance when he bought them, failing to learn of their family history. They are actually the daughters of HRUNGNIR, strongest of the GIANTS, and granddaughters of THJAZZI, a powerful storm giant. The two GIANTESSES also have the gift of being able to see into the future.

Grotti is a very large flour mill, too large for any normal human to operate, so Frodi forces the giant-esses to perform the task. He commands them to grind out gold, peace, and prosperity. When greed for more of these items finally causes Frodi to force the giantesses to grind without rest, they sing a charm on the mill, causing it to generate an army that attacks and conquers the Danish king.

GULLFAXI (Golden Mane)

The giant HRUNGNIR's powerful stallion that was defeated in a race by the god ODIN on his steed, eight-legged SLEIPNIR. Gullfaxi was then given to MAGNI, a son of the god THOR. The story is told in SNORRI STURLUSON's *SKALDSKADARMAL*.

GULLINBURSTI (Golden Bristles)

The golden BOAR made by the DWARFS BROKK and EITI from a pigskin and thousands of pieces of gold wire and given to the god FREY. Frey could ride on the boar or hitch his wagon to it, and Gullinbursti would speed across the EARTH, sky, or sea faster than any horse. Its golden rays shone like the SUN and made plants grow everywhere. With its tusks, Gullinbursti raked the earth and showed men how to plow the land.

Warriors wore the image of Frey's golden boar on helmets and shields as protection and good luck. Archaeologists found a seventh-century helmet topped by a boar in Benty Grange, in Derbyshire, England.

GULLINKAMBI (Golden Comb) The golden cock, or rooster, that crowed to summon the gods and heroes of VALHALLA to the battle at RAGNAROK, the conflict that would end the world of the gods. Gullinkambi's counterpart, FJALAR (1), summoned the GIANTS to the battle. An unnamed rust-red rooster summoned those who dwelt in HEL.

Gullinkambi is named in the Eddic poem *VOLUSPA*.

GULLTOPP (Golden Tuft, Gold Top) One of the 10 horses the AESIR gods rode each day to YGGDRASIL, the World Tree, which grew at the center of the universe. The gods came here on horseback each day to sit in judgment at the spring, or well, named

Odin and his spear, Gungnir. Sculpture by Lee Lawrie on the east entrance of the Library of Congress John Adams Building, Washington, D.C. *(Library of Congress)*

URDARBRUNN. Gulltopp is the only horse to be named in the poems that tell of this journey. According to SNORRI STURLUSON, Gulltopp belongs to HEIMDALL, the god of light and guardian of the gods.

GULLWEIG (GULLVEIG; Power of Gold) The beautiful witch who came to ASGARD and was probably the cause of the AESIR/VANIR WAR. The AESIR burned her three times, but she rose up each time to cause trouble among the gods. Also called HEID (Shining One), Gullweig is thought by most scholars to be an aspect of the VANIR goddess FREYA, who also loved gold and had magical powers.

GUNGNIR ODIN's magic spear, made by the DWARF sons of Ivaldi. Gungnir never missed its mark. It was a symbol of Odin as the god of war. Odin flung his spear at the VANIR gods in the AESIR/VANIR WAR. NORSE warriors threw their spears at the start of a battle to invoke Odin's protection in war.

See "Treasures of the Dwarfs" under LOKI.

GUNLOD (GUNNLOD) Daughter of the giant SUTTUNG, who commanded Gunlod to guard the MEAD of poetry, made from the blood of KVASIR. She became a wife of ODIN when he visited the cave on HNITBJORG Mountain to steal the mead. She bore Odin a child, BRAGI, who went to ASGARD and became the god of poetry and the husband of IDUNN.

GYLFAGINNING (*The Deceiving, or Beguiling, of Gylfi*) One of four main parts of the *PROSE EDDA* written by the 13th-century Icelandic historian, scholar, and chief SNORRI STURLUSON. Some scholars argue that *Gylfaginning* is Snorri's most important work.

The main character, GYLFI, a king of SWEDEN, disguises himself as an old wayfarer when he comes across a magnificent hall. In the hall sit three beings on high chairs. A servant invites Gylfi to stay and talk with the three beings. He sits and begins asking questions of the beings, who, Snorri tells the readers, are actually gods, calling themselves High One, Just-As-High, and Third. Snorri uses the question-and-answer session to teach his readers about the beginnings of all existence, the gods and goddesses, and the end of time.

Snorri draws heavily on the works in the older *POETIC EDDA*, most notably the *VOLUSPA* (or *The Sibyl's Vision*, as Snorri calls it) and *GRIMNISMAL* (*Lay of Grimnir*), to present this account of many NORSE myths.

GYLFI Both a legendary king of SWEDEN and a wise man skilled in magic. Gylfi is named by SNORRI STURLUSON in his great work *GYLFAGINNING*, which means *The Beguiling of Gylfi*.

In the first chapter of this work, Gylfi makes a bargain with the goddess GEFJON: He will give her as much land in Sweden as she can plow in a day. She brings her four sons, giant oxen from JOTUNHEIM, and plows out the island of Zealand.

In the second chapter, Gylfi begins a wandering journey that leads him to ASGARD, the home of the gods, where, disguising himself and using the name Gangleri, he meets three beings called Har (High One), Jaffnhar (Just-As-High), and Thridi (Third). He questions them about the creation of Asgard, the doings of the gods and goddesses, and the end of the world. The three figures answer his questions at length. At the end of the exchange, the great hall and the three speakers vanish and Gylfi is left standing on a wide plain.

Gylfi is the same king of Sweden who, in the *Prologue* to the *PROSE EDDA*, welcomes the men from Asia, led by the great warrior ODIN, who wish to settle in the northland. Gylfi gives Odin all of the land in Sweden that he wants, and Odin then becomes king of Sweden.

GYMIR (1) A JOTUN, or giant, who had a great house in JOTUNHEIM surrounded by dogs. He is the father of the beautiful GIANTESS GERDA, as described in the poem *SKIRNISMAL*, and of her brother, BELI. The poem *HYNDLULJOTH* claims that Gymir was the husband of AURBODA, while SNORRI STURLUSON adds that Gymir was a mountain giant.

GYMIR (2) Another name for the SEA god AEGIR. The prose introduction to the poem *LOKASENNA* says that Gymir is Aegir. SKALDS also used the two names in their poems, according to SNORRI STURLUSON in *SKALDSAPARMAL*, the work in which he explains to students the many KENNINGS, or poetic metaphors, of NORSE poetry.

H

HARBARD (Gray Beard)   One of the god ODIN's many names.

In the *HARBARDSLJOTH*, or *Lay of Harbard*, Harbard is a ferryman with one eye, a big hat, and a cape. He arrogantly refuses to take THOR, who does not recognize him as Odin, across the water on his ferry. The two fling insults and taunts at each other, and in the end Thor has to find another way across. The *Lay of Harbard* appears in the *CODEX REGIUS* and a part of it is in the *ARNAMAGNEAN CODEX*. Both of these works contain parts of the *POETIC EDDA*.

HARBARDSLJOTH (HARBARTHSLJOD; *The Lay of Harbarth*)   A poem in the *POETIC EDDA*. *Harbardsljoth* is the tale of a comical contest between THOR and ODIN, who has disguised himself and goes by the name HARBARD, a ferryman. The contest is a farce, featuring humorous jousting between the two gods.

Harbardsljoth was first written down late in the 11th century, though translators suggest it had a much older history as an oral poem. Copies survive in the *CODEX REGIUS* and the *ARNAMAGNAEAN CODEX*.

HATI HRODUITTNISSON   One of the names given to the terrible WOLF that pursued the chariot of the Moon across the heavens and devoured it at RAGNAROK, the end of the world (see "Sun and Moon," under CREATION). This wolf is also known as MANAGARM. The 13th-century Icelandic historian SNORRI STURLUSON wrote that Hati is the son of Hrodvitnisson. Both names mean "famous wolf," which has led some experts to suggest that Hati, or Managarm, is the offspring of FENRIR, the monster wolf, himself son of the god LOKI. The existing manuscripts of the NORSE myths are unclear on the exact name of the wolf that chases the MOON.

See also SKOLL.

HAUSTLONG   A poem by Thiodor of Hvini, a ninth- or 10th-century Norwegian poet. It describes pictures painted on a shield and thus is called a SKALDIC POEM, or shield poem.

The surviving 20 verses of *Haustlong* are preserved in SNORRI STURLUSON's *PROSE EDDA*. Thirteen of the verses tell the myth of IDUNN and THJAZZI; seven describe THOR's duel with HRUNGNIR. Both stories portray gods carrying out bold exploits against the GIANTS of JOTUNHEIM.

HAVAMAL (*Words of the High One*)   A poem, part of the *POETIC EDDA* found only in the *CODEX REGIUS*. *Havamal* contains many proverbs and advice on good living from the High One, who is the god ODIN. Some of it is addressed to the mortal LODDFAFNIR. *Havamal* also contains the lament of Odin for BILLING's DAUGHTER and the story of how Odin obtained the MEAD of poetry.

HAWK   The hawk, a bird of prey, was often kept by royalty for hunting. In NORSE mythology, hawks are employed as servants of the gods, acting as sharp-eyed informants and symbols of death. In the HEROIC LEGENDS they often precede their masters' arrival at home and signal the family of the nobleman's return from war.

ODIN and FREYA are both known to take the form of a hawk in order to fly out into the world and gain information on the happenings in their realms. In the *HERVARAR SAGA*, Odin shape-shifts into a hawk in order to escape King Heidrek after he defeats the king at a riddle contest. In anger Heidrek hacks at Odin with the great SWORD Tyrfing and cuts off part of Odin's tail. That is why the hawk has a stubby tail, according to Norse mythology.

Another hawk mentioned in the myths is VEDRFOLNIR, which means "storm-pale." According to SNORRI STURLUSON in *GYLFAGINNING*, he sits between the eyes of the EAGLE that sits in the limbs of the world tree YGGDRASIL. Habrok is the best of hawks, according to *GRIMNISMAL*.

HEAVEN

In NORSE mythology, the place above everything else, even above the realm of the gods. Heaven is also known as the sky above the Earth, the place where the SUN and MOON have reign, or the place opposite of the earth: heavenly as opposed to earthly.

The word *hymin* or *himin* in Old Norse means "Heaven," as in HIMINBJORG, which was the dwelling of HEIMDALL and means "cliffs of Heaven." Himinbjorg stood at Heaven's edge according to SNORRI STURLUSON.

Himinvanger, which means "Heaven's field," was an imaginary place, according to the *POETIC EDDA*. The name of one of the daughters of the sea god AEGIR, Himinglaefa, means "transparent," or "that through which one can see Heaven," and refers to looking up through the water.

HEID (GLEAMING ONE; Wise One)

A name often used for a wise woman or seeress. In *VOLUSPA*,

The goat Heidrun. From the 18th-century Icelandic manuscript SÁM 66, in the care of the Árni Magnússon Institute in Iceland.

the first work in the *CODEX REGIUS* of the *POETIC EDDA*, the witch GULLWEIG, who was perhaps a VANIR goddess, is called Heid.

Heid is also the name given by the NORSE people to the women who visit people's homes to perform magic. It occurs frequently in the sagas of ICELAND used in this way. Some scholars suggest Heid may also mean witch.

HEIDRUN (HEIÐRUN; HEITHRUN)

The goat who nibbled the leaves of LAERAD, the tree of VALHALLA. From her udders came an unending flow of mead. Heidrun is included in the list of the creatures of the world of the gods presented in the poem *GRIMINISMAL*.

SNORRI STURLUSON adds to Heidrun's story in *GYLFAGINNING*, explaining that her mead nourishes the fallen human heroes who fight every day in Valhalla and who are fed on the meat from the magical boar SAEHRIMNIR.

HEIMDALL

An AESIR god, known as the WATCHMAN OF THE GODS. Heimdall was mysteriously born of nine mothers and the god ODIN. Heimdall was tall and handsome, with a dazzling smile. He was sometimes called the god of light, the shining god, or the white god. Traveling under the name RIG, Heimdall conceived three sons, the ancestors of the three classes of human society.

Heimdall had a wonderful horn called GJALLARHORN, whose blast could be heard all over the NINE WORLDS. Heimdall blew Gjallarhorn at RAGNAROK, the end of the world. His horse was GULLTOP (Golden Tuft), and his sword was Hofund. He lived in a fortress-like hall called HIMINBJORG (Cliffs of Heaven).

Heimdall had amazing abilities. His eyesight was so sharp that he could see for 100 miles all around him. Some said he could see even farther or that he had "second sight" that allowed him to see into the future. It is certain that he saw all the comings and goings of those who crossed BILROST, the RAINBOW BRIDGE that led from ASGARD, the home of the gods, to MIDGARD (Middle Earth).

Heimdall spotted sly LOKI from afar, after the trickster god had stolen FREYA's necklace and escaped with it into the sea, where he changed himself into a sleek seal. Heimdall, too, was able to change his shape. He dived, seal-like, into the water, barking and nipping. Heimdall vanquished Loki and took the necklace back to Freya. He and Loki were enemies from then on and in the end would kill each other at RAGNAROK.

Heimdall with Gjallarhorn. From the 18th-century Icelandic manuscript SÁM 66, in the care of the Árni Magnússon Institute of Iceland

Heimdall was clever, too. He had the brilliant idea of sending the thunder god, THOR, to JOTUNHEIM dressed as a girl in bridal dress in order to get back Thor's magic hammer from the giant THRYM, who had stolen it.

Heimdall's hearing was so acute and finely tuned that he could hear the grass pushing up from under the earth and the wool growing on a sheep's back. Heimdall needed so little sleep that it seemed he was always awake and alert.

Heimdall's Nine Mothers One obscure and fragmented myth, related in the *HYNDLULJOTH* of the *POETIC EDDA*, told the following story about the origins of Heimdall, the watchman of the bridge Bilrost.

One day when the great god Odin walked along the seashore, he came across nine beautiful giantesses, sound asleep on the sand. They were the wave maidens, daughters of the sea god, AEGIR. Their names were Alta (Fury), Augeia (Sand Strewer), Aurgiafa (Sorrow-Whelmer), Egia (Foamer), GIALP (Howler), GREIP (Gripper), JARNSAXA (Ironstone), Sindur (Dusk), and Ulfrum (She-Wolf). Odin was so enchanted with their beauty that he married all nine of them, and together the nine giantesses brought

forth a beautiful son named Heimdall. (Snorri Sturluson provides a different list of names for Aegir's daughters in his *SKALDSKAPARMAL*, but scholars have not been able to explain the differences in the two lists as they have survived in existing manuscripts.)

The nine mothers nurtured their son on the strength of the earth, the moisture of the sea, and the heat of the Sun. The new god thrived so well on this diet that he was soon tall enough and strong enough to hasten to ASGARD, the home of the gods.

There the gods endowed Heimdall with marvelously keen senses and named him guardian of the Rainbow Bridge.

HEIMSKRINGLA (*The Orb of the Earth*) A compilation of sagas intended to be read as history, compiled by Icelandic leader, historian, and writer SNORRI STURLUSON and probably written between 1223 and 1235 A.D.

In *Hemiskringla*, Snorri set out to create a history of the kings of Norway by compiling many sagas and tales. According to his preface to the work, Snorri relied heavily on the poems of skalds for the information he passes on. These skaldic poems were stories and poems passed by word of mouth from generation to generation and were part of the oral tradition that preceded written manuscripts. An individual poet composed the poems, but many people retold them over time, giving credit to the SKALD as they did so.

Heimskringla begins with *Ynglinga Saga*, which is the story of the Ynglingar, the kings of SWEDEN who were believed to be descendents of the gods, specifically of FREY, who was known in these legends as a son of ODIN. After a brief geographical introduction, Snorri begins this first saga by telling of the life of Odin, a great human warrior. Snorri's version of Odin in *Heimskringla*, is a brave, successful, revered, and even feared leader, but not a god. Here Snorri is trying to show how people turned Odin into a god through their stories, or mythologized him.

According to Snorri, Odin traveled out of Asia and eventually arrived in the northland, founding a kingdom there to leave to his sons. Throughout the rest of the *Heimskringla*, Snorri includes details from mythology. He tells of Odin's preserving MIMIR's (2) severed head so that it can speak prophecies, of Odin's magical feats, of his prophecies, and even of the two ravens that flew out from him each day and brought back to him the news of the land. This is much the same story that Snorri presents in his prologue to *GYLFAGINNING*, his great retelling of NORSE mythology.

HEL (1)

HEL (1) (HELA) The goddess of death and the underworld. Hel was the daughter of the god LOKI and the ogress ANGRBODA. Her brothers were FENRIR, the wolf, and JORMUNGAND, the MIDGARD SERPENT.

According to SNORRI STURLUSON, Hel was terrible to look at, for one-half of her was greenish black and the other a livid white, with flesh that seemed to be rotting like that of a corpse, and her face was gloomy, grim, and sinister.

The great god ODIN cast Hel down to NIFLHEIM, the realm of cold, darkness, and death located under one of the roots of YGGDRASIL. He ordered her to look after all the wicked and miserable souls who had died of sickness, corruption, and old age. (Dead heroes went to Odin's hall VALHALLA or to FRIGG's hall SESSRUMNIR.) Hel's palace was called ELJUDNIR, and here she entertained the dead in a grisly kind of way: Her table was called Hunger; her knife, Starvation; her bed, Sickness; and the curtains around it, Misfortune.

It was said that in times of famine and plague, Hel left her ghastly realm to roam the Earth on her three-legged white horse and to rake up the survivors and sweep them with her broom down to Niflheim.

Although the gods looked upon her with loathing, Hel had more power than Odin. Once someone was in her power, no one, not even Odin, could reclaim that soul unless Hel gave her permission. In the story of BALDER, who was killed and went to Niflheim, Hel refused to give him up, even though Odin and FRIGG sent the god HERMOD to plead and bargain with her.

While Hel is mentioned in the *POETIC EDDA*, most of the details are found in SNORRI STURLUSON's *PROSE EDDA*.

HEL (2)

HEL (2) The world of the dead, a place above NIFLHEIM, the lowest level of the NINE WORLDS connected by the tree YGGDRASIL.

The *PROSE EDDA* and other NORSE manuscripts often refer to Hel as a place to which and out of which gods and GIANTS travel. Some scholars suggest that Hel is an older word for Niflheim and that the word was used first for this place and then for the name of the daughter of LOKI, also known as HEL (1), who came to rule over the place.

HELBINDI

HELBINDI ODIN claims the name Helbindi in the poem *GRIMNISMAL* as one he occasionally uses when he travels in disguise. It is one of the 31 names Odin lists as using in that poem. However, in *GYLFAGINNING*, SNORRI STURLUSON says that the god Loki had two brothers, BYLEIST and Helbindi. No more is known of Helbindi in either use.

HERMOD

HERMOD (HERMOÐ) A son of ODIN. Hermod was bold and brave. It was he who volunteered to go to HEL's underworld and beg her to release his dead brother, BALDER.

Hermod rode off on the great eight-legged horse, SLEIPNIR, passed the test of the maiden guarding the bridge over the river GJOLL, leaped over the gates of HEL (2), and confronted the goddess of the underworld herself. He received from her only the promise that she would release Balder if everyone in all of creation would weep for the fallen god.

This story is told by SNORRI STURLUSON in his *PROSE EDDA*, although Hermod is also named in various poems in the *POETIC EDDA* and in the heroic lays, confusing his identity in some of those tales.

Hermod also stood at Odin's side at the gates of VALHALLA to welcome the dead human heroes brought there from battle by the VALKYRIES.

HEROIC LEGENDS

HEROIC LEGENDS Stories of famous humans that may be based upon actual events but have taken on dramatic features, often involving aspects of mythology and folklore. The NORSE gods are minor characters in the legends. Magic is an important force, and supernatural events occur frequently. Furthermore, humans, not gods, are the central characters of heroic legends and heroic poetry.

Scholars have divided the existing Icelandic manuscripts into several categories. The category of mythological poetry and prose contains the surviving information of the Norse gods, their realms, and their relations with the human world.

Many Icelandic manuscripts contain heroic poems and heroic legends based on the stories that were told about people who probably actually existed. This is another category of works in the manuscripts.

Many of these legends are contained in the SKALDIC POETRY and in the surviving sagas from ICELAND, such as the *HERVARAR SAGA*, which tells of the influence of the great SWORD Tyrfing and the heroes who owned it. The most famous among the heroic legends is the *VOLSUNGA SAGA*, which tells the story of the children of King Volsung, his son, SIGURTH, and his grandson SIGMUND. While humans form the center of these stories, ODIN, DWARFS, VALKYRIE, and other magical creatures and events influence their lives.

The second part of the *CODEX REGIUS* of the *POETIC EDDA* contains 21 poems that most experts consider to be heroic rather than mythical, such as

The First Lay of Helgi Hundingsbane or the two lays involving Atli, which forms the source of the later portion of the *Volsunga Saga*. However, most of these poems, and other heroic poems not in the *Codex Regius*, still relegate the gods to supporting roles.

HERVARAR SAGA (*The Saga of Hervor and King Heidrek*) One of the great NORSE sagas. *Hervarar Saga* tells the story of the SWORD Tyrfing, from the curse at its creation to the final fulfillment of that curse generations later on the battlefields of northern Europe. Two DWARFS, DVALIN (2) and DURINN (2), captured by a human king and forced to forge a sword for him, cursed the weapon as they made it, saying it would kill every time it was unsheathed and specifically that it would kill three of the king's kinsmen.

The sword features most prominently in the life of ANGANTYR (1), the grandson of the king who ordered its creation; in the life of his daughter, Hervor, a warrior maiden; and in the life of ANGANTYR (2), Hervor's descendent and son of King Heidrek.

The saga blends aspects of Norse mythology in its telling, particularly in the role that the curse of the sword plays in the flow of history. In addition to the part of the dwarfs, the saga contains a SEID ritual performed to retrieve the sword from the dead and a long riddle session between King Heidrek and the god ODIN.

HILDISVINI (Battle Boar) The goddess FREYA's BOAR. His golden bristles showed the way in the dark. He was created for Freya by the dwarfs DAIN (1) and NABBI. Freya's human lover, OTTAR, took the form of Hildisvini to visit, with Freya, the giantess HYNDLA in the poem *HYNDLULJOTH*.

HIMINBJORG (Cliffs of Heaven, Heaven Mountain) The eighth great hall, or palace, in ASGARD, kingdom of the AESIR gods. Himinbjorg is the home of the god HEIMDALL. The palace stands near BILROST, the bridge between HEAVEN and Earth. From his vantage point overlooking this passage between the three worlds of the universe, Heimdall carries out his duty to watch over the lives of the other gods.

HIMINBRJOT (Heaven Bellowing) The giant black ox killed by THOR, who then used the ox's head as bait to catch JORMUNGAND, the MIDGARD SERPENT. SNORRI STURLUSON mentions Himinbrjot in *GYLFAGINNING* as one of the herd kept by the giant HYMIR.

HJADNINGAVIG (*Battle of the Followers of Hedin*) A story of endless battle preserved in three separate sources: a SKALDIC POEM written in the ninth century by Bragi Boddason, the 13th-century works of Icelandic writer SNORRI STURLUSON, and most fully in the late 14th-century SAGA *SORLA THATTR*.

Through the magic of the goddess FREYA or an unknown witch, the armies of two kings, Hogni and Hedin Hjarrandason, engage in a battle that goes on day after day for 143 years. The war begins after Hedin abducts Hild, Hogni's beautiful daughter. Hedin is about to return the woman but is too late, for Hogni has already drawn the dread sword, DAINSLEIF, which must kill a man before it can be returned to its sheath. Each day the warriors fight. At night, the magic restores even the most severely injured, those who would normally die in a battle that was not bewitched.

According to some sources, the end of this tedious battle comes at RAGNAROK, the final war between the GIANTS and the gods at the end of time. Others say it ends with the arrival of King Olaf I Tryggvason, who ruled NORWAY from A.D. 995 to 1001 and forced the conversion of many people to Christianity. Modern scholars see parallels or opposites between the horror described in this battle and the glorious life of the EINHERJAR, the souls of HUMAN warriors in VALHALLA.

HLESEY The island under which the sea giant, AEGIR, and his wife, RAN, lived in their coral cave. Experts believe the actual site of Hlesey may be the island of Laeso, in the Kattegat (cat's throat), a strait between the islands of Jutland and Zealand in DENMARK.

HLIDSKJALF (LIDSKIALF; High Seat) ODIN's throne in the high tower of his palace, VALASKJALF, in ASGARD, the home of the gods. From here Odin could see all that occurred in the NINE WORLDS. He had his RAVENS, HUGIN and MUNIN, to help him and the wolves GERI and FREKI to keep him company. No one but Odin was allowed to sit on Hlidskjalf with the exception of his wife, FRIGG. The god FREY, though, once disobeyed the rules. From the high perch he spotted the JOTUN maid GERDA and fell in love with her.

HLIN (Protectress) One of the minor goddesses of the AESIR, according to 13th-century Icelandic historian SNORRI STURLUSON. FRIGG assigned Hlin the job of protecting from danger anyone Frigg chose. The name Hlin appears often in the poem *VOLUSPA*, but her character remains unclear to modern scholars.

HNITBJORG The mountain stronghold where the giant SUTTUNG hid the MEAD of poetry, which he stole from the DWARFS FJALAR and GALAR. Odin used the carpenter's auger, RATI, to drill through the mountain and shape-shifted into a SERPENT in order to slither through the hole.

Although this story is told in the poem *HAVAMAL*, SNORRI STURLUSON mentions the name Hnitbjorg for the mountain in *SKALDSKAPARMAL*. Snorri also says that the KENNING "Liquor of Hnitbjorg" refers to the gift of poetry people receive when they drink the mead protected by the mountain.

HNOSSA (NOSSA) The daughter of the GODDESS FREYA and OD. Her name means "jewel." SNORRI STURLUSON wrote that she was so beautiful that her name could be given to anything that is precious or lovely.

HODDMIMIR'S WOOD Another name for the sacred tree YGGDRASIL, used in *VAFTHRUDNISMAL* (*Lay of Vafthrudnir*). It was from Hoddmimir's Wood that the two humans LIF and LIFTHRASIR emerged at the end of the world, after RAGNAROK.

HODUR (HOD) The blind god. His father was ODIN; his mother, FRIGG; and his brother, BALDER. Hodur unwittingly killed Balder with the help of the trickster god LOKI and a sprig of MISTLETOE. Hodur in turn was killed by VALI, the avenger, another son of Odin. After RAGNAROK (the end of the world), Hodur and Balder were reconciled and together returned from HEL's underworld to the new world.

HOENIR (HONIR) The god of silence. He was one of the three original AESIR gods who, along with his brothers ODIN and LOTHUR, created the world according to the Eddic poem *VOLUSPA*. (See CREATION.) In his *PROSE EDDA*, SNORRI STURLUSON calls Hoenir VILI and Lothur VE.

After the AESIR/VANIR WAR, Hoenir went to live with the VANIR as part of an exchange of gods. With him went the wise MIMIR (2). The Vanir gods became angry when Hoenir appeared to be indecisive and not quick-witted, always relying on Mimir to make decisions. Because Hoenir was Odin's brother, the Vanir did not harm him but instead killed Mimir and sent his head back to Odin.

Hoenir is associated with Odin and LOKI in the stories "Idunn's Apples" (see under IDUNN) and

Hodur in the act of killing Balder with a sprig of mistletoe. From the 18th-century Icelandic manuscript SÁM 66, in the care of the Árni Magnússon Institute in Iceland

"Otr's Ransom" (see under OTR), when he accompanied the two gods on journeys to Earth.

Hoenir survived RAGNAROK, the end of the world. Not much is known about this silent god.

HORSE The horse plays an important role as a helper in NORSE mythology, but archaeological and historical evidence suggests that the ancient people of SCANDINAVIA also worshipped the horse as a divine creature.

The GERMANIC tribes that were the ancestors of the Norse regarded horses as mouthpieces of the gods and tried to learn about the future from their snorts and neighs. Evidence from the MIGRATION PERIOD and the VIKING AGE suggests that the people of the north sacrificed large numbers of horses and even made horses fight one another as a way of determining which one to sacrifice. People also saw a link between horses and fertility.

Horses provided a medium for the gods to travel between the lands of the living and the dead and carried the gods and GIANTS on their journeys.

Famous horses in Norse mythology include SLEIPNIR, ODIN's eight-legged horse; SVADILFARI, the horse of the GIANT MASTER BUILDER and the sire of Sleipnir; and GULLTOPP, the horse HEIMDALL rode to warn the gods of the coming of RAGNAROK.

The poems of the *POETIC EDDA* and the *PROSE EDDA* of SNORRI STURLUSON contain many NAMES of horses.

- *GRIMNISMAL* names the following horses, which the gods ride to YGGDRASIL each day: Falhofnir, Gisl, Gler, Glad, Gulltopp, Gyllir, Lettfeti, Skeidbrimir, Silfrintopp, and Sinir.
- *SKALDSKAPARMAL* includes names of horses that were used by earlier poets. The list begins with: Goti, Gulltop, Hrafn, Lettfeti, Lungr, Marr, Mor, Sleipnir, Soti, Tjaldari, and Valr. This list goes on to name 44 more horses.

HRAESVELG (HRÆSVELG) The creator of the winds, a giant who takes the form of an EAGLE and sits at the northern end of HEAVEN. When Hraesvelg flaps his wings to take flight the movement of the air beneath those wings is so strong it blows the winds into the world of man. Hraesvelg receives credit for this feat in *VAFTHRUDNISMAL*, a poem in the *POETIC EDDA*. SNORRI STURLUSON adds further details when he tells the story of Hraesvelg in *GRIMNISMAL*.

HRAFNAGALDUR ODINS (*Odin's Raven Chant*) An Old NORSE poem that was once considered part of the *POETIC EDDA* but has long been left out of editions and translations of those poems. *Hrafnagaldur Odins* is preserved in several 17th-century manuscripts now in the royal libraries in Stockholm, NORWAY, and Copenhagen, DENMARK. Since the late 1800s, when an expert declared it to be a forgery, *Hrafnagaldur Odins* has received little scholarly attention. Research by Old Norse experts working in the late 20th and early 21st centuries, however, has contradicted that much older opinion. Some modern experts now include this poem as part of the *Poetic Edda*.

Hrafnagaldur Odins is proving to be a confusing poem for scholars to interpret and understand. Essentially, it tells the story of the gods' visit to the underworld and their questioning of a goddess who dwells there.

HREIDMAR (REIDMAR) A master magician. A DWARF, for his sons REGIN, FAFNIR, and OTR are identified as dwarfs. His daughters were LOFNHEID

and LYNGHEID. Otr was killed by the trickster god LOKI. As compensation for his son's death, Hreidmar was given the DWARF ANDVARI's treasure of gold. Hreidmar was killed by Fafnir, who stole the treasure and turned himself into a dragon. The story is told in the poems *REGINSMAL* and *FAFNISMAL* and in *SKALDSKAPARMAL*.

HRIMFAXI (Frosty Mane) The male horse that each day pulls NOTT (night) across the world of the gods. He is named in *VAFTHRUDNISMAL*, part of the *POETIC EDDA*. Each morning, the froth from Hrimfaxi's bit falls as dew upon the valleys of the Earth. Hrimfaxi's counterpart is SKINFAXI, who pulls DAG (day) through the sky.

In *SKALDSAPARMAL*, SNORRI STURLUSON says that another name for this horse is Fjorsvartnir. (See also "Night and Day" under CREATION.)

HRIMGRIMNIR (Frost-Shrouded) The RIME-GIANT invoked by the fertility god SKIRNIR as he tries to persuade the GIANTESS GERDA to marry his master, the god FREY. If Gerda does not give in to Frey's request, Skirnir says Hrimgrimnir will become her mate in HEL (2).

Hrimgrimnir is one of the first giants from whom all others came. The only other mention of him is in the THULUR, one of the many existing lists of the names of characters and events in NORSE mythology. Scholars suggest that Hrimgrimnir represents strong forces of nature, since the curse Skirnir threatens Gerda with is very strong and harsh. Hrimgrimnir is perhaps the personification of the cruel cold of northern winters.

HRIMTHURSSAR The first GIANTS, also known as RIME-GIANTS. The Hrimthurssar represented the changing seasons and the coming of the eternal night, cold, and danger of the long winters of northern climates.

The Hrimthurssar are the children of YMIR, the first great giant, formed from the ice and fire that existed at the beginning of time. Ymir represented, in part, the numbing cold of the Artic.

HRINGHORNI (Ring Horn) The longship of the god BALDER. It was perhaps named for the intricate curving ring designs with which it, like many NORSE ships, was adorned. When Balder was slain, the funeral pyre for his body was built on *Hringhorni*. THOR set the fire ablaze, and the ship was sent out to sea.

See also SHIPS AND SHIP BURIALS.

The Gokstad ship, a Norse burial ship from the late ninth century *(Photo by Holt/Used under a Creative Commons license)*

HRUNGNIR   Strongest of the GIANTS; described as large and stone-headed. Hrungnir bet his horse GULLFAXI (Golden Mane) in a race with ODIN's eight-legged steed SLEIPNIR. He lost the race, then engaged in a duel with THOR, in which he was killed. SNORRI STURLUSON draws upon *HAUSTLONG*, a shield poem, or form of SKALDIC POETRY, for this tale.

HRYM   A giant. Hrym is the leader of the RIME-GIANTS as they take to the battlefields at RAGNAROK, the conflict that ends the world of the gods. With his shield held high in front of him, Hrym stands at the helm of the great ship NAGLFAR and steers it into the final conflict.

Hrym is named in *VOLUSPA*, the first poem in the *CODEX REGIUS* of the *POETIC EDDA*, as the pilot of Naglfar. SNORRI STURLUSON adds further details to the story in *GYLFAGINNING* when he explains that the ship was made from the nails shorn from dead men.

HUGI (Thought)   The young giant who outran fleet-footed THJALFI, servant of the god THOR, at the court of the giant UTGARD-LOKI.

To entertain his visitors when Thor and his servants arrived at his hall, Utgard-Loki asked about Thjalfi's accomplishments. When Thjalfi said he was a very fast runner, Utgard-Loki called upon the youth

Hugi to test him in a foot race. So fast was Hugi that he turned around to watch Thjalfi finish the race. It turned out that Hugi was the embodiment of Utgard-Loki's thoughts and, since no one can move faster than a thought, Thjalfi was bound to lose the race.

SNORRI STURLUSON tells this story in *GYLFAGINNING*, part of the *PROSE EDDA*.

HUGIN (Thought)   One of the god ODIN's two RAVENS. The other was MUNIN (Memory). Each morning Odin sent the two ravens to fly about the NINE WORLDS, then return to HLIDSKJALF, Odin's high seat. They would perch on his shoulders and tell him what they had seen.

HUMANS   According to NORSE mythology, the first humans were carved from trees by ODIN and his brothers VILI and VE (see "The First Humans," under CREATION). They cut down an ASH tree and from it made the first man, ASK. From an elm tree they carved the first woman, EMBLA. Then the three gods gave the first humans spirit and life, understanding and movement, speech, hearing, and sight.

These humans lived in or surrounded by MIDGARD, which was either the land in which they dwelled or the protective wall that surrounded the Earth. The souls of human warriors went to VALHALLA or SESSRUMNIR, the great halls of ODIN and

FREYA, respectively, where they lived until they were called upon to help the gods fight at RAGNAROK, the battle at the end of time.

Many of the surviving manuscripts of Norse mythology include attempts to give the gods human origins, a process known as euhemerism. Thirteenth-century writer SNORRI STURLUSON, for example, writes in his prologue to *GYLFAGINNING* that Odin was first a great leader from Asia who traveled north, settling his sons into kingships in the lands that would become SCANDINAVIA. Members of royal families also attempted to link their ancestry to the gods, often developing elaborate genealogies back to some of these stories and hiring poets to write SAGAS that would show how a human king was actually related to a god.

HVERGELMIR (Roaring Cauldron) The well or spring in NIFLHEIM from which gush the 11 rivers called the ELIVAGAR. The third root of the World Tree, YGGDRASIL, hangs over the poisonous vapor that rises from Hvergelmir. Nearby lives NITHOG, the corpse-eating dragon that nibbles on the roots of the sacred tree.

HYMIR (Dark One) A fierce giant. Hymir owned a large cauldron that the gods wanted for brewing their beer. THOR and TYR journey to Hymir's hall to steal the cauldron.

The oldest source of this conflict between Hymir and Thor is found in the Eddic Poem *HYMISKVITHA*, which is translated into English as *The Lay of Hymir*. SNORRI STURLUSON retells the story in greater detail in *GYLFAGINNING*, the first section of the *PROSE EDDA*.

In *Hymiskvitha*, Tyr, the NORSE god of war, says that Hymir is his father, but scholars are unclear why he makes such a claim, since many more sources say that ODIN is Tyr's father.

HYMISKVITHA (HYMISKVIÐA; *The Lay of Hymir*) The poem in the *POETIC EDDA* that tells the story of THOR and TYR's visit to the giant HYMIR and of their quest to fish for the MIDGARD SERPENT, JORMUNGAND. The purpose of Thor's journey to Hymir was to steal a cauldron from him, which the gods wanted to use to brew their beer.

While debate exits over the dating and composition of the poem, it appears to have been first written down in Iceland in the late 1100s. Some experts suggest that the scribe who wrote it down condensed several poems into one. The main story of *Hymiskvitha*, however, which is that of Thor killing

Odin with his ravens Hugin and Munin. From the 18th-century Icelandic manuscript SÁM 66, in the care of the Árni Magnússon Institute in Iceland

the Midgard serpent, is much older and dates well back into the 900s. *Hymiskvitha* is found in the *CODEX REGIUS* and in the *ARNAMAGNÆAN CODEX*.

HYNDLA The GIANTESS visited by the goddess FREYA, who asked Hyndla to reveal the lineage of her human lover, OTTAR. The story is told in the *POETIC EDDA* in *HYNDLULJOTH* (*Lay of Hyndla*).

HYNDLULJOTH (*HYNDLJIOÐ; HYNDLULJOD*; Lay of Hyndla) A poem found in the *POETIC EDDA*. This poem was included in an Icelandic manuscript compiled in the late 14th century, but it was most likely written down in the 12th century.

Hyndluljoth contains many stories. One is of FREYA's visit to HYNDLA, who is apparently the bride of a giant, lives in a cave, and rides a WOLF. It also presents information on the main AESIR gods.

Part of this poem is known as the "Shorter Voluspa." *Hyndluljoth*, like the full *VOLUSPA*, perhaps the most important poem in the *Poetic Edda*, contains a question-and-answer session and tells a story of LOKI, the trickster god.

HYROKKIN (Fire Smoke) The giantess who launched the longship HRINGHORNI, the funeral pyre of the slain god BALDER. She rode an enormous WOLF, using serpents as reins. The BERSERKERS killed the wolf, but Hyrokkin pushed the ship into the water with her own strength. SNORRI STURLUSON tells Hyrokkin's story in *GYLFAGINNING*, but she is also mentioned in SKALDIC POETRY.

ICELAND An island nation in the Arctic and North Atlantic oceans, about 570 miles west of Norway. Iceland is considered part of Scandinavia and the Nordic nations, and as such it shares language and cultural histories with Norway, Sweden, and Denmark. Norwegians settled this volcanic island in the middle of the ninth century A.D. The settlers took with them their old religion and the stories of the gods and goddesses of the Norse. In their isolation, the peoples of this rugged land maintained their beliefs in the old gods longer than their relatives in Europe, who converted to Christianity in the 10th century. Iceland became a Christian land during the 11th century. However, for some reason unclear to modern historians and literary experts, the stories of the old Norse gods thrived in Iceland until well into the 13th century, long after they had faded from the cultures of Norway, Sweden, and Denmark.

Most of the surviving manuscripts about the mythology of the Norse were created by artists living in the ninth and 10th centuries and recorded by scribes living in Iceland in the 13th, 14th, and later centuries. The great stories in the *POETIC EDDA* were composed by anonymous poets and later written down by people skilled in the new art of writing and manuscript creation. These poems are part of the *CODEX REGIUS*, a manuscript written in the late 13th century and found in a farmhouse in Iceland in the 17th century. Snorri Sturluson, the author of the *PROSE EDDA*, was a scholar, historian, and chieftain in Iceland who wrote his works in the early 1200s in an effort to preserve the stories for later generations. He based his work on old poems and prose sagas, stories of heroes from Scandinavia that provide clues and details concerning the beliefs of these people.

The language of these manuscripts, known as Old Norse or Old Icelandic, is closely related to the modern languages of Scandinavia, particularly modern Icelandic.

Very little archaeological evidence of the beliefs in the Aesir and Vanir gods remains in Iceland, for it was settled late in the age of the Nordic people. While rock carvings and burial sites in Norway, Sweden, and Denmark from the Bronze Age (3500–1000 B.C.) and more recently provide scientists with additional evidence of the beliefs of these people, very few such carvings exist in Iceland.

IDAVOLL The plain or field in Asgard where the shining palaces of the Aesir gods stood. It was here that the young gods played games such as chess, and it was here that the god Balder was slain by his blind brother, Hodur. After Ragnarok (the end of the world), Idavoll became green again at the Regeneration. New halls were built by the surviving gods. It is said that they found the golden chess pieces of their slaughtered friends and looked at them in wonder as they remembered the past.

IDI One of the rime-giants, or frost giants. Idi was the brother of Thjazzi and Gang and the son of Olvaldi, who left piles of gold to be divided among his sons. The brothers, in choosing how to divide the treasure, decided that each should take as much as his mouth would hold. Idi is said to have given fine speeches.

Idi is mentioned only in *SKALDSKAPARMAL*, by the poet and historian Snorri Sturluson, most notably in *GROTTASONG*, a poem Sturluson quotes in full. (See also "Skade and Njord" under skade.)

IDUNN (IDUNA) The golden-haired goddess who supplied the Aesir gods with apples that gave them eternal youth. Idunn was the wife of Bragi, the god of poetry.

She was probably an important goddess, but the only myth that survives about Idunn is the one in which she is kidnapped by the giant Thjazzi. In the

PROSE EDDA, SNORRI STURLUSON bases his retelling of the myth partially on the poem *HAUSTLONG*, by mid-ninth- to early-10th-century Norwegian poet Thiodor of Hvini.

Idunn's Apples The goddess Idunn supplied the gods with the apples that kept them forever young. One day Idunn and her apples were stolen.

According to Snorri, the great god ODIN, his brother HOENIR, and LOKI, the sly one, went exploring. When they became hungry, they killed an ox, built a fire, and started to cook the meat. But no matter what they did, the meat remained raw and inedible.

A huge EAGLE landed on a tree nearby and said he would make their fire burn like a furnace to cook the meat if only he could have a share of the food. The hungry travelers agreed to the bargain, the fire burned bright, the meat cooked, and the eagle ate almost all of it in the gulp.

Loki, quick to anger, swiped at the eagle but got carried away in its talons. The eagle dragged Loki over rocks and thorns until he begged for mercy.

Painting of Idunn and Bragi (1846) by Nils Johan Olsson Blommér (1816–1853)

The eagle would not let Loki go until he promised to deliver to him Idunn and her apples of youth. Loki agreed at once, and the eagle dropped him back to Earth. After Loki limped back to his companions, he did not tell them of his promise to the eagle, who he had realized was the giant Thjazzi in disguise.

Back in ASGARD, Loki wasted no time, for he was terrified of the fierce Thjazzi and knew he must somehow keep his promise. Loki ran to the peaceful orchard that Idunn tended with her husband, Bragi. He told her that he had found some apples in MIDGARD that looked just like hers. He urged her to bring her basket of apples and accompany him to Midgard so they might compare apples.

Idunn was glad to follow Loki. She would be very happy to find more apples for the gods to eat.

As soon as Idunn and Loki were across BILROST, the RAINBOW BRIDGE, and into Midgard, the giant eagle swooped down, seized Idunn, and carried her away. Once in THRYMHEIM, his fortress, Thjazzi shut the golden maiden in the highest tower.

Without the magic apples, the faces of the Aesir and ASYNJUR—the gods and goddesses—began to wrinkle and sag, their rosy cheeks faded, their hair grew white and thin, and their joints stiff and creaky, for these gods and goddesses were ancient. The gods and goddesses met to decide what to do. Everyone was there except Loki. The gods immediately concluded that Loki must have been up to some mischief. They searched for him and found him. Odin ordered Loki to bring back Idunn and her apples under threat to his life.

Loki fled in terror to the goddess FREYA to borrow her flying suit of FALCON feathers. With this, he flew off to Thrymheim. Fortunately for Loki, Thjazzi had gone fishing, and Idunn was unguarded. Loki used his magic to turn the maiden and her basket of apples into a small nut, which he grasped in his claws and flew toward Asgard. Odin, the all-seeing, caught sight of the falcon from afar and saw that behind him came an enormous eagle—Thjazzi.

Odin commanded that everyone build a great fire at the gates of Asgard.

Just in time, Loki flew over the walls of Asgard. The eagle was so close behind that he got caught in the flames that roared up when the dry kindling was lit. The eagle fell to the ground, and the gods killed him. Then Loki said the magic words, and Idunn stood before them once more, offering her wonderful apples with a happy smile.

It is of particular interest to mythologists that Loki turns Idunn into a nut. This symbol of eternal youth is often found in old Scandinavian burial sites. Idunn may have been a *VANIR* goddess of fertility, youth, and death. This is the only surviving myth about her.

IFING The river that separates the world of the AESIR from the world of the GIANTS, JOTUNHEIM, according to *VAFTHRUDNISMAL*. Ifing's waters always ran free and ice never formed on its surface. Ifing was also most likely the river where THOR fought GIANTS in the poem *HARBARTHSLJOTH*.

ING In NORSE mythology, Ing was a name associated with the god FREY, who was a god of the VANIR until he was sent to ASGARD as part of the exchange that ended the AESIR/VANIR WAR. Ing was a term of respect that preceded Frey's name, as in Ingunar Frey, which is found in the surviving Norse literature.

Ing is also a hero of an Old English RUNE poem and the name of the Norse rune that represented the "ng" sound (see YNGVI). The word is a common element in many place names in SCANDINAVIA.

Scholars suggest that Ing was a GERMANIC god or hero. One old tale tells of the wagon of Ing traveling eastward over the ocean waves. Some suggest that the wagon carried the Sun through the underworld during the night to return it to the east, where it would rise the next morning.

Other scholars suggest that Ing was a son of MANNUS, who was the first human in Old German mythology, a source of Norse mythology. Ing may have been a name of the Germanic people known as the Ingvaeones or Ingaevones.

JARL (nobly born; earl)   Jarl was the third and last son conceived by the god HEIMDALL on his journey through the land of HUMANS. Heimdall travelled in the disguise of a man named RIG, according to the poem *RIGSTHULA*.

After having conceived THRALL and the race of slaves and KARL and the race of free men, Heimdall slept between the wealthy and gracious Fadir and Modir (father and mother). Nine months later, Modir gave birth to a blond, bright-eyed son she named Jarl.

Jarl learned to use lances, shields, and the bow and arrow. He rode horses, brandished swords, and raised dogs. Rig claimed Jarl as his son and taught him the mysteries of the RUNES. Jarl married Erna the wise, the beautiful daughter of a distant lord, a girl of noble birth. Jarl and Erna gave birth to the race of the nobles, the rulers of the people sired by his brothers Karl and Thrall.

JARNSAXA (Iron Sword)   A GIANTESS. Jarnsaxa was the mistress of the thunder god THOR and said by some scholars to be one of his two wives (the other being SIF). Jarnsaxa was the mother of Thor's sons MAGNI and MODI. This relationship is mentioned in SKALDIC POETRY and by SNORRI STURLUSON in *SKALDSKAPARMAL*.

Jarnsaxa is also named as one of the nine giantess mothers of the AESIR god HEIMDALL, according to *HYNDLULJOTH*, a work in the *POETIC EDDA*. As Heimdall's mother, Jarnsaxa is a grandmother of the classes of humans.

JARNVID (JARNVIÐ; Ironwood)   The home of a GIANTESS, witch, crone, or old lady who raises her offspring, the wild, monstrous wolves that are the children of the great wolf FENRIR. One of these is the wolf SKOLL, who eats the Sun from the sky at

RAGNAROK. This story is according to the *VOLUSPA*, the first poem in the *POETIC EDDA*.

Some scholars argue that if the hag who lives in Jarnvid is a giantess, then her children by Fenrir are themselves GIANTS.

Jarnvid is also mentioned in *GRIMNISMAL*, another poem in the *Poetic Edda*, as a place to which Skoll often runs.

JORD (JÖRÐ; JORTH; Earth)   A GIANTESS and the mother of the thunder god THOR and wife of his father, ODIN. Jord was the daughter of NOTT and her second husband Annar. SNORRI STURLUSON says Jord was included among the ASYNJUR. Her name occurs most often in SKALDIC POETRY and Eddic poetry in phrases that refer to Thor as "the son of Jord."

Some confusion exists, however, for in some places in the *POETIC EDDA*, the word *FJORGYN* appears in phrases referring to Thor, such as in the poem *VOLUSPA*, where Thor is described as the "son of Fjorgyn." Scholars explain the confusion by pointing out that *fjorgyn*, as an Old NORSE noun, means "Earth" when used in the feminine form and refers to Odin when used in the masculine form.

JORMUNGAND   The giant SERPENT—also known as the MIDGARD SERPENT, Midgard Snake, or Midgard Worm—offspring of LOKI and the ogress ANGRBODA. Jormungand is the brother of the WOLF FENRIR and HEL, the goddess of death.

The huge serpent was cast into the sea by ODIN and doomed to encircle the Earth, his tail in his mouth. Jormungand and THOR were mortal enemies. On one occasion, Thor caught the serpent using an ox head for bait, but the giant HYMIR snipped the line and the serpent disappeared beneath the waves. The serpent appeared again at RAGNAROK and made his way onto the land, spewing VENOM. Thor killed the serpent but was himself poisoned by the deadly venom.

JOTUN (Giant)   The beings who lived in JOTUN-HEIM, which was the land of the GIANTS. Jotun were the main enemies of the AESIR gods and goddesses, although the two races often intermarried.

The first generation of giants was formed from the original giant, YMIR. They were known as the RIME-GIANTS, HRIMTHURSSAR (*thursar* means "giant"), or frost giants. Among the people of the north, they were said to represent the threat of winter, darkness, and sterility. The Jotun are the descendents of one of these first giants, BERGELMIR, and his wife. This single rime-giant and his family survived the flood that killed all the other giants when the divine brothers, ODIN, VILI, and VE, killed Ymir.

Famous characters among the Jotun are: GERDA, beloved of the god FREY; JARNSAXA, a wife or mistress of THOR; HRUNGNIR, who duels with Thor; and HYMIR, with whom Thor goes fishing for the MIDGARD SERPENT.

JOTUNHEIM (JOTUNNHEIMAR; Giant Land)   The mountainous, freezing lands of the JOTUN, a race of GIANTS. Many manuscripts of NORSE myths use the plural form, Jotunnheimar, to refer to the lands of these giants. Some scholars suggest that people viewed the giants as living in places that surrounded the edges of the world of HUMANS. Others say that people saw Jotunheim as one single place, just as they regarded ASGARD, the realm of the gods, as one place.

One of the three huge roots of the World Tree, YGGDRASIL, reached into Jotunheim. The great thunder god, THOR, traveled often to Jotunheim to battle the giants.

K

KARL (Freeman) The second son conceived by the god HEIMDALL as he journeyed through MIDGARD, the land of HUMANS, according to the poem RIGSTHULA. In his second stop, Heimdall, using the name RIG, slept between Afi and Amma (grandfather and grandmother) and nine months later Amma bore a son, Karl. He was red of face with flashing eyes. He raised oxen and built houses and barns. He married Snot, and they gave birth to the human race of working-class people. (See also THRALL and JARL.)

KENNING A poetic technique used most frequently by the NORSE writers of SKALDIC POETRY, who created their art from about A.D. 700 to 1100. Essentially a kenning is a type of metaphor, using a set of words to represent a common noun. For example, for SWORD, the poet might use the NAME of a famous sword such as DAINSLEIF, which means "Dain's heirloom." Or a poet might refer to gold as "Sif's hair," which would remind the audience of the myth of the golden hair the god LOKI had the DWARFS make after he cut off the locks of the goddess SIF, wife of THOR.

Many kennings contain names and objects important to Norse mythology and provide scholars with hints and clues of stories that have been lost over time. At the same time, however, kennings are often the only mention of a name, and modern scholars and students have no other information to understand the meaning of that kenning. Kennings at the very least provide experts with the understanding that much about Norse mythology is lost to modern audiences.

KORMT AND ORMT Two of the four rivers that THOR must wade through each day as he travels to ASGARD to sit in judgment and at RAGNAROK, the end time, according to GRIMNISMAL, a section of the POETIC EDDA. The other two rivers are the Kerlaugs. SNORRI STURLUSON quotes this poem in the PROSE EDDA.

The location of these rivers is unclear, though scholars suggest they, like the river IFING, separate the land of the JOTUN from the lands of the AESIR, since Thor spends much of his time fighting the GIANTS, the enemies of the gods.

KVASIR (1) (Spittle) A wise man who was created from the spit of the AESIR and the VANIR gods after their battle (see AESIR/VANIR WAR). Kvasir walked the world spreading his great wisdom to any who asked for it. He was slain by two DWARFS, FJALAR (2) and GALAR, who mixed his blood with honey to make a powerful MEAD that inspired any who drank it to talk with wisdom and poetry (see "The Mead of Poetry," under ODIN).

KVASIR (2) A VANIR god known for his great wisdom. With the gods NJORD, FREY, and FREYA, Kvasir went to live in ASGARD as part of the peace settlement after the AESIR/VANIR WAR. He was a symbol of the pledge for peace and of the end of the fighting between the two great races of gods. (MIMIR (2) and HOENIR were the Aesir gods sent to the Vanir.)

Kvasir went with ODIN and a party of gods to capture LOKI, who was hiding as a salmon after mocking the gods at the feast in AEGIR's hall. Kvasir deduced from the ashes in the fire of the hut where Loki had been hiding that the trickster god had been making a fishing net. The gods immediately knew that they had to make a similar device to catch Loki.

SNORRI STURLUSON includes this story of Kvasir in his PROSE EDDA.

L

LAEDING (LÆDING) The first of three chains with which the gods tried to muzzle and secure the dangerous WOLF FENRIR. Laeding and the second chain, DROMI, were made of ordinary metal, and Fenrir broke them easily. Only the magical third chain, GLEIPNER, was strong enough to hold the wolf. Fenrir remained chained until the time of RAGNAROK, the battle that brought an end to the world of the gods. The story is preserved by SNORRI STURLUSON in GYLFAGINNING.

LAERAD (LÆRAD) The great tree around which ODIN's hall, VALHALLA, was built. The GOAT HEIDRUN, who produced an endless supply of MEAD for the gods

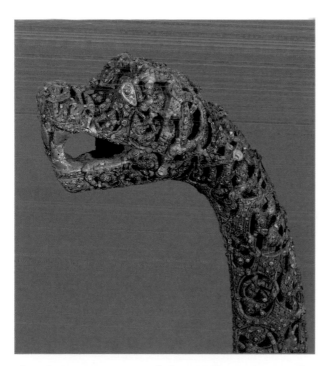

The decorative prow of the Oseberg ship in the Viking Ship Museum, Oslo, Norway *(Museum of Cultural History, University of Oslo, Norway)*

and heroes, and the stag EIKTHYRNIR nibbled at its branches.

LANDVAETTIR (LANDVÆTTIR; Land Wights) Spirits that protected the land (that is, the soil or ground). According to stories, huge crowds of Landvaettir might inhabit a place. They were invisible to people unless someone looked very closely in the right light at the right time. A law in ICELAND prohibited ships with dragonhead carvings on their bows from coming toward shore in case the huge monsters frightened away the Landvaettir. These wights (creatures that are neither mortals nor gods) are similar to land ELVES, though more connected to the soil than to an area.

LANDVIDI (VIDI; Wide Land) The land in which the silent god VIDAR made his home. According to the poem GRIMNISMAL, the land was filled with growing trees, branches, and tall grasses. Some scholars suggest that it was a clearing in a forest and that Vidar himself was a forest deity who lived in the silence of the deep forest.

LAUFEY (Tree Island) A GIANTESS and mother of LOKI, whose father, FARBAUTI, was also a giant. Some stories say Laufey gave birth to Loki when a lightning bolt thrown by Farbauti struck her. Laufey apparently did not raise Loki, since Icelandic author SNORRI STURLUSON and others say that the trickster god was a foster brother of ODIN, the most powerful NORSE god.

In SORLA THATTRA, a Norse SAGA more ancient than Snorri's 13th-century PROSE EDDA, Loki's mother is named Nal, which means "needle." In this story, his mother is slender and weak.

LAY A short lyric or narrative (storytelling) poem, especially one intended to be sung, usually by traveling minstrels. These minstrels thus kept alive ancient stories dealing with mythology, history, or legendary adventures. In NORSE mythology many of the poems in the *POETIC EDDA* are lays, such as the *Lay of Thrym* or *THRYMSKVITHA*.

LIF (Life) The man who with his wife, LIFTHRA-SIR, survived RAGNAROK and repeopled the Earth. During the fearful holocaust, they took shelter in HODDMIMIR'S WOOD, which may be another name for the World Tree, YGGDRASIL. They were nourished by the morning dew. They emerged from the tree unhurt when they saw the new SUN shining. They had children and started a new life for humankind. The story appears in *VAFTHRUDNISMAL*.

LIFTHRASIR (Sturdy for Life) The woman, wife of LIF, who survived RAGNAROK and with Lif began to repeople the Earth. Lif and Lifthrasir hid in HODDMIMIR'S WOOD, which may be another name for YGGDRASIL, during the holocaust that caused the end of the world. The myth forms part of *VAFTHRUD-NISMAL*.

LIGHT-ELVES The creatures who dwelled in the land of ALFHEIM. Fairer than the SUN, they lived in the upper world of the world tree YGGDRASIL.

After RAGNAROK, the final battle between the gods and the GIANTS, only the light-elves remained to dwell in VIDBLAIN, the highest of all of the worlds of the gods. This information about elves comes only from *GYLFAGINNING*, the first part of SNORRI STURLUSON'S *PROSE EDDA*. Little else is known of the light-elves from NORSE mythology, although they are often referred to in the *POETIC EDDA* as being connected to the AESIR gods.

The Icelandic sagas, stories of the lives of the people of that island nation, frequently mention ELVES, or *alfar*, as nature spirits that bring fertility to men and women.

LIT The DWARF who suddenly appeared at BALDER'S funeral and got in the way of THOR, who was consecrating the funeral pyre with his magic hammer, MJOLLNIR. Hot-tempered as always and stricken with sorrow at Balder's death, Thor kicked Lit into the flames of the pyre. Lit gained immortality in mythology by being burned to ashes along with the god Balder and his wife, NANNA.

LODDFAFNIR A man from MIDGARD (Middle Earth), that is, a human. In the *Lay of Loddfafnir*, part of the poem *HAVAMAL* from the *POETIC EDDA*, Lodd-fafnir tells his fellow men many words of wisdom. He had somehow found his way to URDARBRUNN, the sacred well, where he heard the words of the High One (ODIN). Loddfafnir recounted these words to fellow mortals. The words contained much good advice. For example, beware of a witch's sweet words, always carry food if you have to cross a mountain, cherish your friends and be loyal to them, stay away from evil people, doing good deeds will make you feel happy, hold to your promises, and respect the wisdom of the elderly. There were also words full of ancient superstitions, such as those for warding off the curses made by witches.

LOFN A minor GODDESS, counted by SNORRI STURLUSON among the main ASYNJUR, or goddesses of the AESIR. Lofn was portrayed as gentle and good. ODIN and FRIGG gave her permission to help people find love. In many ways, Lofn served as a matchmaker. She might help young people tell each other of their love or fulfill the dreams of a man or woman whose love of another was not returned. Lofn means "praise" or "praised."

LOFNHEID One of two daughters of HREIDMAR, a farmer who receives from the gods gold in compensation for their killing of Hreidmar's son OTR. The other daughter is LYNGHEID. Though the story of Hreidmar is also told in the legendary *VOLSUNGA SAGA*, Lofnheid and her sister are named only in the poem *REGINSMAL*, part of the *POETIC EDDA*. Another of Hreidmar's sons, FAFNIR, kills his father as his sisters look on. Their father begs his daughters for help, but they declare themselves powerless against their brother. REGIN is their third brother.

LOGI (Flame) The young giant who defeated the trickster god LOKI in an eating contest at the court of the giant UTGARD-LOKI. It turned out that Logi was the embodiment of fire, which can consume anything and everything quickly.

(See also "Thor's Journey to Utgard," under THOR.)

LOKASENNA (*Loki's Verbal Duel; Loki's Wrangling*) A poem in the *POETIC EDDA*, found only in the *CODEX REGIUS* manuscript. *Lokasenna* features the nasty banter between the trickster god LOKI and the guests of a feast held by the SEA god, AEGIR.

Lokasenna is an important work to NORSE mythology, for its characters are the prominent gods and the banter reveals many details about the stories of the gods. For instance, it reveals more details about Loki and his relationship to the gods than any other source in Norse mythology.

Lokasenna was most likely composed in the 10th century and passed along orally for more than 200 years before being written down by the scribe who compiled the *Codex Regius*. The version of the tale found in the manuscript contains a prose introduction, and throughout the poem prose statements have been inserted, much like stage directions in a play. Experts who study the manuscripts of ICELAND believe that the scribe added these prose insertions as a storyteller would have inserted explanations for his or her audience in earlier times.

LOKI Loki is known as the trickster god, the mischief-maker, the father of lies and deceit, and the SHAPE-SHIFTER. He is the personification of both aspects of fire: the merry but potentially dangerous hearth fire and the destructive fire of forest and volcano.

Loki was the son of the giant FARBAUTI and of the giantess LAUFEY or Nal. He had two wives. The first was the fearful ogress ANGRBODA, with whom he had three monstrous offspring: HEL (I), the GODDESS of death and the underworld; JORMUNGAND, the MIDGARD SERPENT who encircled the world; and FENRIR the wolf. His wife in ASGARD was SIGYN, with whom he had two sons, NARFI and VALI (I).

Loki was counted among the AESIR gods, but he was not one of them, as he was born among the JOTUN, the gods' enemies. Some say that he and the great god ODIN were blood brothers, which is why none of the gods dared to harm Loki, no matter how mischievous and malevolent he became.

Loki was handsome and could be amusing. He made the goddess SKADE laugh even while she mourned for her father, THJAZZI. Loki was sometimes helpful to the gods, for he was quick-witted and always had an answer for everything, but often the gods would regret taking his advice.

It was Loki who accompanied THOR to JOTUNHEIM to retrieve Thor's magic hammer. Loki also thought of a way to outwit the giant who built Asgard's wall (see GIANT MASTER BUILDER). However, his solution was nothing but fraud and resulted in Thor committing murder within Asgard; such behavior was against the code of the Aesir.

Loki stole FREYA's necklace and cut off SIF's golden hair, yet it was he who went down to the underground caves of the DWARFS and brought back wonderful treasures for the gods. Loki double-crossed both the giant Thjazzi and the Aesir when he delivered IDUNN and her apples to the giant and then, disguised as a FALCON, carried Idunn back to Asgard, leading Thjazzi to his death.

Not only could Loki change himself into other creatures at will, such as a seal, a salmon, a fly, a falcon, he could also change his sex. As a mare, he was the mother of SLEIPNIR, Odin's eight-legged steed. He became an old crone when he tricked FRIGG into telling him that MISTLETOE was the only object on Earth that could harm the gentle god BALDER. Even though Loki was the principal cause of Balder's death, the Aesir took no action against him.

However, when Loki came to AEGIR's banquet and flung vicious insults at all the gods and goddesses, the Aesir finally decided to punish the evil creature that Loki had become. At RAGNAROK (the day of doom), Loki led the forces of evil against the gods, and he and HEIMDALL killed each other.

Treasures of the Dwarfs This story tells how the gods came to acquire some of the great treasures for which they were famous. It is told most completely by SNORRI STURLUSON, the 13th-century poet, in his *SKALDSKAPARMAL*.

One night, Loki snuck into the bedroom of Sif, Thor's wife, and cut off her golden hair while she slept. When Thor discovered that Loki had stolen his wife's precious hair, he threatened to tear Loki to pieces. The trickster god put on a show of remorse and promised to bring back not only hair made of real gold for Sif but other treasures for the gods as well, so Thor let him go.

After being released, Loki immediately made his way to SVARTALFHIEM, the realm of the dark-elves, which was the underworld home of the dwarfs. While ugly and bad-tempered, these undersized creatures were master craftsmen and worked with gold and other metals found in their dark world.

Loki went to the cave of the sons of Ivaldi, BROKK and EITRI, and begged them to make golden strands so real that they would grow out of Sif's head. The dwarfs easily accomplished this feat with their great magic, and while the furnace was still hot, they made other magical treasures for Loki to carry back to the gods.

They made SKIDBLADNER, a marvelous ship, for FREY. It could be folded up small enough to fit into a pouch and yet expand to a size large enough to carry all of the Aesir gods and their equipment. It could sail on land, water, or air. And for Odin, they made GUNGNIR, the mighty spear, strong and slender. It always flew straight to its target.

Once the creation of these fine gifts was finished, Loki still wanted more. With Brokk, Loki bet his own head that the dwarf's brother, Eitri, could not make three finer treasures. The dwarf accepted the bet. While Brokk worked the bellows to keep the fire hot, Eitri went to work using his magic to make three precious objects: GULLINBURSTI, a BOAR with golden bristles and mane which Loki would give to Frey; DRAUPNIR, a magical arm ring of gold for Odin that every ninth night would produce eight more rings; and finally, MJOLLNIR, a massive iron hammer for Thor.

All the time that Eitri worked, Loki pestered Brokk, trying to interrupt his steady work on the bellows and win the bet through trickery. The god transformed himself into a fly and buzzed around the dwarf's head and bit him several times, but Brokk was not bothered. Finally, while Mjollnir was forming in the fire, Loki stung Brokk's eyelid so hard that blood dripped into the dwarf's eye. Swiftly Brokk reached up to wipe it, taking only one hand from the handle of the bellows and only for a brief moment. That moment was long enough to spoil the handle of the great hammer. Thus Thor's hammer has a short handle, although it still had the ability to always return to its master after he threw it. Brokk, proud of his work, felt he had won the bet, but Loki, using fast talk and cunning, escaped with nothing worse than sore lips when Brokk tried to sew up his wicked mouth.

Loki took the six precious gifts and presented them to the gods, who marveled at their beauty and attributes, but they all agreed that the hammer with the stunted handle was the best for it would help protect them from the GIANTS of JOTUNHEIM.

Loki's Mocking Loki could be playful and charming, but as time went on, he became sinister, evil, and bad-tempered. The story of Loki's mocking of the gods and goddesses, part of the *LOKASENNA* in the *POETIC EDDA*, shows Loki at his worst.

Aegir, the lord of the sea, invited the gods to a banquet in his coral caves under the island of HLESEY. He brewed the ale in the huge cauldron that Thor and TYR had taken from the giant HYMIR.

It was soon after the death of BALDER and the gods were subdued, talking quietly among themselves. Loki listened impatiently as they praised Aegir's servants, FIMAFENG and ELDIR. Suddenly Loki sprang up and stabbed Fimafeng with his knife, then fled. He soon returned, and this time his targets were the gods and goddesses and his weapons were poisonous words.

He insulted BRAGI, the god of poetry, by calling him a soft coward. One by one he accused each of the goddesses, Idunn, GEFJON, Frigg, FREYA, and Sif, of being deceitful and unvirtuous. He laughed at NJORD for being a hostage from the VANIR gods and at Tyr for losing his hand in the jaws of the wolf Fenrir. No one escaped, not even FREY's servants, BYGGVIR and his wife BEYLA, nor HEIMDALL, who was mocked as being a mere servant of the gods. Even the great god Odin did not escape Loki's evil tongue. Loki sneered at him for once having turned himself into a witch, "a woman through and through."

At last Thor, who had been absent, entered the hall. His eyes glowed with rage, and his whiskers bristled when he heard Loki's vicious insults. He threatened to kill Loki there and then with his hammer, and Loki swiftly left.

The Pursuit of Loki-Salmon After Loki insulted the gods and goddesses at a feast given by Aegir, the sea god, he fled from the wrath of the gods and built himself a hut in the mountains. The hut had doors on all four sides so Loki could escape easily, for he knew the gods wanted to punish him for his evil words and also for the death of the gentle god Balder.

By day Loki, the shape-shifter, turned himself into a salmon and swam in the mountain torrent at Franang's Falls. To distract himself in the evening, he fashioned a fine net—some say, the first fishing net. (In other poems the sea ogress RAN, Aegir's wife, invented the fishing net to catch drowning sailors and bring them to her domain under the waves.)

From his high seat, HLIDSKJALF, Odin could see far and wide over all NINE WORLDS. When he finally saw where Loki was hiding and in what guise, Odin went with a party of gods to capture the troublemaker. Loki saw them coming and quickly threw the fishing net into the fire, then sprinted down to the stream and leapt in as a salmon.

The gods entered the hut and saw the remains of the net. KVASIR (2), a very wise god, concluded that a finished net might be very useful to the gods for catching slippery Loki-Salmon. The gods sat up all night repairing and completing the net. At dawn they set out to catch Loki.

Loki escaped their clutches for quite a while, as they used the net to drag the stream, but in the end Thor caught him in midair as he made a flying leap over the net. To this day, the salmon is noted for its slender tail, a reminder, Northmen say, of how strongly Thor had held Loki in his powerful hand.

This story of Loki is told at the end of *Lokasenna* and in Snorri Sturluson's *Gylfaginning*.

Loki's Punishment After the gods captured Loki, they dragged him into a dark cave. They changed Loki's son Vali into a wolf, which immediately attacked his brother, Narfi, and killed him. The gods took Narfi's intestines and bound Loki with them. Once Loki was firmly bound, they changed the horrid bonds into iron. Then the icy goddess Skade placed a serpent over Loki's upturned face so that its venom would drip onto him.

Only Sigyn, Loki's faithful wife, stayed with Loki in the miserable cave. She held a bowl to catch the drops of venom, but when she turned aside to empty the poison, the drops fell on Loki's twisted face. He writhed with pain and terror, causing the Earth to tremble and quake. So Loki, the Norse myths say, is the cause of earthquakes.

Loki remained a prisoner until Ragnarok, when he took his revenge on the gods and they on him.

LOTHUR (Loður) According to the *Voluspa*, part of the *Poetic Edda*, one of the three original Aesir gods who, along with his brothers Odin and Hoenir, created the world (see "The First Humans," under creation). In his *Prose Edda*, Snorri Sturluson identifies Lothur as Ve and Hoenir as Vili.

Some mythologists have tried to identify Lothur with Loki, but virtually nothing is known about this god.

LUT (Lit) A giant, perhaps the father of a family of giants or the leader of a group of giants, apparently killed by Thor. Little is known of Lut. His name is used in kennings by early skalds who praise Thor for his defeat of this giant. In some of the manuscripts of these poems, this giant is named Lit,

Loki's Punishment (1923) by Ida Matton *(Photo by Hedning/Used under a Creative Commons license)*

which is also the name of the DWARF Thor kicked into the fire during BALDER's funeral.

LYNGHEID A daughter of the farmer, master magician and dwarf HREIDMAR. Lyngheid looked on with her sister, LOFNHEID, as their brother FAFNIR killed their father for the hoard of gold he protected. The gods had given the gold to Hreidmar as compensation for their killing OTR, another son of Hreidmar. Lyngheid and her sister are mentioned only in *REGINSMAL*, part of the *POETIC EDDA*, though the story of Otr and Hreidmar is also told in the legendary *VOLSUNGA SAGA*.

LYNGVI (Heathery) The island in the middle of the lake AMSVARTNIR (Red-Black) where ODIN and the gods bound the WOLF FENRIR. On Lyngvi, Fenrir waited for RAGNAROK, the battle at the end of time, when he would be freed to fight on the side of the GIANTS. The island and the lake are named by SNORRI STURLUSON in *GYLFAGINNING*.

MAGNI (Mighty) One of the two sons of the god THOR and the giantess JARNSAXA. His brother is MODI. At an early age, Magni was strong enough to rescue his father from under the leg of the giant HRUNGNIR. As a reward, Thor gave him the magnificent horse GULLFAXI, which had belonged to the giant. Magni was one of the seven AESIR who survived RAGNAROK, the end of the world, and inherited, with his brother, Thor's hammer, MJOLLNIR. Magni's story is in SNORRI STURLUSON's *PROSE EDDA*, though he quotes the 10th-century poem *VAFTHRUDNISMAL*.

MANAGARM (Moon Dog) A name used by 13th-century Icelandic historian SNORRI STURLUSON for one of the horrible wolves that destroy the SUN AND MOON at the time of RAGNAROK. The other wolf was SKOLL. Managarm was also known as HATI HROD-VITNISSON. Managarm was one of the many sons of an old GIANTESS who lived in JARNVID, all of whom were wolves.

MANI The man who drove the chariot that carried the Moon across the sky. He is the son of MUNDILFARI and the brother of SOL. For company, Mani stole two children from MIDGARD (Middle Earth). Their names were BIL AND HJUKI (Waning and Waxing). Some say that on a clear night the children in the Moon can be seen as dark shapes on the Moon's face, as they eternally carry a pail of water on a pole (see "Sun and Moon," under CREATION). At RAGNAROK, the WOLF HATI HRODVITNISSON, which pursues the chariot across the skies, will devour the Moon.

MEAD An alcoholic drink made by fermenting honey and water. The creators of the NORSE myths considered mead superior to the usual beer and ale (made by fermenting cereals flavored with hops) drunk by ordinary people. In VALHALLA, mead was supplied in a never-ending flow by the GOAT HEIDRUN, and the gods and heroes never lacked the heavenly brew.

See also "The Mead of Poetry," under ODIN.

MEGINGJARDIR (MEGINGJORĐ, MEGINGIORĐ, Power Belt) The name SNORRI STURLUSON gave to the god THOR's magic belt. When the thunder god fastens it on, his already great powers become twice as strong. Megingjardir was one of three of Thor's great treasures, which included his mighty hammer, MJOLLNIR, and iron gloves. The belt is

Depiction of warriors drinking mead on a rune-stone *(Photo by Berig/Used under a Creative Commons license)*

described in older NORSE sagas, but only Snorri calls it Megingjardir.

MEILI A brother of THOR and son of ODIN about which little information remains in the surviving manuscripts of NORSE mythology. Meili is referred to three times in SNORRI STURLUSON's *SKALDSKAPARMAL*. Sturluson uses the KENNING "Meili's brother" twice to refer to Thor, and once he uses the kenning "Meili's sire" to refer to Odin.

MENGLOD (MENGLOTH; Necklace-Happy) A very beautiful GIANTESS who was served by eight maiden goddesses, including EIR. SVIPDAG fell in love with Menglod and traveled to the underworld to learn from his dead mother how to win the love of this maiden. She is part of the story in the poem *SVIPDAGSMAL*.

MENJA See FENJA AND MENJA.

MIDGARD (Middle Earth) The world of HUMANS formed from the body of the giant YMIR. It was midway between ASGARD, the home of the gods, and JOTUNHEIM, the home of the GIANTS. Midgard was connected to Asgard by BILROST, the RAINBOW BRIDGE. It was surrounded by an ocean in which lived JORMUNGAND, the MIDGARD SERPENT. The first man and woman to live in Midgard were ASK and EMBLA. One of the three roots of the sacred tree, YGGDRASIL, was embedded in Midgard.

MIGRATION PERIOD In Scandinavian and GERMANIC history, the time from about 400 A.D. to approximately 575 A.D. when the Germanic peoples of northern Europe moved and shifted their territory, spreading their influence and culture as the Roman Empire collapsed. The Migration Period, also known as the Merovingian Era, was a time of change throughout northern Europe and, based on archaeological and written evidence, historians believe there was a great mixing of the tribes of northern Europe.

Those peoples most connected with the mythology now known as NORSE were well established on the Scandinavian peninsula and in DENMARK at the beginning of this period. They spread with other tribes, extending their reach to GREAT BRITAIN, the FAROE ISLANDS, ICELAND, and even Ireland. This migration was recorded by Roman writers such as the historian Tacitus and later by the Danish historian SAXO GRAMMATICUS.

A Migration Period iron helmet excavated from a boat grave in Vendel, Uppland, Sweden *(Photo by Mararie/Used under a Creative Commons license)*

Rock carvings, burial sites, and artifacts suggest that the gods of Norse mythology were worshiped by the people in SCANDINAVIA as early as the Bronze Age, from 1000 B.C. Saxo describes a cult to ODIN existing during the Migration Period.

Human remains discovered in peat bogs in Denmark and SWEDEN from the Migration Period indicate the cause of death was ritual hanging. Other evidence at these burial sites suggests that hanging people was a common sacrifice to the prominent Norse gods. Rock carvings that date to the Migration Period in Sodermanland and Gotland, Sweden, show a monster or SERPENT devouring a human, a symbol associated with the worship of Odin.

By the end of the Migration Period, the communities that had spread at its beginning had settled into larger recognizable kingdoms. In Scandinavia, the Migration Period ends with the beginning of the VIKING AGE and the rise of the influence of these seafaring people throughout the North and Baltic seas and as far away as the Mediterranean Sea.

MIMIR (1) Mimir was a nature spirit and the guardian and owner of the well of wisdom and knowledge, which was known as MIMIR'S WELL. Mimir drinks MEAD daily from the well, using the GJALLARHORN as a cup. The well and Mimir's abode lie beneath a root of YGGDRASIL, the World Tree, and Mimir fed Yggdrasil daily on the waters from this well.

Odin became the one-eyed god by giving an eye to Mimir to put in the well. The loss of one eye was the price Odin paid for the wisdom and foresight for which he was famous. This act led to expressions in poetry associating Mimir and his well with the one-eyed god.

This version of Mimir is often mentioned in the poems of the *POETIC EDDA*, particularly in phrases referring to wisdom, but the water spirit's name is also used in reference to a wise god and member of the AESIR (see MIMIR [2]), leading to questions by translators and scholars as to which Mimir each poet may have been referring to.

MIMIR (2) A wise god, sent as a peace hostage by the AESIR to the VANIR as part of a pact to end the AESIR/VANIR WAR. The god HOENIR, stout and handsome but rather slow-witted and a brother of the great god ODIN, went with Mimir in this peace trade. (FREY, FREYA, and KVASIR (2) were the Vanir gods sent to the Aesir.)

The Vanir made Hoenir a chief, but he never spoke for himself, always trusting to Mimir's advice. The Vanir grew suspicious of the truce between the gods and, thinking they had been tricked, beheaded Mimir and sent his head back to Odin and the Aesir.

Odin used his magic to preserve Mimir's head and often consulted the beheaded god for advice and wisdom.

This story is told only in SNORRI STURLUSON's *Ynglinga Saga*, the first part of *HEIMSKRINGLA*, a history of the kings of NORWAY. Scholars suggest that Snorri either quoted poems that have not survived in the manuscripts or that he invented the story to explain such phrases in the work of the skalds as "Mimir's head."

MIMIR'S WELL The well of wisdom under the second root of the tree YGGDRASIL in JOTUNHEIM. The head of MIMIR (2) resides beside the well. The god ODIN visited the well seeking wisdom. HEIMDALL, the WATCHMAN OF THE GODS, left his horn there until he needed it to announce RAGNAROK, the end of the world.

MISTLETOE A European plant (*Viscum album*) that grows as a parasite on trees. In NORSE mythology, it is known as the sprig that was hurled at the god BALDER by his blind brother, HODUR. Because mistletoe has weak stems, some scholars suggest that the trickster god LOKI used his magic arts on the mistletoe to make it strong and sharp enough to kill Balder.

MJOLLNIR The hammer of the god THOR. It was made by the DWARFS BROKK and EITRI. The hammer was a symbol of Thor's strength and of the thunderbolt he personified.

The hammer had a massive head and a short handle and was shaped somewhat like a cross. While Eitri was shaping the hammer in the foundry, LOKI, who had changed himself into a gadfly, pestered Brokk, who worked the bellows for his brother. At a crucial point in the making of the hammer, Loki stung Brokk on his eyelid; the dwarf was distracted and let go of the bellows. The fire died and Eitri did not have enough heat to finish the handle.

For many centuries, Norsemen wore the hammer's likeness as an amulet. Many of these amulets have been discovered in archaeological digs in SCANDINAVIA and Great Britain. Many ancient gravestones and RUNE stones also depict Thor's hammer.

Mistletoe plant growing in a tree. Hodur used a sprig of mistletoe to kill the god Balder. *(Photo by David Monniaux/Used uder a Creative Commons license)*

The gods considered Mjollnir to be their greatest treasure, for it alone could be used to defend ASGARD against the GIANTS. When Thor hurled it, it always struck its mark and returned instantly into his hand, like a boomerang. Although mighty in size, it could be magically shrunk to fit inside Thor's shirt.

The hammer was a symbol of fertility. In "The Theft of Thor's Hammer," Thor dressed himself as a bride when he went to visit the giant THRYM, who had stolen the hammer. Thor knew that at some point in the wedding ceremony a hammer was always placed in the lap of the bride, for such was the custom of the Norse. When Thrym placed Mjollnir in Thor's lap, Thor retrieved his hammer.

Mjollnir was also a symbol of resurrection. In "Thor's Journey to Utgard," when Thor waves Mjollnir over the skin and bones of his dead goats, the goats spring back to life.

Mjollnir was used at funerals as well. When BALDER lay on his funeral pyre, Thor consecrated the funeral with his hammer.

With Mjollnir, Thor killed the giant HRUNGNIR and also the GIANT MASTER BUILDER, who built Asgard's wall.

A decorative reproduction of Thor's hammer, Mjollnir
(Photo by Uwe H. Friese/Used under a Creative Commons license)

The only time that the hammer seemed to be ineffectual was when Thor struck the giant SKRYMIR with it. Skrymir said that he thought he was being assaulted by delicate leaves and twigs. However, it turned out that the hammer had made huge dents in a hillside instead of in Skrymir's head, thanks to the giant's clever magic.

After RAGNAROK, the end of the world, Thor's sons, MAGNI and MODI, inherited Mjollnir.

MODGUD The maiden who guards GIALLARBRU, the bridge that crosses the river GJOLL (2). When HERMOD journeyed to HEL (2) to bargain for the return of the slain god BALDER, Modgud stopped him and challenged him, as she did everyone who wanted to cross the bridge. She described Hermod's approach as louder than the thunder made by more than five companies of dead men who had passed the bridge to Hel the day before. She confirmed that Balder, too, had crossed her bridge. After Hermod explained his mission, Modgud allowed him to pass, telling him that Hel was farther down the road and to the north.

Modgud is only mentioned in *GYLFAGINNING* by SNORRI STURLUSON, and some scholars suggest that she serves as a typical challenger of the gods.

MODI (MODI; Courage) The lesser known of the two sons of the god THOR and the GIANTESS JARNSAXA. Along with his brother, MAGNI, Modi was one of the seven AESIR gods to survive RAGNAROK. According to the poem *VAFTHRUDNISMAL*, Modi and Magni inherited Thor's hammer, MJOLLNIR.

MOKKURKALFI (Mist Calf) The clay monster made by the JOTUN as a second, or substitute, for HRUNGNIR in his duel with the god THOR. Mokkurkalfi was nine leagues tall, or about nine miles. The Jotun equipped Mokkurkalfi with the heart of a mare. Thor's servant, THJALFI, hacked the clay figure to pieces. The story is in SNORRI STURLUSON's *SKALDSKAPARGMAL*.

MOON See CREATION; SUN AND MOON.

MOTSOGNIR The first of two DWARFS created by the Aesir from the maggots that oozed from the body of the first giant, YMIR, at the time of CREATION. The gods were in the process of creating all of the objects and creatures of their realms, after they had created their worlds from the proto-giant's body. After sitting and thinking for a short time, they decided dwarfs should resemble humans and transformed a maggot into Motsognir. Next they made DURINN (1).

Together, these two dwarfs themselves created many more dwarfs, all in the likeness of man. This story is told first in the *VOLUSPA*, part of the *POETIC EDDA*, which contains a lengthy list of dwarf names. SNORRI STURLUSON retells it in *GYLFAGINNING*.

MUNDILFARI (Turner) A man from MIDGARD who named his daughter SOL (Sun) and his son MANI (Moon). The gods stole the children and set them to driving the chariots of the Sun and the Moon eternally through the heavens (see "Sun and Moon," under CREATION; SUN AND MOON).

MUNIN (Memory) One of the god ODIN's two RAVENS. The other was HUGIN (Thought). Each morning Odin sent the two ravens to fly about the NINE WORLDS. Then they returned to HLIDSKJALF, Odin's high seat, perched on his shoulders, and told him what they had seen.

MUSPELL A group of people or creatures from the fiery lands of MUSPELLHEIM, who would ride their horses against the gods at RAGNAROK, the battle at the end of time. SNORRI STURLUSON tells of "the sons of Muspell" and "the people of Muspell" in the *PROSE EDDA*. He also says that *NAGLFAR* is Muspell's ship.

The fact that the name Muspell is also used to refer to the same groups in some works of the *POETIC EDDA* suggests to modern experts that Muspell was an important figure in ancient NORSE myths. Some say Muspell was apparently a giant who ruled over a vast world of evil creatures. He may have ruled a land of heat and flame and thrown fire as his weapon in battle. Surviving stories do not contain enough information to answer these questions.

Muspell's sons are many—enough to form a vast army or a horde of warriors at the end battle between the gods and giants. They fight with the weapons of the land in which they lived: fire, light, and heat.

In the early 20th century, scholars believed Muspell referred to a place and that that place was named after this old mythical giant.

MUSPELLHEIM (Home of Destruction) The realm of fire. Heat from MUSPELL's fires and ice from NIFLHEIM helped to form the first living beings at the CREATION of the world.

Muspellheim was ruled by the fire giant, SURT, who guarded it with a flaming sword. At RAGNAROK, the end of the world, Surt burst through a crack in the dome of the sky and destroyed the world by fire. The forces of evil that fought the gods at Ragnarok came from Muspellheim and are called the sons of Muspell.

N

NABBI A dwarf mentioned only in *HYNDLULJOTH*, a section of the *POETIC EDDA*, as one of the creators of the gold-bristled BOAR HILDISVINI. According to this poem, Nabbi and his brother, DAIN (1), made the magical boar.

NAGLFAR (Conveyance Made of Nails) The ship made from dead men's nails. It carried the GIANTS into battle against the gods at RAGNAROK. *Naglfar's* size would depend on how many men had been buried with untrimmed fingernails. According to SNORRI STURLUSON, an ancient superstition said that the nails of the dead must be cut to keep the size of the fatal ship small and thus give the gods a better chance in battle.

NAGLFARI (Darkling) A giant, the first husband of NOTT (night). They had a son named AUD. The only information about this giant comes from the stories of 13th-century Icelandic poet SNORRI STUR-LUSON in *GYLFAGINNING*.

NAMES NORSE mythology is rich with meaningful names. Gods may have dozens of names; the supreme god ODIN, for example, was known by more than 150 names or titles. Each character, whether human or supernatural, received his or her own name and often many different names. In Norse poetry, SWORDS, chains, wells, animals, and even bridges received names.

Many names of the gods, DWARFS, and GIANTS reflect what scholars see as a strong tradition among the Norse to give significant names to the objects of mythology. Scholars, however, suggest that some of the names in the manuscripts that have survived to modern times reflect a tendency among some editors and scribes of the stories to poke fun at the Norse tradition of naming objects.

NANNA An AESIR goddess, wife of BALDER and mother of FORSETI. After Balder's death, Nanna died of grief, and the gods placed her on his funeral pyre to burn with him. She accompanied Balder to NIFL-HEIM, the realm of HEL (1), and gave gifts to HERMOD for him to take back to ASGARD.

NARFI (NARI) A son of LOKI, the trickster god, and his wife SIGYN. Brother of VALI (1).

The manuscripts containing the stories of NORSE mythology contradict one another in regards to Narfi. The prose conclusion of *LOKASENNA*, a 10th-century poem found in the *POETIC EDDA*, claims that the gods turned Narfi into a WOLF and used the intestines of his brother, Vali, to bind Loki to a boulder. However, SNORRI STURLUSON, who wrote his *PROSE EDDA* in the 13th century and likely used *Lokasenna* as a source, says that the gods turned Vali into a wolf that then killed Narfi. The gods then used Narfi's intestines, not Vali's, to bind Loki to the rock.

NASTROND (Strand of Corpses) The gruesome shore in HEL (2) where the corpses of the evil dead washed up and where the dragon NITHOG feasted. After RAGNAROK (the end of the world), there was still a Nastrond and a Nithog to feed upon the bodies of the dead.

NERTHUS (HERTHA; Earth) A north German goddess, an EARTH MOTHER, worshipped as a goddess of fertility. Some say that she was the sister-wife of the god NJORD and the mother of FREY and FREYA. The Roman historian Tacitus wrote that when Nerthus appeared in her wagon, drawn by oxen, it was a cause for rejoicing throughout the land, and sacrifices were made in her honor.

NIDAFJOLL (Dark Mountains) Two interpreta-tions for this name exist in NORSE poetry. One is a mountain range in the underworld, a place from which the dragon NITHOG flew, carrying corpses in his claws.

The other interpretation, from the works of SNORRI STURLUSON, is that Nidafjoll was the shining land that survived the devastation of RAGNAROK, the final battle between the AESIR gods and the GIANTS. In this land stood the magnificent hall known as SINDRI. The righteous people who survived the conflict would dwell in Nidafjoll, a new world.

NIFLHEIM (World of Fog) A vast waste of frozen fog, brutal cold, and endless night. Niflheim was the lowest region of the underworld. From its poisonous fountain, HVERGELMIR, flowed 11 ice-cold rivers, the ELIVAGIR. The rivers poured into the huge chasm, GINNUNGAGAP, and froze. Fiery clouds from MUSPELLHEIM melted the ice and turned it into mist. From the whirling mist and fire came the first proto-giant, YMIR (see CREATION).

The goddess HEL ruled over this land of the dead. Niflheim was the home of the dragon NITHOG and other serpents. They nibbled on one of the roots of the World Tree, YGGDRASIL, that reached into the underworld.

After MIDGARD (Middle Earth) was created, the gods pushed Niflheim deep into the ground so its terrible cold would not freeze the Earth.

NINE WORLDS In NORSE mythology the Nine Worlds connected by the world tree, YGGDRASIL, were broken into three levels.

- At the top level were ASGARD, the home of the AESIR; VANAHEIM, the home of the VANIR; and ALFHEIM, the home of the LIGHT-ELVES.
- At the middle level, and connected to Asgard by BILROST, the RAINBOW BRIDGE, were MIDGARD (Middle Earth), the home of HUMANS; JOTUN-HEIM, the home of the JOTUN, or GIANTS; and SVARTALFHEIM, the home of the DARK-ELVES.
- At the bottom level, the underworld, were NIFLHEIM, world of the dead, cold, and misty, whose citadel was HEL (2), home of HEL (1), queen of the dead; and MUSPELLHEIM, world of fire, presided over by the fire god, SURT.

In some tellings of the myths, there was also NIDAVELLIR at the middle level; it was cited as the home of the DWARFS and may have been part of Svartalfheim.

From his high seat, HLIDSKJALF, the great god ODIN could see what was happening in all Nine Worlds and with the help of his ravens HUGIN and MUNIN learned each day the events happening in them. (See also RAVEN.)

NITHOG (NIÐHOGGR; NITHOGG; Corpse Tearer) The DRAGON that lived in NIFLHEIM at the foot of the World Tree, YGGDRASIL, and gnawed at its roots. The squirrel RATATOSK brought gossipy messages between the EAGLE at the top of the tree and the dragon at the roots. As well as feeding upon the roots of the sacred tree, Nithog fed on the corpses washed down from NASTROND into the bubbling cauldron of HVERGELMIR. At RAGNAROK, the end of the world, Nithog would harvest many corpses and survive to live in the new world. The Eddic poems *GRIMNISMAL* and *VOLUSPA* describe Nidhogg's roles in the myths, and SNORRI STURLUSON adds details in *GYLFAGINNING*.

NJORD (NIORD) The NORSE god of the sea and seafarers, and also a fertility god. Njord was a VANIR god. He went to live in ASGARD after the AESIR/VANIR WAR. He took with him his twin children, FREY and FREYA, both fertility gods. In some tellings, Njord's first wife and the mother of the twins was NERTHUS, his sister. As the AESIR did not approve of marriage between brother and sister, Njord had to leave Nerthus behind. According to SNORRI STURLUSON, Njord's second wife was SKADE, goddess and GIANT-ESS of winter. Njord's home was NOATUN, a bustling shipyard, noisy with the sound of the wind and the sea and the seabirds. Skade and Njord could not live happily together, for Skade hated the cheerful shipyard, while Njord felt unhappy at Skade's grim, cold mountain home. After spending nine nights together in each other's lands, the two decided to live apart.

NOATUN (BOATHOUSE; Ships' Haven) Home of the VANIR god NJORD after he came to live in ASGARD. Noatun stood on the seashore and was made of great timbers. Njord, god of seafarers, loved the sound of the waves, the seabirds, and the noises of the shipyard.

In a story told by SNORRI STURLUSON in *GYLFAGIN-NING*, the giantess SKADE chose Njord as her husband by looking at his feet only. When the time came to live with her husband, they each agreed to spend nine nights in the other's realm, but Njord missed the sounds of the sea and Skade could not abide the movement and noises at Noatun. As a result, they went their separate ways.

NORDI (NORTH)   One of the four DWARFS who held up the sky. The other three are SUDRI (south), AUSTRI (east), and VESTRI (west). These dwarfs are named in early NORSE poetry, but only 13th-century Icelandic poet SNORRI STURLUSON assigned Nordi and his three companions the job of holding up the four corners of the sky.

NORFI (NARFI; NOR)   A giant who lived in JOTUNHEIM and, according to SNORRI STURLUSON in *GYLFAGINNING*, was the father of NOTT. However, in several works in the *POETIC EDDA*, Nott's father was named Nor. In those works, he is not described as a giant.

"Daughter of Nor," however, was a popular KENNING, or poetic metaphor, for the night.

NORNS (NORNIR; Fates)   The three spirits of destiny who spun a thread of life for every living being, including gods, HUMANS, GIANTS, and DWARFS. They shaped the life of each one from the first day to the last.

The names of the three sisters were URD (Past), VERDANDI (Present), and SKULD (Future). Urd is the oldest of the sisters; often she is pictured as looking backward. Verdande looks straight before her. Skuld usually wears a mysterious veil and carries a scroll in her hands.

The three sisters lived near the URDARBRUNN (Well of Urd) at the foot of the World Tree, YGGDRASIL. Each day they watered the roots of Yggdrasil with the well's sacred water.

The three sisters were more powerful than the gods, for the thread they spun was the destiny of the universe. They measured time and controlled it, and the gods were helpless against them. The gods held all their important meetings by the Well of Urd, a sacred place to them.

In northern folklore, the Norns sometimes appear as spinners, and the spider is therefore associated with them.

The Norns are mentioned in both the *PROSE EDDA* and the *POETIC EDDA*.

NORSE   The name of a specific language group and the people who spoke the languages in that group. Old Norse is a dead language; no group of people speaks it today as its first language. It is part of the North GERMANIC group of languages in the Indo-European language family; this group is also known as the Norse, or Scandinavian, languages. Old Norse is related to modern Danish, Norwegian, Swedish, Icelandic, and Faeroese, the language of the FAROE ISLANDS. Most of the surviving manuscripts of the mythology of SCANDINAVIA, such as the *CODEX REGIUS*, were written in Old Norse.

Norse also refers to ancient peoples who lived in the region of northwest Europe known as Scandinavia, particularly those who spoke Old Norse or one of its dialects. One group of Norse people were known as Norsemen or VIKINGS.

NORWAY   One of the three principal nations of SCANDINAVIA, Norway occupies the western side of the Scandinavian peninsula in northwestern Europe. People have made this land their home since the last great ice age ended more than 13,000 years ago.

Norway features many archaeological sites to provide evidence of the worship of the NORSE gods. Bronze Age rock carvings near Kalnes, Norway, show men in boats and Sun images. At least three burial ships from the VIKING AGE (about A.D. 800–1000) have been uncovered near Oslo. The Oseberg ship,

The Oseberg ship in Oslo, Norway *(Photo by Sagitseagal/Used under a Creative Commons license)*

considered the oldest Viking ship yet found, was built between 850 and 900. It was buried for about 1,000 years and discovered by archaeologists in the early 1900s. The boat itself was elaborately carved. It contained small wagons for carrying "gods," an ornately decorated sleigh or sled, and a narrow tapestry portraying scenes from mythology. An elaborate bucket onboard contained APPLES, a symbol of fertility. Many of these artifacts are on display in museums in Oslo. Churches in Hallingdal and Hegge, meanwhile, contain evidence of the "gods," including carvings that experts believe are representations of ODIN.

Some of Norway's contributions to NORSE history and literature are actually preserved in the manuscripts from ICELAND. The SAGAS, lays, and poems found in Iceland tell of Norway's kings and warrior heroes. Few manuscripts of the Norse age have been found in Norway itself.

NOTT (NIGHT) The dark-haired daughter of NORFI, one of the first GIANTS of JOTUNHEIM. She married three times. Her first husband was NAGLFARI (Darkling); their son was AUD. Her second husband was Annar (Another); their daughter was JORD. Her third husband was DELLING (Dawn); their son was DAG (Day).

The gods gave Nott and her son Dag each a chariot to ride through the heavens (see "Night and Day," under CREATION). Nott's lead horse was HRIMFAXI.

OAK The largest tree of the forests that covered northern Europe, the oak was sacred to THOR, god of thunder and lightning, and a symbol of strength and endurance. There were no great oaks in Iceland, but early settlers from Scandinavia brought oak pillars with them and set up shrines to Thor. Early Christian missionaries such as Boniface (eighth century) considered it their duty to destroy oak trees and groves where the pagan gods had been worshipped.

OD (OÐR; ODUR) The husband of FREYA and father of HNOSSA. Od left Freya to roam the Earth; it is said that Freya wept golden tears for her lost husband. Some scholars think Od may have been the god ODIN in one of his many guises.

ODIN (OÐN) Chief of the AESIR gods. The god of war and death, as well as a sky god and the god of wisdom and poetry. Odin is sometimes called ALFODR, the father of the gods.

He was descended from one of the earliest gods, BOR, and the GIANTESS BESTLA. His brothers were VILI and VE (also called HOENIR and LOTHUR, respectively). (See CREATION.) Odin's Aesir wife was FRIGG. His sons included THOR, VALI, and possibly TYR. Odin had many other wives and children.

Odin's hall in ASGARD was VALASKJALF. From his throne, HLIDSKJALF, in the hall's high tower, Odin could survey all NINE WORLDS of NORSE mythology.

His RAVENS, HUGIN and MUNIN, brought Odin news. He gave his food to his two wolves, GERI and FREKI (see WOLF), for Odin needed nothing but the sacred MEAD for nourishment. Odin's eight-legged steed was called SLEIPNIR.

GUNGNIR was Odin's spear. On his arm Odin wore the marvelous ring DRAUPNIR, from which dropped eight other rings every nine nights. When he rode into battle, he wore an EAGLE helmet and armor. When he wandered peacefully on Earth (as he

often did), Odin wore a sky-blue cape and a broad-brimmed hat.

Odin had only one eye, for he gave his other eye to MIMIR (1) in exchange for wisdom. Odin could compose poetry, for he had drunk the MEAD of poetry.

Odin was also thought of as a magician, for he was a master of the magic songs known as GALDRAR. He knew the secrets of the RUNES (the earliest alphabet used by the Norse), which he had obtained by hanging himself from the World Tree, YGGDRASIL. For this reason he is sometimes called Lord of the Gallows (see below).

Odin (1825–1827) by H.E. Freund in Copenhagen, Denmark

Odin had another palace, named VALHALLA, where he entertained heroes who had fallen in battle and who would help him fight the JOTUN at RAGNAROK, the end of the world. But Odin and most of his warriors would be killed at Ragnarok—Odin, by the monster-wolf, FENRIR. Many wonderful tales are told of Odin, the greatest of the gods. He had as many as 200 different NAMES and attributes.

Odin, along with Thor, FREY, and Tyr, was worshipped for many years after the coming of Christianity to northern Europe.

Lord of the Gallows Odin was called Lord of the Gallows, God of the Hanged, and God of the Spear, among many other names. Odin was the god of knowledge but paid dearly for his wisdom. In one poem (*HAVAMAL*, or *Words of the High One*), Odin hanged himself from the branches of Yggdrasil, the sacred tree. He wounded himself with his spear and hung there for nine days and nine nights, without nourishment. At the end of that time, he came back to life and picked up the magic runes that had dropped from the tree. The runes brought secret knowledge to Odin. He passed on this wisdom to both gods and humans.

Men would make human sacrifices to Odin by hanging prisoners and victims on gallows. It was said that Odin and his ravens would visit the victims and talk to them.

The Mead of Poetry The mead of poetry was the wondrous liquid created by the gods after the AESIR/VANIR WAR. Whoever drank the mead would acquire wisdom and the inspiration to make poetry.

After the truce between the two races of gods (the Aesir and the VANIR), each god and goddess spat into a great jar to put a seal on their friendship. According to a myth in the *PROSE EDDA* and *Havamal* in the *POETIC EDDA*, the Aesir then carried off the jar, and out of the spittle they fashioned a man, KVASIR (1), who walked the world spreading great wisdom to all who asked for it.

The wicked DWARFS FJALAR (2) and GALAR killed Kvasir, collected his blood in three vats, and mixed it with honey to make a powerful mead, which they shared with no one. One day, in a fit of rage, the dwarfs murdered the giant GILLING and his wife. They were forced to give the mead to Gilling's angry son, SUTTUNG, in exchange for their lives.

Suttung built a strong underground cave in the mountain HNITBJORG, where he lived. There he placed the three containers of mead and entrusted his daughter, GUNLOD, to guard them.

Because Suttung was a boastful, bragging kind of giant, it was not long before the Aesir heard what had happened to the divine mead. Odin, a master of disguise, turned himself into a giant of a man and went to JOTUNHEIM, calling himself BOLVERK. There, he sharpened the scythes of nine slaves who were at work in the fields owned by the giant BAUGI, Suttung's brother. The slaves managed to kill one another with their carefully honed scythes.

As Baugi now had no field hands, he agreed to let Odin-Bolverk work for him, for the one-eyed man looked very strong and seemed to need no rest. Odin put his magic to use. He worked better than nine men, for Baugi had promised to try to persuade his brother to allow Odin a sip of the famous mead as a reward for his work.

When the work was done, Baugi talked to his brother, but Suttung refused to part with even one drop of mead. Baugi then drilled a hole into the mountain with the auger RATI, and Odin quickly turned himself into a serpent and slithered into the chamber where Gunlod guarded the treasure.

When lonely Gunlod saw Odin, once more in the shape of a tall, handsome man, she forgot all the promises she had made to her father and entertained Odin for three days and three nights. At the end, she even offered Odin a sip of the precious mead from each of the three containers, BODN, ODRERIR, and SON. To her dismay, Odin gulped down the entire contents of the vats, turned himself into an EAGLE, and flew off to Asgard. He was closely pursued by Suttung, who had tasted the mead and so knew some magic and could change his shape to that of a powerful eagle. But the gods had lit a great fire just outside the walls of Asgard. Suttung fell into this and was burned to death.

Odin spat the precious mead into the vessels that the gods eagerly held out, but in his haste to escape Suttung, he spilled some of the mead, which fell to Earth (MIDGARD). That is how some lucky humans acquired the gift of poetry. This story is in the poem *HAVAMAL* and in SNORRI STURLUSON's *GYLFAGINNING*.

Mimir: How Odin Lost His Eye Mimir was an ancient being noted for his wisdom. According to one myth, Mimir was the guardian of a sacred well (known as MIMIR's WELL) that gave knowledge to those who drank from it. Odin so coveted wisdom that he gave up one of his eyes to Mimir to gain the privilege of drinking from the well. Mimir placed the eye in the well, where it shone as brilliantly as the Moon. This story is referred to in the poem *VOLUSPA* and told by Sturluson in *GYLFAGINNING*.

Odin's Names   Odin had more than 150 names and attributes. Here are just a few of them:

Alfodr—All-Father, Father of the Gods
Baleyg—Flaming-Eyed
Bileyg—Shifty-Eyed
Fjolnir—Wide in Wisdom
GRIMNIR—Hooded One
Valfodr—Father of the Slain
Ygg—Awful

ODRERIR (OÐRÆRIR; ODRORIR; OTHRORIR)
Either the kettle or vat in which the MEAD of poetry was made or the name given to the mead itself.

In the oldest source, the poem *HAVAMAL*, which is part of the *POETIC EDDA*, Odrerir is initially the name of the mead of poetry, the great drink that gives to the drinker the art of being able to create poetry. Later in the poem, Odrerir is a vessel from which a god or person drinks this precious beverage.

SNORRI STURLUSON, in *SKALDSAPARMAL*, explicitly says that Odrerir is the name of the kettle in which the DWARFS let flow the blood of KVASIR (1), a wise man and poet who was made from the spit of the gods, and from whose blood the dwarfs brew the mead of poetry. Two vessels, large vats or barrels named BODN and SON by Sturluson, contained this magical mead.

Sturluson quotes several KENNINGS, or poetic metaphors, that mention Odrerir, but it is unclear if they refer to the drink or the kettle. (See also "The Mead of Poetry" under ODIN.)

OLVALDI   JOTUN father of storm giants THJAZZI, IDI, and GANG. Olvaldi left such a large amount of gold to his sons that no scales could weigh it, so the sons measured it out in giant mouthfuls after their father's death.

See also "Skade and Njord," under SKADE.

OTR (OÐR)   Son of HREIDMAR (a dwarf) and brother of REGIN and FAFNIR. Otr was a SHAPE-SHIFTER and usually took the form of an otter. He was killed by the trickster god, LOKI. Hreidmar demanded as ransom enough gold to cover the dead otter's pelt and to fill its insides.

This myth is told by SNORRI STURLUSON in the *PROSE EDDA* and is mentioned in the *POETIC EDDA* and the late 13th-century *VOLSUNGA SAGA*.

In the *REGINSMAL*, part of the *Poetic Edda*, the story of Otr also forms a preface to the SIGURD legends, in which Hreidmar is murdered by his sons REGIN and FAFNIR. Fafnir then steals the dwarf's treasure for himself and turns himself into a frightful DRAGON, the better to guard it. In the end, the hero Sigurd slays the dragon.

Otr's Ransom   Something of a magician, Otr often took the form of an otter. One day ODIN, his brother HOENIR, and his blood brother LOKI were walking by a stream in MIDGARD. They saw an otter. Loki threw a stone at it and killed it. Then he picked up the otter and flung it over his shoulder.

The three came to the prosperous farmhouse of Hreidmar and asked for shelter for the night. At first Hreidmar was welcoming enough, but when he saw the otter, he shouted in rage and grief, for the dead creature was his son.

Hreidmar summoned his other two sons, Regin and Fafnir. Then, with his magic spells, he disarmed the gods and bound them. Now the gods recognized Hreidmar as the master magician of the TROLLS and DWARFS. He was very powerful indeed.

Odin told Hreidmar that he and his companions would pay whatever ransom he asked, for they had slain his son—but unknowingly, thinking that the creature was a real otter.

Calmed by Odin's fairness, Hreidmar and his sons demanded that the otter's skin should be stuffed with gold inside and the outside covered with gold until not a whisker could be seen.

Odin and Hoenir agreed among themselves that, sly and cunning as he was, Loki would be the best one to find enough gold for the awesome task, for the otter skin was growing bigger by the minute.

Freed of his bonds, Loki went straight to the place where he had killed the otter and stared down into the water. Soon he saw what he was looking for, an enormous pike guarding the entrance to an underwater cave that gleamed with gold. The pike was the dwarf ANDVARI, keeper of the fabled treasure.

Quickly Loki raced to the island of HLESEY, where RAN, the ogress of the oceans, lived with her husband, AEGIR, god of the sea. Loki borrowed from her the cruel net with which she dragged drowning sailors to her underwater realm. With the net, Loki had no difficulty scooping up the pike. He landed it on the bank, where it lay gasping and gradually changed into the ungainly shape of the dwarf.

To save his life, Andvari gave up his entire hoard of gold but for a single ring, ANDVARANAUT. This he begged Loki not to take from him. Loki snatched the ring and put it on his finger. Andvari laid a terrible curse upon the ring, vowing that anyone who wore it would be smitten with ill fortune and death.

The eyes of Hreidmar and his sons glittered greedily when they saw the gold. Odin, Hoenir, and Loki stuffed the otter's pelt and then made a blanket of gold all around the outside of it. Hreidmar examined it critically, then pointed out a whisker that was exposed. Odin had seen Andvari's ring on Loki's finger. Loki pulled it off and laid it on the whisker.

Thus was Otr's ransom paid and the three travelers allowed to go, but not without a parting shot from Loki. He told Hreidmar that he and his sons were doomed to ill fortune and death, for that was the curse of Andvari.

OTTAR The human lover of the goddess FREYA. He built an altar to Freya and offered sacrifices. Freya helped him win a bet by turning him into her BOAR, HILDISVINI, and taking him to visit the GIANTESS and seeress HYNDLA. Hyndla revealed that Ottar was the son of Instein and the priestess Hledis and that SIGURD, the greatest of GERMANIC heroes, was among his ancestors. This story is told in the poem *HYNDLULJODTH*.

POETIC EDDA A collection of poems about the mythological and legendary themes of the NORSE people, written down from the oral tradition by many different poets and scribes at different times between the eighth and 13th centuries. The *Poetic Edda* was, for many years, known as the Elder Edda because most of its material is hundreds of years older than the *PROSE EDDA*, the manuscript written by 13th-century poet and historian SNORRI STURLUSON. The *Poetic Edda* was often the source material for Snorri's work.

The primary and oldest manuscripts that contain some of the poems considered to form the *Poetic Edda* are:

- The *CODEX REGIUS* (GK 2365 4to). The original manuscript is in the Árni Magnússon Institute in Reykjavik, ICELAND. It was written down about 1280 A.D. and appears to be a copy of an even older manuscript. The *Codex Regius* contains 31 mythical and heroic poems important to the study of Norse mythology.

- The *ARNAMAGNAEAN CODEX* (AM 748 Ia 4to). A manuscript that contains some or portions of the poems in the *Poetic Edda*. The section with these poems is only six handwritten pages long. It contains the only copy of the poem *BALDRS DRAUMAR* (*Balder's Dreams*). This document is in the Árni Magnússon Institute Collection at the Universit of Copenhagen in Denmark.

- *FLATEYJARBOK* (GKS 1005 fol.) A late 14th-century manuscript concerning historical sagas of SCANDINAVIA, it contains the *SORLA THATTR* and the only source of the poem *HYNDLULJOTH*. It, too, is in the Arni Magnusson Institute in Reykjavik.

The mythological poems commonly included in published versions of the *Poetic Edda* are:

- *VOLUSPA* (*Prophecy of the Seeress*)
- *HAVAMAL* (*The Words of the High One*)
- *VAFTHRUDNISMAL* (*The Words of Vafthrudnir*)
- *GRIMNISMAL* (*The Lay of Grimnir*)

Title page of a manuscript of the *Prose Edda*, showing Odin, Heimdall, Sleipnir, and other mythological figures. From the 18th-century Icelandic manuscript IB 299 4to, in the care of the Icelandic National Library

- *SKIRNISMAL* (*The Words of Skirnir*)
- *HARBARDSLJUTH* (*The Song of Harbard*)
- *HYMISKVITHA* (*The Lay of Hymir*)
- *LOKASENNA* (*Loki's Verbal Duel*)
- *THRYMSKVITHA* (*The Lay of Thrym*)
- *ALVISSMAL* (*The Words of the All-Wise; The Ballad of Alvis*)
- *BALDRS DRAUMAR* (*Balder's Dreams*)
- *RIGSTHULA* (*The Song of Rig; Rig's Rhymed List*)
- *HYNDLULJODTH* (*The Poem of Hyndla*)

Some translations include *HRAFNAGALDUR ODINS* and *SVIPDAGSMAL* in the *Poetic Edda*, although these poems survive only in paper manuscripts created well after the *Codex Regius* and the *Arnamagnaean Codex* were written. These translators suggest that the content and poetic style of these additional works is so similar to the other poems in the *Poetic Edda* that they should be included.

The poems in the second half of the *Poetic Edda* deal with mortal human heroes whose lives are occasionally interfered with by the Norse gods, DWARFS, GIANTS and TROLLS. Among them, *REGINSMAL* (*The Ballad of Regin*) and *Fafnismal* (*The Lay of Fafnir*) have the strongest connections of the myths of the gods.

PROSE EDDA   The work of Icelandic historian, poet, and politician SNORRI STURLUSON (1179–1241 A.D.) written in the early part of the 13th century. The *Prose Edda* is contained in three vellum manuscripts preserved in SCANDINAVIA; these are called *CODEX REGIUS*, *Codex Upsaliensis*, and *Codex Wormianus*. The manuscripts have been copied onto paper manuscripts several times since the older vellum manuscripts were created in the 13th and 14th centuries.

Three separate works make up the *Prose Edda* and come together to create a handbook of NORSE mythology, written as a guide for poets to encourage them to use the style of the poets of the VIKING AGE, particularly SKALDIC POETRY. These works include:

- *GYLFAGINNING* (*The Deceiving of Gylfi*) tells the myths of the Norse gods and the worlds they lived in. In this section, Snorri borrowed heavily from the works in the *Poetic Edda* and other poems that did not survive in manuscripts. *Gylfaginning* is an important, and sometimes a unique, source of many Norse myths. Snorri's prologue to *Gylfaginning* presents his attempt to create a human history for the Norse gods or an explanation other than a myth for how the Norse pantheon and all of its beings came into existence.
- *SKALDSKAPARMAL* (*Prose Diction*), mostly a listing of the NAMES and KENNINGS, poetic metaphors or sayings frequently used in Norse poetry. This work also contains many of the mythological and historical tales.
- *Hattatal* (*The Meters of Poetry*), a poem by Snorri about King Haakon and Duke Skuli of NORWAY during the years 1221–1223 A.D.

Snorri, himself a Christian, wrote this guide to Old Icelandic poetry and Norse mythology after Christianity was well established in ICELAND and knowledge about the old gods and their adventures was dying out. He sought to preserve the old knowledge as well as the poetic form that he practiced.

R

RAGNAROK (Judgment of the Gods) The final battle between the gods, headed by ODIN and the EINHERJAR on the side of good, and LOKI and the JOTUN on the side of evil. It took place on the plain called VIGRID. Nearly all the participants were slain. The SUN AND MOON were swallowed by wolves, the stars vanished, the sacred tree YGGDRASIL trembled, the ocean boiled, and SURT set the world on fire so that everything was reduced to cinders. However, BALDER and HODUR rose up from the underworld; VALI, VIDAR, MODI, MAGNI, and some others survived to live in a regenerated world. A HUMAN couple, LIF and LIFTHRASIR, also survived and repeopled Earth.

Ragnarok is described in detail in the Icelandic poem *VOLUSPA* (*Sibyl's Prophecy*) and in the *PROSE EDDA*.

Ragnarok, the Day of Doom Ragnarok was the end of the world, the twilight of the gods, the final battle between the forces of good (the gods) and the forces of evil (the GIANTS and the monsters of the underworld). After the death of Balder, the gods banished Loki, the evil one, to MIDGARD (Middle Earth), but it was too late. The god of light and innocence had been killed. The gods knew that the day of doom was at hand and that they and all their worlds would perish.

First came a wave of ghastly crimes and bloody wars in Midgard. Brothers fought against brothers; murder and looting and other evil deeds were committed. Then came FIMBULVETR, the worst of all winters. It brought bitter cold and driving snow, screeching winds and black darkness. The Fimbulvetr lasted three years. People shivered and starved and lost all hope and goodness.

From JARNVID came the ravenous wolves SKOLL and HATI. Skoll caught up with SOL's chariot and swallowed the Sun, spilling her blood on the Earth.

Hati devoured the Moon. The stars fell out of the sky, and the darkness was complete.

Then the Earth began to tremble and quake, and the WOLF FENRIR broke from his bonds, ready to seek vengeance on the gods who had tricked him. Loki, too, broke free. GARM, HEL's hound, was set free. Evil and destruction were loose on the land.

EGGTHER, the watchman of the giants, struck a note on his harp. The red cock FJALAR (1) crowed to the giants, while GULLINKAMBI screeched to the gods in VALHALLA and a third rooster, rust red, awakened all the dead in NIFLHEIM.

HEIMDALL, the WATCHMAN OF THE GODS, lifted his horn, GJALLERHORN, and blew it. All the AESIR and the Einherjar sprang up and donned their armor, ready for the battle to end all battles. First Odin galloped off on SLEIPNIR to MIMIR's WELL to seek his wisdom. The NORNS regarded him with veiled faces, their web of life torn into shreds. No one knew what Odin learned from MIMIR the Wise. He rejoined the waiting army with a grim, sad face and led them into battle, holding aloft his magic spear, GUNGNIR.

The sea began to boil like a cauldron, and its waves crashed on the shore, for JORMUNGAND, the MIDGARD SERPENT, had risen up from the deep and was lashing and writhing his way toward the land, spewing VENOM from his jaws.

The horrid ship *NAGLFAR*, made from dead men's fingernails, drifted loose, packed with giants, and steered by HRYM. It headed toward the battlefield. The crew and passengers of Loki's ship were all the pale dead from the underworld.

Hel, the goddess of death, left Niflheim to join the fray, followed by the hound Garm and the dragon NITHOG, who flew over the battlefield gathering corpses for his sustenance.

Loki led the terrible army of evil. As they crossed BILROST, the RAINBOW BRIDGE, it trembled and broke beneath them, but not before they had reached Vigrid.

Odin, the mighty leader of the gods, attacked first. He joined battle with the monster-wolf, Fenrir, whose slavering jaws grew wider and wider, stretching from heaven to Earth, until they swallowed up Odin.

Nearby, THOR, the god of thunder, wrestled with Jormungand. In the deathly struggle, Thor killed the serpent, but Thor, too, died a gasping death from the beast's fatal venom.

Loki and Heimdall, lifelong enemies, killed each other.

FREY, the god of fertility, grappled with the fire god, SURT, in a lengthy battle. Frey had given away his magic sword long ago for love of GERDA, and now, without it, he was killed by the fire demon.

TYR, who had only one hand, fought bravely against Garm, and the two killed each other.

All around the battle raged, and all were doomed to perish. But Vidar, a son of Odin, avenged his father. On his foot he wore a boot made from all the strips of leather snipped off and saved by good cobblers for just this purpose. Vidar crushed his magic boot onto the lower jaw of Fenrir, and, using all his strength, tore the wolf apart.

With Odin and most of the other gods, heroes, giants, and monsters dead, Surt flung his brands of fire all over Earth so that there was a great and terrible conflagration. All NINE WORLDS went up in flames, and at last the Earth sank into the boiling sea.

The idea of Ragnarok is similar to Christian and Asian conceptions of Judgment Day or doomsday. However, the dramatic descriptions of darkness, earthquakes, flood, fire, and ashes undoubtedly came straight from the Icelandic poets' own experiences of volcanic eruptions in their native land.

The Regeneration After the terrible destruction of Ragnarok, all was not lost, for there was a rebirth: Two HUMANS emerged, some of the gods survived, green plants grew, and a new world was born.

Before she was devoured by the wolf, Sol had given birth to a daughter, as brilliant and burning as she. As this new sun appeared, darkness vanished, and a new day dawned in a world that gradually, magically, became green and pleasant, with fields of corn growing where no seeds had been planted.

From the remains of the sacred tree, Yggdrasil, stepped a human man, Lif, and a human woman, Lifthrasir. They had been nourished by dew and were unhurt by Surt's fire. They would repeople the Earth.

Vidar and Vali survived, as did Modi and Magni, Thor's sons, who inherited his hammer, MJOLLNIR. Balder came back from the dead, leading his blind brother, Hodur. HOENIR (VILI) appeared and so did LOTHUR (VE), Odin's brothers. They went to IDAVOLL, which had remained unscorched, and there they built new mansions, the greatest of which was GIMLE, roofed with gold. Another was Brimir, on the place called Okolnir (Never Cold). SINDRI rose up in the mountains of NIDAFJOLL. All these places were good.

But there was also a hall on NASTROND, the shore of corpses. All its doors faced north to greet the shrieking winds. The walls were made of writhing snakes that poured their venom into a river that flowed through the hall. This was the new underworld, full of murderers and thieves, and when they died, Nidhoss, who had survived, was there to feed upon the corpses.

The Aesir walked on the new green grass of Idavoll and talked about the past and their dear, perished friends. They played chess with the golden pieces that they found on the ground, and they thought with wonder about the new life of the Earth.

RAINBOW BRIDGE The common name for BILROST, the bridge that stretched between the human world and the world of the gods, between Earth and Heaven. This bridge was made by the gods in three colors—red, blue, and green—giving Bilrost its common nickname.

Only in the writings of 13th-century Icelandic historian SNORRI STURLUSON was the image of the rainbow associated with Bilrost, according to Old NORSE experts. Earlier forms of this Norse myth refer to the Milky Way as the bridge that joins Heaven and Earth.

RAN (Robber) The wife of AEGIR, JOTUN lord of the sea. She lived with Aegir beneath the island of HLESEY, in coral caves. She dragged drowning sailors down to her realm in her fishing net, which either she or LOKI invented. Her halls were lighted only by the gleam of gold, reminiscent of the phosphorescent glow of the sea. It is said that Ran felt kindly toward dead sailors who had some gold in their possession to help her light her halls. In "Otr's Ransom" (under OTR), Loki borrows Ran's net to catch the DWARF ANDVARI.

RATATOSK The squirrel that scampered up and down the World Tree, YGGDRASIL. He spread gossip and carried insults between NITHOG, the dragon who nibbled at the roots of the tree, and the EAGLE that sat in the topmost branches.

RATI (Traveler) The carpenter's tool, known as an auger or drill, which ODIN, in disguise, uses to drill a hole through the mountain HNITBJORG. Odin produces Rati as he is trying to trick the giant BAUGI into helping him get a drink of the MEAD of poetry. Odin commands Baugi to drill a hole through Hnitbjorg so Odin may enter the place where the giant SUTTUNG keeps the mead. Though Baugi tries to hide the hole, Odin finds it, turns into a serpent, and quickly slithers through the mountain. Baugi throws Rati at Odin but misses, and Odin succeeds in getting the mead.

SNORRI STURLUSON tells the story in the beginning of *SKALDSKAPARMAL*, part of his *PROSE EDDA*. (See also "The Mead of Poetry" under Odin.)

RAVEN A large, black bird, *Corvus corax*, a member of the crow family. The raven is commonly found in northern Europe, North America, and northern Asia. The raven was a symbol of ODIN, chief god among the AESIR gods. Odin kept two ravens, HUGIN (Thought) and MUNIN (Mind). Odin sent these ravens out into the world each daybreak, and they returned by breakfast time to tell Odin of what they had seen and learned. In an early NORSE poem, *HRAFNAGALDUR ODINS* (*Odin's Raven Chant*), Odin sends the ravens to the underworld to investigate the disappearance of the goddess IDUNN.

The raven was a common symbol in many mythologies, sometimes as a sign of evil owing to its habits as a scavenger and sometimes as a sign of good. In Norse mythology, ravens played both roles. As representatives of Odin's mind and thoughts, ravens symbolized his power to see into the future. As symbols of the battlefield, they represented Odin's welcoming to his palace, VALHALLA, the spirits of slain HUMAN heroes who died in battle. Viking war flags carried symbols of ravens as Odin's servants.

REGIN Son of the magician HREIDMAR and brother of FAFNIR and OTR. Regin was a wise and fierce dwarf, skilled in magic.

After Fafnir killed Hreidmar and stole the hoard of gold the family had received from the gods ODIN, HOENIR, and LOKI as payment for Otr's death, Regin spent his life seeking his deceitful brother. In the poem *REGINSMAL*, Regin journeys to the court of Hjalpreck, where he meets the young hero SIGURD. Regin raises the boy to be strong and fierce, with the intention of having Sigurd hunt down Fafnir, now in dragon form, and kill him. In the poem *FAFNISMAL*, this plan of revenge comes to fruition when Sigurd slays the dragon. However, Sigurd also kills Regin after he learns that the dwarf has only used him for the long-awaited vengeance.

SNORRI STURLUSON tells the story of the killing of Otr, Regin's brother, in *SKALDSKAPARMAL*. The story is depicted in a famous RUNESTONE, or rock carving, found in Sodermanland, SWEDEN.

REGINSMAL (*The Ballad of Regin; Regin's Poem*) A poem within the *CODEX REGIUS* of the *POETIC EDDA*. *Reginsmal* tells part of the story of REGIN, a dwarf and foster father to the hero SIGURD, whose story is also told in the *VOLSUNGA SAGA*. It is one of the heroic poems (see HEROIC LEGENDS) in the later portion of the *Poetic Edda*.

Reginsmal begins with the mythical tale of the death of Regin's brother OTR at the hands of the gods ODIN, LOKI, and HOENIR. It continues with the story of Loki's theft of ANDVARI's gold and the death of Regin's father, HREIDMAR, at the hands of his son and the brother of Otr and Regin, FAFNIR. Fafnir hoards the gold in which the gods had wrapped Otr's body, the treasure of the family, and turns himself into a DRAGON to guard it. Regin tells Sigurd all of this in *Reginsmal*.

Then Regin encourages Sigurd to ask the king for a HORSE and a SWORD. Finally, Regin tells Sigurd to seek out and kill the dragon, Fafnir, a successful feat for which Sigurd becomes famous.

The poems *Fafnismal* and *Sigrdifuml*, also parts of the *POETIC EDDA*, continue the story of Sigurd, paralleling the story told in the *Volsunga Saga*. Some translators and scholars believe that these three poems were originally one work and were broken up by the medieval scribes who worked with and copied the manuscripts that became the *Codex Regius*.

RIG The main character in *RIGSTHULA*, an ancient poem, part of the *POETIC EDDA*. The introduction to this poem in the surviving manuscripts says Rig is the god HEIMDALL, but modern scholars agree that an editor of the manuscript made that assumption and addition.

Rig-Heimdall and the Races of Men Heimdall was the WATCHMAN OF THE GODS. He seldom left his post on BILROST, the RAINBOW BRIDGE. One day, at ODIN's suggestion, Heimdall went down to MIDGARD

(Middle Earth) disguised as a mortal man. He left behind his horn, GJALLERHORN, his sword, and his golden-topped steed, and took the name Rig.

Rig wandered along the seashore at the edge of the world. When evening came, he saw a rickety old hut. Rig knocked and the door creaked open. It was dark and smoky inside, but Rig-Heimdall with his keen eyes could see Ai and Edda (great-grandfather and great-grandmother) and gave them his golden smile. They shared their miserable meal with him. Rig was so courteous and friendly that they shared their bed, too, allowing the sweet-talking god to sleep warmly between their two thin bodies. He shared their food and their bed for three days and three nights, then went on his way.

Nine months after the god's visit, Edda gave birth to a son. His parents named him THRALL. The boy was sturdy and strong and grew to be very good at all the hard and heavy chores that laborers must do: chopping wood, digging the earth, building huts, tending the pigs and GOATS, gathering food, burning peat. When Thrall grew up, he married Thir, another hard worker, and their children and their children's children were the peasants, laborers, and slaves of the world.

The evening after leaving Ai and Edda, Rig came to a big farm, where he found Afi and Amma (grandfather and grandmother). Afi's beard was neatly trimmed and Amma's hair was smooth and silvery. They both wore clean and simple clothes. Rig gave them his golden smile. They shared their nourishing meal with him. Rig was so courteous and friendly that they shared their bed, too, allowing the sweet-talking god to sleep warmly between their sturdy bodies. He shared their food and their bed for three days and three nights, then went on his way.

Nine months after the god's visit, Amma gave birth to a son. The parents named him KARL (Freeman). The boy was healthy and ruddy, and he grew to be very good at all the work that a proud farmer must do: building fine houses and sturdy barns and learning the skills of the blacksmith, the reaper of corn, and the tender of fine animals. When Karl grew up, he married a strapping girl named Snot. She knew how to spin and weave; she sewed a fine seam and baked good bread. Their children and their children's children became the farmers, landholders, and craftsmen of the world.

The evening after leaving Afi and Amma, Rig came to a great mansion, where he found Fodir and Modir.

Their clothes were rich and glittering with jewels. Rig gave them his golden smile, and the handsome couple invited him to dinner. A long table was covered with a linen cloth and set with silver wine jugs, goblets, and pewter platters. The servants brought in mounds of delicious meats and fruits. Rig was so courteous and friendly that Fodir and Modir shared their luxurious bed with him, allowing the sweet-talking god to sleep warmly between their two shapely bodies. Rig shared their food and their bed for three days and three nights, then went on his way.

Nine months after the god's visit, Modir gave birth to a son. The parents named him JARL (nobly born). The boy was tall and handsome, with golden hair and a golden smile, and he grew to be a fine horseman, skilled with both spear and sword as well as with a bow and arrow. When Jarl grew up, he married a rich and graceful girl named Erna. Her skin was soft and her fingers long. She played beautifully on the lute and her voice was the envy of the nightingale. Their children and their children's children became the kings and queens of many lands of the world.

Rig-Heimdall transported himself to the time when Jarl was still a young lad. The god appeared before Jarl in a forest grove, bringing with him some sticks with strangely carved markings on them. Rig taught Jarl, his son, the secrets of the RUNES and much wisdom about the good and evil in the world so that Jarl and his children and grandchildren could become fine and just rulers of their kingdoms.

RIGSTHULA (RIGSPULA) A poem of questionable found only in a manuscript that also contains SNORRI STURLUSON's work. It's the source of the story RIG, who may have been HEIMDALL in disguise.

The importance of this poem in understanding NORSE mythology is heavily debated among scholars and experts. The introduction to the 14th-century manuscript in which this poem was found says that Rig, the main character, is actually the god Heimdall, who watched over the land of the gods. However, nowhere in the poem itself is Rig identified with Heimdall, and many scholars question why others say Rig is Heimdall. Modern experts also suggest that the poem is older than its introduction and that the editor of the manuscript chose to give Heimdall credit for being Rig. In the manuscript in which it was found, the *Codex Wormanius* the end of the *Rigsthula* is missing.

Experts are unsure of the age of the poem. Some say it was written as early as the ninth century A.D., others as late as the 13th century.

RIME-GIANTS A common name for the first GIANTS, also known as the proto-giants or frost giants. They preceded the JOTUN in NORSE mythology and represent a period of mythology even older than that of the VIKING AGE.

Some translators use the term rime-giant for the term HRIMTHURSSAR, which means rime or frost giant. Both rime and frost refer to the ice crystals of VENOM that were formed by the spring HVERGELMIR. That poisonous frost, when melted in GINNUNGAGAP by the heat from MUSPELLHEIM, created AUGLEMIR, the first of this earliest race of giants. According to SNORRI STURLUSON, Auglemer is the name the rime-giants themselves gave to YMIR, the father of their race and the proto-giant killed by the gods to create the universe.

RINDA (RIND) Daughter of Billing, king of the Ruthenians; mate of the god ODIN; mother of VALI (2). She appears only once in the existing NORSE manuscripts, as the temporary wife of Odin. Rinda is a personification of the hard, frozen rind of the Earth. At first, she resists the wooing of Odin (the Sun) but finally succumbs to his warmth and gives birth to Vali, the light god of spring. See also BILLING'S DAUGHTER.

RIVERS Rivers in NORSE mythology provided barriers between worlds, marked the boundaries of realms, and provided challenges to the gods.

The river IFING separates the world of the gods from the world of the GIANTS, while the river GJOLL (2) divides the land of the living from the land of the dead.

From the middle of the river VIMUR, Thor battles the GIANTESS GIALP, who seeks to drown the mighty god by adding her own bodily fluids to the powerful flow of the water. Each day, Thor must wade across the mighty rivers KORMT AND ORMT to arrive at the gathering of the AESIR.

In one ancient story, all of the rivers of the world flow from the spring HVERGELMIR, which lies in the center of NIFLHEIM, the lowest of the three levels of the underworld. In two places in *GYLFAGINNING*, SNORRI STURLUSON names the rivers that flow from Hvergelmir. According to Snorri, the spring itself is fed by water that drips from the horns of EIKTHYRNIR, the male DEER that nibbles at the tree that grows next to ASGARD.

Two mighty rivers, the Horn and Ruth, flow into HEL (2) and seem to represent the dangers of rivers that overflow during the spring melt.

The poet who composed *GRIMNISMAL* included a list of 48 rivers in his work. Scholars researching these names have worked to identify them with the many rivers of SCANDINAVIA.

ROSKVA The farmer EGIL's daughter, who becomes the god THOR's servant, along with her brother THJALFI. Thor took the brother and sister to be his eternal servants after Thjalfi had disobeyed his command not to mutilate the bones of his GOATS. The story is told in SNORRI STURLUSON's *GYLFAGINNING*.

ROWAN A mountain tree of the rose family, not related to the common ASH tree. A sturdy tree, it has dense white blossoms and clusters of red fruit well loved by birds. Old superstitions say that the tree has protective qualities, especially against witches. In NORSE mythology it is called "Thor's Salvation" or "Thor's Tree of Deliverance" because it saved THOR from drowning in the VIMUR River.

RUNES (That Which Is Secret) Ancient letters or symbols used in the earliest alphabets of the GERMANIC tribes of northern Europe, including the NORSE, from the second to the 12th centuries. Runic inscriptions occur most commonly in SCANDINAVIA and parts of GREAT BRITAIN. The characters consisted of perpendicular, slanting, and curved lines, well adapted to being carved on wood, stone, and metal. Magical and mysterious powers were associated with runes.

According to Norse mythology, knowledge of runes was introduced by the god ODIN, who hanged himself from the branches of the sacred tree, YGGDRASIL, for nine days and nine nights until fallen twigs from the tree spelled out the secrets of the runes.

After the establishment of Christianity in the north, runes were looked down upon as pagan. Nonetheless, in Scandinavia their use continued after the Middle Ages in manuscripts as well as in inscriptions on stone, metal, and wood.

RUNESTONES (picture stones) Stones across much of SWEDEN, portions of NORWAY and DENMARK, and the islands in the Baltic and North seas that contain carvings of tributes and verses in RUNES, some with illustrations of people, snakes, birds, ships, and more. Many runestones are huge boulders that stand in fields. While many are now in museums in

SCANDINAVIA, others are still standing in the fields, most likely in their original locations.

Runestones are the original documents of the VIKING AGE (700 to 1200 A.D.) and earlier. They provide archaeologists and scholars with the names of men who fought in Viking wars and of their gods and heroes. They tell of good, kind women, of rulers and their lands, and of the people who believed in the stories that are now NORSE mythology.

The oldest stone art in Scandinavia was made during the region's Bronze Age, from 1600 to 450 B.C. These carvings, known as petroglyphs, show crude people, ships, reindeer, bulls, and other objects; examples of petroglyphs can be found in the Tanum area in GOTLAND, Sweden. While some experts see links between these drawings and the gods and stories of Norse myths, others do not support those conclusions.

By about 750 A.D., simple carvings of one or two words written in runes appeared on stones. These evolved into elaborate carvings of runic verse. During much of the Viking Age, artisans were creating impressive memorials to their deceased ancestors and their cultures. More recent runestones tell of the Nordic conversion to Christianity in the 10th and 11th centuries and peoples' beliefs in that religion.

Among the most famous runestone is the story of SIGURD, slayer of the dragon FAFNIR, carved on bedrock near Ramsundberg, Sodermanland, Sweden. Another is the Altuna stone near Uppland, Sweden, which tells the story of THOR's battle with JORMUNGAND, the MIDGARD SERPENT.

Some of the older stones tell their stories through pictures and contain no runes. Among these, the most famous picture stones are the memorial stone from Alskog, Tjanngvide, Gotland, which depicts ODIN riding his eight-legged HORSE, SLEIPNIR, and the memorial stone in Bunge, Gotland, which shows scenes of a journey to HEL (2).

SAEGR   The bucket the children BIL AND HJUKI used to carry water from the well, according to SNORRI STURLUSON in *GYLFAGINNING*, part of his *PROSE EDDA*. While carrying the bucket, the children were taken up to HEAVEN by the MOON so that they could forever follow him.

SAEHRIMNIR (SÆHRIMNIR; Sooty)   The magical BOAR of VALHALLA that each day was killed and cooked by the gods' chef ANDHRIMNIR in the giant kettle ELDHRIMNIR. Saehrimnir returned to life each night, only to be butchered the next day.

Saehrimnir was the best of pigs, and later the best of hams, but few knew, according to the poem *GRIMNISMAL*, that he was the food source of the daily banquet held for the EINHERJAR, the dead human warriors who had fought in battle all day. According to SNORRI STURLUSON in *GYLFAGINNING*, never would there be so many fallen heroes in Valhalla that Saehrimnir would not have enough flesh to feed them.

SAEMING   A son of the great NORSE god ODIN, perhaps invented by the 13th-century Icelandic historian SNORRI STURLUSON or by rulers of ancient NORWAY.

According to Snorri in the introduction to three of his great works, Odin was a powerful leader from central Asia who traveled north through Europe to SWEDEN, establishing two of his sons as rulers of kingdoms along the way. Near the end of his journey, Odin traveled north to the coast. There he made his son, Saeming, king. This interpretation of myths as the stories of real HUMANS is known as euhemerism.

Many historical rulers of Norway traced their ancestry to Saeming, and he became a father figure, a great ancestor, to the powerful families in that region. Scholars believe the rulers of the lands in SCANDINAVIA may have created the stories of Saeming and his

brothers to connect their histories to the legends of the gods.

In another part of his *PROSE EDDA*, Snorri also wrote that SKADE, daughter of the frost giant THJAZZI, was Saeming's mother.

SAEMUND SIGFÚSSON (SÆMUND SIGFUSSON; Saemund the Learned) (1056–1133) Icelandic historian and Catholic priest; author of an important history of the kings of NORWAY that has been lost. Later authors made use of Saemund's history and discussed its importance in their own works.

Before 1900, literary scholars and experts believed Saemund wrote the *POETIC EDDA*, a collection of ancient NORSE poetry found in the *CODEX REGIUS* and other manuscripts. They referred to these poems as *Saemund's Edda*. Based on detailed studies of the language and style of these old poems, experts no longer believe that Saemund had any connection to the *Poetic Edda*. Many books in libraries, however, still list him as the author.

SAGA (1)   An Old NORSE word meaning "story." The sagas were stories in prose or verse dating from the early 11th to the mid-14th centuries, first written down about 1200. There were family sagas about early Icelandic settlers; sagas of the kings, which were semihistorical stories about the kings of NORWAY; and heroic sagas, which told of legendary heroes and fantastic adventures. The *VOLSUNGA SAGA* (late 13th century) is a good example of a heroic saga. Many are now available in English in books and on the Internet.

SAGA (2)   A female goddess, one of the ASYNJUR. (The first *a* in her name is a long *a*, making the pronunciation different from SAGA [1], a type of story.) Little is known of Saga except that she lived in the great hall known as SOKKVABEKK, where she often spent the day drinking from golden goblets with ODIN. Some scholars suggest that Saga was another name for FRIGG, Odin's wife, for Saga means "she who knows all things" and this was a trait Frigg shared with her husband.

SAXO GRAMMATICUS
Danish scholar of the 13th century who wrote in Latin *GESTA DANORUM*, a multivolume, partly mythical history of the Danes. In it Saxo recounts many myths of DENMARK (including that of Hamlet) and NORWAY. Saxo's approach to the myths and the people in them was rather harsh and unsympathetic compared to that of the Icelandic writer SNORRI STURLUSON.

SCANDINAVIA
A region in northwestern Europe. NORWAY and SWEDEN form the great peninsula once known as Scandia and now known as the Scandinavian peninsula. DENMARK's Jutland peninsula and the islands that lie between it and the Scandinavian peninsula, as well as the FAROE ISLANDS and ICELAND, which lie in the Atlantic Ocean to the west and northwest of Norway, are often considered part of the region.

The people of Scandinavia share similar languages, histories, and cultures. Norwegian, Swedish, Danish, and Icelandic all share roots with the GERMANIC languages. Their ancestors spoke Old NORSE, a name that has often been used to refer to the people of Scandinavia as well as the ancient language. In 400 B.C., the Germanic peoples of north central Europe began moving northward and building settlements in Scandinavia, living next to or pushing aside the native people of those lands. By A.D. 600, nation-states had begun to take shape in these regions, and language changes separated these immigrant peoples from the cultures of their origins. Around this time the VIKINGS, a powerful people, began centuries of conquest across northern Europe, including GREAT BRITAIN, Finland, and parts of eastern Russia.

Much of the information of the mythology of the Norse has survived in the records and manuscripts of the Scandinavian nations and on the intricate and complex stone carvings known as RUNESTONES or picture stones found throughout the region. Scholars have pieced together the stories of the gods, goddesses, enemies, and kingdoms of this mythology from scattered sources. From Iceland to the west and Finland to the east, the Arctic Circle to the north and the bogs of low-lying Denmark to the south, archaeologists have for almost two centuries uncovered the story of Scandinavia's past, including the spectacular finds of SHIPS AND SHIP BURIALS near Oseberg, Norway, in 1904 and at Sutton Hoo in East Anglia, England, first excavated in 1939.

SEA
The sea was important to NORSE mythology as a threat, a danger, and an everyday part of life.

The sea represented a realm of passage between the land of the living and the land of the dead. The story of the death of BALDER, the son of ODIN, as well as the many SHIP BURIALS found across SCANDINAVIA show how important the sea was in the journey beyond death. After his brother HODUR kills Balder, the AESIR take Balder's body to the sea and put him in a great ship which a GIANTESS then pushes into the water. Archaeologists have found burial sites in NORWAY, SWEDEN, and GREAT BRITAIN that resemble the scene described in this tale.

Though very dangerous, the sea was also a source of food for the people of the VIKING AGE. Fishing trips are frequent in the myths and the heroic legends. The most famous fishing trip is THOR's journey out to sea with HYMIR to fish for JORMUNGAND, the MIDGARD SERPENT, who lived in the sea that surrounded the world.

SNORRI STURLUSON included a long list of terms for the sea in *SKALDSKAPARMAL*, his work of advice and instruction to poets.

Two sea kings are named in the surviving manuscripts of Norse mythology. AEGIR was a giant who lived by and ruled the sea. With his wife, RAN, he had nine daughters, and each of them had a name that represented a characteristic of the sea: Himinglaefa means transparent, that through which one can see Heaven; Dufa means wave or the pitching one; Blodughadda means bloody hair or red sea foam; Hefring means riser; Udr or Unn means frothing wave; Hronn means welling wave; Bylgja means to billow; Drofn (or Bara) means foam fleck or wave; Kolga means cool wave. SNORRI lists these daughters twice in *Skaldsaparmal*. An older poem, *HYNDLULJOTH*, gives a different sent of names for these nine daughters of Aegir; scholars cannot explain these differences. See "Heimdall's Nine Mothers" under HEIMDALL.

SEID
A special form of magic or witchcraft, often socially objectionable, containing highly ritualistic ceremonies and oaths. In powerful cultic ceremonies, priestesses summoned this magic so they could see into the future; arrange bad luck, illness, or death for an enemy; or transfer the mind and strength of one person into another. Often leaders would seek out the help of people with these magical powers in times of crisis.

Women were the primary practitioners of seid, which reportedly had a strong sexual impact on the magicians. In the ceremonies, the priestess wore a special costume made of fur and featuring a prominent headdress.

According to NORSE mythology, FREYA, a VANIR goddess, shared the gift of seid with the great AESIR god ODIN and the other gods and goddesses. Odin became the chief practitioner of this magic among all of the Aesir gods. Freya is said to have never used her powers.

SERPENT   A word often used in mythology, religion, and folklore to denote nonspecific reptiles, such as snakes, dragons, or SEA monsters. Serpent is used as a poetic metaphor, or KENNING, in the SKALDIC POETRY of ICELAND. It was a symbol of protection for warriors, a guardian of great treasures, and may have been a symbol of fertility and healing. In some instances, the serpent was an opponent of the gods.

In NORSE mythology, the DRAGON NITHOG chewed at the roots of the sacred tree, YGGDRASIL and JORMUNGAND, the MIDGARD SERPENT, encircled the

The figure of a serpent is depicted on this runestone in Lifsinge, Sweden, a commemoration of a Viking sailor who died in Ingvar the Far-Travelled's expedition to the Caspian Sea. *(Photo by Berig/Used under a Creative Commons license)*

earth with his tail in his mouth and spewed poisonous VENOM during RAGNAROK. ODIN turned himself into a serpent to enter the cave where he found the MEAD of poetry. FAFNIR turned himself into a dragon to guard his treasure. The gods placed a serpent over LOKI's head after they had bound him to a rock.

The serpent is a common figure on the RUNESTONE carvings found across SCANDINAVIA. It is often depicted wound around the stone, sometimes surrounding the primary message, and usually containing RUNES itself. It is also found decorating woodcarvings such as the wagon found in the SHIP BURIAL in Oseberg, NORWAY.

SESSRUMNIR (Rich in Seats)   The hall of the goddess FREYA where she welcomed the spirits of slain warriors and heroes, whom she shared with the war god, ODIN. Sessrumnir was located in the part of ASGARD known as FOLKVANG, the realm of Freya. It is said to have had as much room for its guests as did VALHALLA, the palace where Odin welcomed his share of fallen warriors.

SHAPE-SHIFTER (Shape Changer)   Gods and GIANTS magically change form often within the stories of NORSE mythology. This was a complete physical transformation, not merely a surface disguise. Most commonly they took the shape of EAGLES or FALCONS to fly swiftly over land.

The supreme god ODIN had the power to change shape at will and took on many different identities to walk among HUMANS. He and FREYA preferred the form of the hawk for their supernatural travels. LOKI, though, was the most famous shape-shifter, for he would change gender as well as form. In the story of the GIANT MASTER BUILDER, Loki became a mare to lure away the giant's stallion. In the story "Treasures of the dwarfs," he became a fly to pester the dwarfs.

Giants, too, changed shape. One became an eagle to steal the gods' dinner. Another took the shape of a man to trick the gods.

SHIPS AND SHIP BURIALS   Ships were an important part of NORSE culture. The Norse depended on ships not only for fishing and trading but for expanding their empires. The VIKING seafarers roamed from their northern strongholds as far south as the Iberian peninsula (modern Spain and Portugal), Italy, and Sicily and as far east as Russia, Constantinople, and Baghdad. A Viking navigator, Leif Eriksson, sailed to North America in about the year 1000, almost five centuries before Christopher Columbus set foot in the Americas. The Vikings also colonized ICELAND and Greenland.

Viking ships were long ships, with graceful, upward-curving bows and sterns, often carved with elaborate designs. They were powered by oarsmen and sails.

Ships were so venerated that when a distinguished person died, he was put aboard his ship, which was then set afire and sent out to sea. In the myth of BALDER, the god was set aboard his ship, *HRINGHORNI*, along with his dead wife, his horse, and some of his treasures. *Hringhorni* was then set afire and sent out to sea.

In recent years, archaeological digs have uncovered various burial ships in SCANDINAVIA and GREAT BRITAIN. Along with the bones of dead people and animals, they contained ancient weapons, chariots, jewelry, ornaments, food, and utensils—all the necessities for the comfort of the dead in the afterlife. In Sutton Hoo, in East Anglia, England, the remains of an 80-foot ship were uncovered along with treasures but no bones of the dead. It is thought that the hero may have disappeared at sea, or perhaps he had been given a Christian burial while his treasures were buried according to a more ancient pagan custom. The Sutton Hoo ship dates from the seventh century. Many other graves found in East Anglia were the tombs of humble people, including children who were buried with toy-like ships. In early English literature the account in *Beowulf* (recorded about A.D. 1000) describes the voyage of Skyld, first king of the Danes, on his funeral ship.

The ship was so important in Norse culture that it was carried as a symbol in processions long after Christianity had become established. Medieval craftsmen built mock ships (symbols of life and of death and of the journey in between) to be carried in religious processions. So beautiful and elaborate were these ships that eventually they were made collapsible to be folded up and stored inside the church until the next procession. It is thought that this medieval practice may have influenced the description of *SKID-BLADNIR*, the marvelous ship made for the god FREY. *Skinbladnir* could be shrunk and folded to fit inside a pouch when not in use.

SIF THOR's golden-haired wife, goddess of grain and of fertility. She was the mother of ULL, Thor's stepson. The mischief-maker LOKI cut off Sif's hair while she slept. He was forced to replace it with strands of gold crafted by the DWARFS (see BROKK and EITRI).

SIGMUND The son of Volsung and the father of the hero SIGURD. Sigmund's story is from the first chapters of the *VOLSUNGA SAGA*, a NORSE legend that has strong connections to mythology. Starting with his parentage, Sigmund's life is influenced by the gods.

On his father's side, Sigmund is the great-grandson of ODIN, chief of the AESIR gods. The goddess FREYA delivered a magical apple to Sigmund's grandmother to help her conceive Volsung. Sigmund's mother, wife of Volsung, was Ljod, daughter of the giant Hrimnir.

When Sigmund was a young man, Odin visited Volsung and his family in disguise at a wedding feast and drove his mighty SWORD into the tree that grew within the king's hall. Then he dared anyone to pull the sword from the tree, saying that he who could achieve this feat would have the mighty sword as his own. Only Sigmund proved strong enough, and he easily removed the sword.

This is the beginning of a long, tormented journey for Sigmund, who eventually dies in battle at the hands of Odin, again in disguise, in a fight that shatters the mighty sword. Before he dies, Sigmund tells his wife that she is pregnant with Sigurd and that their son will be the noblest and most famous of all his family.

SIGURD A human hero of GERMANIC legend, possibly of historical origin. He is the chief character in the 13th-century *VOLSUNGA SAGA* and in *REGINSMAL*. The Sigurd stories are prefaced by the NORSE myth "Otr's Ransom" (see under OTR), though it is believed that originally there was no connection between the two.

SIGYN (SIGUNN, SIGRYN, SIGUNA; Victory Giver) The wife of the trickster god, LOKI, and the mother of NARFI and VALI (1).

When the gods finally trapped Loki and bound him, placing a SERPENT over his head, Sigyn stayed by her husband's side. In a bowl she caught the VENOM that dripped from the serpent's jaws. When she turned aside to empty the bowl, some venom fell on Loki, and he writhed with pain, causing earthquakes on MIDGARD. Sigyn stayed with Loki until RAGNAROK, the end of the world.

SIMUL The pole on which the children BIL AND HJUKI carried the bucket, SAEGER, full of water from the well, according to SNORRI STURLUSON in *GYLFAGINNING*. While carrying the bucket, the children were taken up to HEAVEN by the MOON so they could forever follow him.

SINDRI (Sparky, Slag) The name of the magnificent golden hall that will stand shining upon a mountain after RAGNAROK, the final battle between the gods and the GIANTS at the end of time. Sindri also refers to the good and righteous people who will dwell within this splendid palace.

SJOFN A female goddess named by 13th-century Icelandic historian SNORRI STURLUSON in his prose work *GYLFAGINNING*. Very little is known of Sjofn except that, according to Sturlusor, she had the job of influencing people to fall in love with each other.

SKADE (SKADI; Destruction) Daughter of the HRIMTHURSSAR THJAZZI and wife of NJORD, the VANIR god of the SEA and of sailors and fishermen. Skade was the goddess of winter, skiers, and hunters. After her father's death, she went to ASGARD, the home of the gods, to choose a husband from among them. She chose Njord, but she and Njord found that they could not live happily together, for Skade did not like Njord's seashore home, NOATUN, and Njord did not like the bleak cold of THRYMHEIM, Skade's home.

In the story "Loki's Punishment" (see under LOKI), Skade placed a venomous SERPENT over the head of the trickster god. She is the personification of the cold-hearted northern winter that can be touched only briefly by the warmth of the summer sun (Njord) and the cheerful hearth fire (Loki).

Skade and Njord In SNORRI STURLUSON's *PROSE EDDA*, the story of the marriage between Skade, goddess of winter, and Njord, the god associated with the seas and seafarers, immediately follows "Idunn's Apples" (see under IDUNN), in which Thjazzi, Skade's father, is killed by the gods after stealing the apples. At the news of his death, Skade was full of rage. She put on her shining armor and her weapons and strode across BILROST to ASGARD, the home of the AESIR.

The gods were at peace, glad to feel young again now that Idunn was back with her magic apples of youth. They asked Skade if she would take gold in payment for her father's death, for such was the custom of the NORSE.

Skade scornfully replied that she had all the gold she needed. When OLVALDI had died, he had left much gold to his sons, Thjazzi, GANG, and IDI, and now she had all of Thjazzi's share. Instead, she demanded a husband from among the gods.

The gods conferred and agreed it would be wise to let the icy GIANTESS have her way. There was one condition: Skade must choose her husband by the look of his feet, not by his face. Skade agreed, but she, too, had a condition. The gods must make her laugh, for she was full of rage and her heart was cold.

The strange bargain was struck, and the gods stood barefoot behind a curtain that hid all but their feet. One pair of feet at once struck Skade as more beautiful than the rest. They must belong to the beautiful god BALDER, she thought. She announced her choice.

Out stepped Njord, the VANIR god, lord of the seas and of seafarers, and the father of FREY and FREYA. Skade was disappointed. Bitterly, she asked the gods to make her laugh.

LOKI, the trickster god who had been partially responsible for Thjazzi's death, had set his quick mind to work as soon as he had heard Skade's requests. Now he led forward one of THOR's rambunctious billy GOATS, and the two played such lively and hilarious antics that Skade and all the gods laughed until their sides ached.

As a wedding present for Skade, ODIN took Thjazzi's eyes from his pouch and hurled them into the heavens, where they shone brightly as twin stars.

Njord took his new wife to his home, Noatun, by the seashore. Skade did not like the sunshine, the sea, the sound of the waves, or the cry of the gulls. Njord then went with Skade to Thrymheim, her sunless, freezing mountain home, but Njord did not like the howling of the wolves, the wind, the bare mountains, or the terrible cold.

The two tried to divide their time between the two homes: nine days in Njord's Noatun and nine in Skade's Thrymheim. But Skade spent more and more time in the cold mountains, a dark shape speeding over the snow in her snowshoes, bringing death to wolves and bears from her quiver full of arrows. She is the goddess of skiers and hunters.

SKALD (SCALD) In Old NORSE, a poet. In the study of Norse mythology, the term refers to a specialist among poets who served in the courts of kings, powerful rulers, and chieftains. These poets often wrote about the great deeds of their leaders and of the gifts the leaders gave them. Skalds used complex, elaborate patterns and KENNINGS to create a distinct form known today as SKALDIC POETRY.

The oldest of the known skalds, Bragi Boddason inn gamli (Bragi Boddason the Old), lived in the ninth century A.D. Scholars believe he was the court poet of the Swedish king Björn. His poem *Ragnars-drapa* describes scenes from mythology as portrayed on a shield, including THOR fishing for JORMUNGAND, the MIDGARD SERPENT; GEFJON plowing away part of SWEDEN; and the story of Hild encouraging her father Hogni and Hedin, her abductor, to fight, as told in the *HJADNINGAVIG*.

SKALDIC POETRY A complex form of NORSE poetry that relies on precise numbers and stresses of syllables in each half-line of the poem. Skaldic poetry mainly consists of KENNINGS, or poetic, often mythical, metaphors, to present meaning to the audience. Much information about Norse mythology is preserved in this form of poetry.

Skaldic poems are distinct from the works in the *POETIC EDDA* in several important ways. Most skaldic poems are the works of named SKALDS, or specialist poets. Eddic poems, on the other hand, are anonymous and timeless. Skaldic poets counted syllables carefully, while Eddic poets wrote in a freer verse. Skaldic poets used myth to praise real heroes, and Eddic poems are about the myths themselves.

Existing skaldic poetry is preserved in ancient manuscripts written down centuries after the lives of the poets, who were part of a preliterate oral tradition. Some poems have survived in full, but of others only a stanza has survived.

SKALDSKAPARMAL (*Poetical Diction; The Poesy of the Skalds*) The second section of SNORRI STURLUSON's *PROSE EDDA*. The first is *GYLFAGINNING* and the third is *Hattatal*.

The first portion of *Skaldskaparmal* is a dialogue between a magician named AEGIR (2) and the god BRAGI. When Aegir visits the AESIR in ASGARD, he is seated next to Bragi at a feast. He questions the god and Bragi recounts many of the stories of NORSE mythology.

In the second portion of *Skaldskaparmal*, Bragi provides Aegir with many examples of poetic descriptions, or KENNINGS, and lists of names, THULUR, of the gods, creatures, and objects of this northern mythology. Both parts of *Skaldsaparmal* provide an in-depth lesson to young skalds, or poets, in how to use the stories of the gods in their work.

SKIDBLADNIR (Wooden-Bladed) The magic ship made by the DWARF sons of Ivaldi and brought to FREY by LOKI. The ship was big enough to hold all the gods and their horses and equipment, yet small enough to be folded up and put away in a pouch when not in use. It could sail over land or through the air,

as well as on the sea and has been compared to a swift-moving cloud or a magic carpet.

See also SHIPS AND SHIP BURIALS and "Treasures of the Dwarfs" under LOKI.

SKINFAXI (Shining Mane) The horse that each day pulls DAG (day) across the worlds of the gods. Skinfaxi was considered to be the best of horses. His gleaming mane lit up the heavens and the Earth. He is identified in *GRIMNISMAL*, a poem in the *POETIC EDDA*. Skinfaxi's counterpart is HRIMFAXI, the horse that pulls NOTT (night) through the sky. (See also "Night and Day" under CREATION.)

SKIRNIR (Shining) The servant of the shining god, FREY. He borrowed Frey's horse and sword and went on a long journey to woo the JOTUN maid GERDA for his lovesick master. In another myth, Skirnir was sent by the gods to ask the DWARFS to make them a magic chain with which to bind the wolf, FENRIR.

SKIRNISMAL (*THE LAY OF SKIRNIR; THE BALLAD OF SKIRNIR*) A poem in the *POETIC EDDA*, complete in the *CODEX REGIUS*, where it is also known as *Skirnir's Journey*, and in part in the *ARNAMAGNAEAN CODEX*. The poem tells the story of the journey of FREY's servant SKIRNIR to woo the GIANTESS GERDA for his master.

Skirnismal may have been created as early as the beginning of the 10th century. It contains details that allow scholars to gain a more complete understanding of many stories in NORSE mythology.

SKOLL The terrible WOLF born in JARNVID to a GIANTESS and the great wolf monster, FENRIR. Skoll steadfastly pursues the chariot of the SUN and in the end, at RAGNAROK, he devours it. His brother, HATI HRODVITNISSON, pursues the MOON.

Skoll is named as this wolf in *GRIMNISMAL*, a poem in the *POETIC EDDA*. SNORRI STURLUSON also identifies Skoll as the wolf that the Sun fears. (See also "Sun and Moon" under CREATION.)

SKRYMIR (Big Fellow) A very large GIANT encountered by THOR and LOKI and their servants on their way to UTGARD. Skrymir, sometimes called Vasty in English retellings, was most likely UTGARD-LOKI in disguise. He was so huge that Thor and his companions mistook his mitten for a large cabin, where they spent the night.

SKULD (Future) One of the three principle NORNS, or Fates, of NORSE mythology. They are named in the *POETIC EDDA*. Her sisters are URD (Past) and VERDANDI (Present). While many Norns in the form of spirits who determine the fates of gods and humans are often referred to in the Eddic and skaldic poetry, only these three sisters are named specifically.

Skuld's name is associated with the Old Norse verb *skulu*, which means "shall" or "should." Some translators interpret this broadly as "something that will happen." Skuld is often pictured wearing a veil and carrying a scroll.

SKY In the NORSE CREATION myth, the sky was made from the dome of the giant YMIR's skull. It was held up at the corners by four DWARFS, NORDI, SUDRI, AUSTRI, and VESTRI. It was lit by the SUN and the MOON (see "Sun and Moon," under CREATION); the stars were created from sparks borrowed from MUSPELLHEIM, the land of fire; and it was shaded by clouds made from Ymir's brains.

The upper right corner of this runestone depicts Odin riding the eight-legged horse, Sleipner. *(Photo by Berig/Used under a Creative Commons license)*

SLEIPNIR (Glider) ODIN's eight-legged horse, the offspring of SVADILFARI and LOKI, the SHAPE-SHIFTER god who disguised himself as a mare to tempt Svadilfari away from his work for the GIANT MASTER BUILDER (see "Asgard's Wall and the Giant Master Builder," under ASGARD).

Sleipnir was no ordinary horse. He could gallop over the sea and through the air as well as on land and could outrun any horse in all the NINE WORLDS, including GULLFAXI. Sleipnir was able to journey to the world of the dead; he carried both HERMOD and ODIN there. At RAGNAROK, the end of the world, Sleipnir carried Odin into battle.

SNORRI STURLUSON (1179–1241) A leading figure in NORSE literature, Snorri Sturluson was ICELAND's most distinguished author. He was the author of the *PROSE EDDA*, of *Heimskringla* (a history of Norwegian kings), and of *Hattatal* (a poem in praise of King Haakon and Duke Skuli of NORWAY), plus various sagas. One of Iceland's greatest chieftains, Snorri came from the powerful Sturlung dynasty. He was educated at Iceland's foremost cultural center, Oddi, where he received strong training in law, history, poetry, and the telling of sagas. He became renowned as a lawyer and a SKALD, or poet. Politically ambitious, Snorri was welcomed at all the Scandinavian courts. He acquired great wealth and power but was involved in numerous disputes and battles. He was finally assassinated in a political coup at the command of the king of Norway.

It would be difficult to exaggerate the importance of the *Prose Edda*, sometimes called the *Younger Edda* or the *Snorra Edda*. It gives the most complete picture of Norse mythology dating from the Middle Ages. The *Prose Edda* had great influence on medieval Icelandic literature and helped to preserve the ancient skaldic tradition.

SNOTRA (Clever) A minor GODDESS named by SNORRI STURLUSON, who described her as clever and well-behaved. Scholars suspect that she might have been created by Snorri.

SOKKVABEKK The great home of ODIN and the goddess SAGA in ASGARD, according to the poem *GRIMNISMAL*. It stood "where cool waves flow" and is identified by different scholars as on a farm and near a deep stream. It may be another name for FENSALIR, the home of FRIGG, who was Odin's wife.

Statue of Snorri Sturluson by Gustav Vigeland, in Bergen, Norway

SOL (Sun) According to 13th-century Icelandic poet SNORRI STURLUSON, a servant of the SUN. Sol was the daughter of the human MUNDILFARI and the sister of MANI. The gods stole Sol and Mani from their father when they were children—or perhaps young adults, since Snorri says Sol was married to a man named GLEN. The gods were offended that a HUMAN, Mundilfari, had named his children after the Sun and the Moon.

In Snorri's telling of their story, the gods put Sol to work in the heavens, where she drove the chariot that carried the Sun through the sky. Two horses, ARVAKR and ALSVID, pulled the chariot. To protect the horses and Sol from the flaming heat of the Sun, which would burn up anything that came too close to it, the gods placed the shield SVALIN between them and the Sun.

The huge, evil WOLF SKOLL chased Sol and the Sun's chariot through the sky until RAGNAROK, when he caught and devoured the Sun.

Sol is rarely given human characteristics in Norse poetry. Only Snorri tells the story of her work in the heavens. An older poem, part of the *POETIC EDDA*, identifies Sol as the Sun, not a servant, and only names her and the Moon as children of Mundilfari. The Sun played only a small role in Norse mythology.

SON (Reconciliation) The vessel used by the DWARFS to hold the blood of the wise poet KVASIR (1) after they killed him in order to brew the MEAD of poetry. Son was one of two such containers; the other is BODN. A kettle, ODRERIR, was also used by the dwarfs in this story.

SNORRI STURLUSON gives the names Son and Bodn to these two vessels in *SKALDSAPARMAL*. The names are not found anywhere else in the manuscripts of NORSE mythology. Some scholars suggest that Snorri chose Son, which means reconciliation, as the name for one vessel to suggest that the mead of poetry would bring peace between the AESIR and VANIR gods. (See "The Mead of Poetry" under ODIN.)

SORLA THATTR (SORLA ÞATTR; *The Tale of Hogni and Hedinn*) *Sorla thattr* is the tale of the conflict between two kings, Hogni and Hedinn, which includes the story of the making of the golden BRISINGA MEN, a necklace of great beauty and value.

The beginning of the *Sorla thattr* describes the bargain FREYA makes with four dwarfs to get the marvelous golden necklace she sees them creating. It then describes the trickery LOKI used to steal the necklace from the sleeping goddess and the mighty ODIN's bargain with Freya required for her to get the necklace back from her husband.

The *Sorla thattr* is found only in the manuscript known as *FLATEYJARBOK*.

STARKAD A famous NORSE hero who was both blessed and cursed by the gods. Starkad was the name of the main character of many heroic legends, and scholars suggest there may have been several different heroes with the same name. In the stories that survive, there are two Starkads. One was the descendent of GIANTS who himself had six or eight arms. This Starkad, who had the last name Aludreng, was the grandfather of the most famous Starkad, a divine hero and the foster son of the god ODIN.

Odin remained in disguise as he helped raise the younger Starkad. Once Starkad witnessed a gathering of the gods, 12 of them sitting in chairs with an empty chair in the gathering. Only when Odin joined the gathering and sat in the empty chair did Starkad recognize his foster father for the god he was.

The mighty thunder god, THOR, hated Starkad. On one occasion, Odin wanted to honor the bravery of the warrior Starkad, but Thor wanted to harm the hero he so hated. Odin bestowed many blessings upon Starkad, among them success in battle, invincibility, great wealth, and great skill as a poet. Thor countered each positive gift with a negative consequence, causing Starkad to be seriously hurt in every battle, to never enjoy his wealth, and to never have anyone know of his poetry.

As a result of the conflicting favor and disfavor bestowed on him by the two gods, Starkad lived to be very old, but he committed notorious deeds, including killing the king whom he had earlier served with much honor.

Many sagas from ICELAND tell of the adventures of Starkad. In them, he is portrayed as old, misshapen, and gray-haired. The *GESTA DANORUM* by SAXO GRAMMATICUS contains the most information on Starkad, though he is featured in SAGAS as well.

STARS After they had created the Earth and the SKY, ODIN and his brothers caught glowing embers and sparks from MUSPELLHEIM and threw them up into the sky to be stars (see "The Sky," under CREATION). As time went on, they created new stars.

See also THJAZZI.

SUDRI (South) One of the four DWARFS named after the four cardinal compass directions. The others are AUSTRI (east), VESTRI (west), and NORDI (north). These four dwarfs are mentioned in early NORSE poetry, but only SNORRI STURLUSON gave Sudri and his companions the job of holding up the four corners of the sky.

SUN The Sun is mentioned frequently in NORSE mythology but only in one poem in the *POETIC EDDA*. In SNORRI STURLUSON's *PROSE EDDA*, is it given the name SOL. Only Snorri tells the story of Sol's life, and in that story, she is a servant of the Sun.

The Sun disk, however, was a popular image in rock carvings and on brooches and ornaments from the Norse age. The disk was also carved into memorial stones. The Sun is often represented as a wheel, both in objects made during the VIKING AGE and in the surviving poetry from that time. The Sun is referred to as the "wheel of heaven."

FREY appears to be the god most closely connected to the Sun. Scholars often see his courtship of and marriage to the GIANTESS GERDA as a legend of the Sun pursuing the frozen Earth (see CREATION).

SUN AND MOON The children of MUNDILFARI, who named his daughter SOL, which means "sun," and his son MANI, which means "moon." Older NORSE poems identify Mundilfari as the father of these children but do not discuss where he lived or what type of being he was. The 13th-century Icelandic poet SNORRI STURLUSON in his *PROSE EDDA* described Mundilfari as a HUMAN father. According to Snorri, the gods grew angry with this presumptuous human, stealing his children and putting them to work in the sky.

SURT (Black) Surt was a giant and a central character in the story of RAGNAROK, the great conflict that ends the worlds of the NORSE gods.

Surt ruled over MUSPELLHEIM, the realm of fire near the roots of the World Tree, YGGDRASIL. He was the watchman for the GIANTS, as HEIMDALL was the WATCHMAN OF THE GODS; both waited for the time they would announce the beginning of the final conflict between the two mighty forces.

At Ragnarok, Surt came forth from Muspellheim, leading a troop of warriors that included the great wolves that would devour the SUN and MOON. He carried a SWORD that flashed flames and with it he set fire to all of the worlds. While the gods fell around them, the giant Surt fought the god FREY in a long battle. Surt finally killed Frey. The fire Surt spread created one of the strongest images of this final battle and is referenced in the Eddic and skaldic poetry as "the fires of Surt."

The story of Surt and his central role in Ragnarok is described in the *VOLUSPA*, the first poem in the *CODEX REGIUS* of the *POETIC EDDA*, and is also retold by SNORRI STURLUSON in *GYLFAGINNING*.

SURTSEY An island south of and belonging to ICELAND, named for the NORSE fire god, SURT. It was formed by a volcanic eruption from an underwater volcano, Sutur. The eruption began in 1963 and ended in 1967. Surtsey, the newest island on Earth, is now a nature reserve.

SUTTUNG (Heavy with Broth) A giant. Suttung was the son of GILLING, who was murdered by the DWARFS FJALAR (2) and GALAR, and the brother of BAUGI. His daughter was GUNLOD, the guardian of the MEAD of poetry (see under ODIN). Suttung hid the three containers of the MEAD in an underground cave of the mountain HNITBJORG, where he and Gunlod lived. He would share it with no one. Odin, using his magic, succeeded in getting into the cave and stealing the mead. Suttung was able to change himself into an EAGLE to chase Odin (who was also in eagle form), but Suttung fell into a fire that the gods had made at the walls of ASGARD, their home, and perished.

Surtsey Island *(Photo by Pinpin/Used under a Creative Commons license)*

SVADILFARI The stallion belonging to the GIANT MASTER BUILDER who built the ASGARD wall. Svadilfari was a mighty animal, immensely powerful. He was lured from his task of helping the builder by a pretty mare (LOKI in disguise) and became the sire of SLEIPNIR, ODIN's eight-legged horse.

SVALIN (The Cooling) The shield in front of "the shining god," whom scholars say refers to SOL, the SUN goddess. The shield protects the mountains, the seas, and the Earth from the heat of Sol's flames.

The shield Svalin is named in the poem GRIM-NISMAL and is referred to in *Sigrdrifumol*, a HEROIC LEGEND in the POETIC EDDA. (See also "Sun and Moon" under CREATION.)

SVARTALFHEIM (DARK ALFHEIM) The realm of the black, or dark, elves, who were also called DWARFS. It lay deep underground, beneath the roots of the World Tree, YGGDRASIL. It was there that LOKI went to ask the dwarfs, who were skilled craftsmen, to produce treasures for the gods (see "Treasures of the Dwarf" under Loki).

SVIPDAG (Swift Day) The human son of the seeress GROA and the hero of SVIPDAGSMAL (*Ballad of Svipdag*) in the POETIC EDDA. Svipdag goes to NIFL-HEIM to seek the advice of Groa. He summoned her from the grave to ask her the best way to woo and win MENGLOD, the fair maiden he loves. Groa chants him a series of charms that will protect him in his travels. Svipdag sets off to seek Menglod. In JOTUNHEIM he finds a massive gate guarded by the giant FJOLSVID. After a series of questions and answers in which Svipdag learns about the gods and giants and their worlds, the giant finally lets Svipdag enter the gates, where he finds the beautiful Menglod waiting for him with open arms.

SVIPDAGSMAL (*Lay of Svipdag*) A poem or combination of poems included in some translations of the POETIC EDDA. *Svipdagsmal* is found only in the paper manuscripts of the *Poetic Edda*, all of which were copied in the 17th century or later.

Svipdagsmal tells the story of SVIPDAG, the human son of the witch GROA, who seeks help from his dead mother to win the love of the beautiful giantess

MENGLOD. The story combines elements of mythology with elements of the HEROIC LEGEND, and some scholars point out that the scribes who created the manuscripts containing *Svipdagsmal* often made errors in recounting the NORSE myths.

Modern experts believe that the existing manuscripts combine two older poems, *Grogald* (*Groa's Spell*) and *Fjolsvinnsmal* (*The Lay of Fjolsvith*), into one story, but even these poems appear to have been composed later than the VIKING AGE, in which Norse mythology had its strongest expression.

While experts on Old Norse mythology still disagree on the origins of *Svipdagsmal*, they do agree that the story of Svipdag and Menglod became extremely popular in SCANDINAVIA and became the subject of many ballads and legends.

SWAN   The swan appears in NORSE mythology as a symbol of grace, beauty, and mystery. The feathers of the swan bring magical power, as do the feathers of the HAWK and EAGLE.

Two swans lived near URDARBRUNN (Urd's Well), feeding on its dew. They were, according to SNORRI STURLUSON, the parents of the species of swan.

The song of the swan was seen as a sign of death, since the swan was believed never to make a sound during its life but only as it was dying. However, the song of the swan was beautiful music to SKADE, who refused to leave her mountain home to live by the SEA with her husband, NJORD.

Swan maidens appear in several of the heroic poems of the *POETIC EDDA*. In some, such as that of VOLUND in *Volundarkvitha*, they are believed to be VALKYRIES in disguise. In order to discard their warrior nature, these women put on swans' feathers and fly away. When they take off these robes of feathers, they appear to be human. Experts on Norse and GERMANIC mythology believe that these tales of swan maidens began south of SCANDINAVIA and were later blended into the tales of Norse legends and mythology.

SWEDEN   A nation in northern Europe forming the eastern half of the Scandinavian peninsula. Sweden is part of SCANDINAVIA, which includes NORWAY, making up the western part of the peninsula, DENMARK, ICELAND, and the FAROE ISLANDS. Together these nations form the home of the NORSE culture and its mythology.

Archaeological finds and a significant number of NORSE artifacts from Sweden have helped scholars

Burial site from about A.D. 500 in Anundshog, Sweden (*Photo by Christer Johansson/Used under a Creative Commons license*)

piece together the stories of the gods and goddesses of the northlands. Huge burial mounds of ancient kings of Sweden—three located in OLD UPPSALA, about 50 miles north of Stockholm—have provided scientists with significant information about the Nordic people and their religious beliefs. Even farm fields in Sweden have been rich sources of information. Amulets, brooches, and stone carvings have been plowed up, uncovered, and preserved to provide information and greater understanding of the age of Norse mythology.

One of the richest sites of archaeological information is the Swedish island of GOTLAND, which lies in the Baltic Sea near the southern end of the peninsula. Here outlines of ships made with huge rocks still dot the landscape, and some of the most prominent rock carvings of ancient Scandinavia stand as reminders of this earlier age.

SWORD   The sword was a symbol of power throughout NORSE mythology and the HEROIC LEGENDS of SCANDINAVIA. It was the weapon of the king and the leader. The sword was essential during the VIKING AGE to defend one's life and possessions.

Odin, though the leader of the AESIR, did not carry a sword himself. His weapon was the spear, GUNGNIR. He did drive a great sword into the huge OAK tree that

Burial mound in the shape of a sailing ship in Anundshog, Sweden *(Photo by Christer Johansson/ Used under a Creative Commons license)*

grew within King Volsung's hall. Only SIGMUND, son of Volsung, could draw the sword from the tree. After the sword was broken into shards in a battle between Odin and Sigmund, the dwarf REGIN put the pieces together to form yet another great sword, Gram, the weapon used by the hero SIGURD. The story is told in the *VOLSUNGA SAGA*.

The dwarfs DVALIN and DURINN made the legendary sword Tyrfing at the command of a king who held them prisoner. They cursed the sword before the king took it away. Tyrfing brought havoc to the family and killed three of the king's descendents before losing its powers. This story is told in the Icelandic *HERVARAR SAGA*.

In *GRIMINISMAL*, after learning that the man he has been torturing is Odin, King GEIRROD (2) tries to cut the god free from the ropes that are suspending him over a fire, but the king falls on his own sword and dies.

Other swords are mentioned by name in the Icelandic manuscripts; these include Refill, Regin's sword, and Laevateinn, a sword inscribed with RUNES and made by LOKI near the gates of HEL (2) that will kill the cock at the beginning of RAGNAROK.

SYN (Refusal, Denial) One of the ASYNJUR, or female goddesses. Syn guarded the door of FRIGG's great hall, SESSRUMNIR, keeping out all unwelcome visitors. Syn also was called upon to guide or protect defendants in trials.

T

TANNGNIOST (Tooth Gnasher) One of the two fierce billy goats that drew the cart of the god THOR. The other GOAT was TANNGRISNIR (Tooth Grinder). To people on Earth, the rumble of the cart was heard as thunder. Thor's goats could be killed and eaten and then revived again the next day.

TANNGRISNIR (Tooth Grinder) One of the two fierce billy goats that drew the cart of the god THOR. The other GOAT was TANNGNIOST (Tooth Gnasher). Thor's goats could be killed and eaten and then revived again the next day.

THJALFI (ÞJALFI) Son of the farmer EGIL and brother of ROSKVA. He became THOR's servant because he had disobeyed Thor's command not to break any of the bones of the GOATS on which he and his family were feasting in "Thor's Journey to Utgard." Thjalfi was long-legged and fleet of foot, but he was outrun in a race with HUGI (Thought) in UTGARD. Thjalfi was also Thor's companion in the duel with the giant HRUNGNIR. He easily vanquished the clay giant, MOKKURKALFI, which the stone-headed giants had created in an attempt to frighten Thor.

THJAZZI (ÞJAZI, THIAZZI) A powerful storm giant. He was the son of OLVALDI, brother of GANG and IDI, and father of SKADE. He lived in THRYMHEIM. Disguised as an EAGLE, Thjazzi tricked LOKI into helping him kidnap IDUNN, the goddess in charge of the magic apples of youth. In turn, Loki tricked the giant and returned Idunn to ASGARD. Thjazzi was killed at the gates of Asgard. His daughter, Skade, was given as a husband the VANIR god NJORD as compensation for her father's death. The great god ODIN threw Thjazzi's eyes into the heavens to stay there forever as gleaming stars.

THOKK (Coal) The GIANTESS who refused to weep for BALDER, thus ensuring that he would remain in HEL's (1) realm until RAGNAROK. Some mythologists believe that Thokk was LOKI, the trickster god, in disguise. Thokk personifies the darkness of the underground (where coal is formed) that will not weep for the light of the Sun (Balder).

THOR (Thunderer) The god of thunder and storms. His father was ODIN, his mother JORD (Earth). Thor had two wives: JARNSAXA (Ironstone), who bore him two sons, MODI and MAGNI; and golden-haired SIF, who gave him two daughters, Lora and THRUD. His realm was THRUDHEIM. His hall was BILSKIRNIR (Lightning), which had 540 rooms, fittingly large for this giant of a god who loved to feast and entertain. Thor was strong and fiery of temper, but he was well loved by the gods, respected by the GIANTS, and worshipped by the ordinary people.

Thor did not ride a horse; instead he had a chariot pulled by two enormous billy GOATS, TANNGNIOST and TANNGRISNIR. The wheels of the chariot made a noise like thunder when Thor raced across the heavens.

Thor's greatest possession was his hammer, MJOLLNIR. When he hurled it, the hammer always hit its mark and then returned to Thor like a boomerang. Mjollnir was not only a weapon but a symbol of fertility, used at weddings, and of resurrection, used at burials. Thor also had iron gloves with which he could crush rocks, and a belt, MEGINGJARDIR, which doubled his mighty strength.

At RAGNAROK, the end of the world, Thor killed JORMUNGAND, the MIDGARD SERPENT, his ancient enemy, but himself was killed by the poisonous VENOM of the dying serpent.

Worship of Thor continued for centuries after the coming of Christianity to SCANDINAVIA in the late 900s A.D. The great OAK trees of central and western Europe were sacred to the god. Worshippers of Thor

An illustration of Thor with his hammer Mjollnir. From the 18th-century Icelandic manuscript SÁM 66, in the care of the Árni Magnússon Institute in Iceland

made wooden oak chairs with high backs, called "high seats," to ensure Thor's blessing on the house (protecting it from lightning) and the well-being and fruitfulness of the family and its lands. As well as bringing thunder and lightning and storms, Thor sent the rain that made the fields fertile.

Evidence of Thor's popularity is found in the name THURSDAY (the fifth day of the week) and in numerous English place names, such as Thundersley, in Essex; Thunderfield, Surrey; and many others in England and elsewhere.

There are many myths about Thor taken from the *POETIC EDDA* and the *PROSE EDDA*. In Richard Wagner's opera *Der Ring des Nibelungen*, Thor appears as Donner. Thor is also found in Henry Wadsworth Longfellow's "Saga of King Olaf," part of *Tales of a Wayside Inn*.

The only source of the myth of the theft of Thor's hammer is the poem *THRYMSKVITHA* (*Lay of Thrym*) from the *Poetic Edda*. It is considered a masterpiece of burlesque.

The Theft of Thor's Hammer Thor, the god of thunder, was the personification of strength and manliness. His hammer, Mjollnir, was a potent weapon, the gods' only real defense against the giants. Thor was seldom separated from his hammer, so it is not surprising that he went into a fury when the hammer disappeared.

LOKI, the trickster god, heard Thor's shouts and knew that for once he must be helpful rather than mischievous. He rushed to FREYA, the beautiful goddess, and borrowed her suit of FALCON feathers. Then Loki flew to JOTUNHEIM, the home of the giants.

THRYM, the huge and ugly king of the HRIMMTURSSAR, was in a good mood, plaiting gold thread to make leashes for his colossal hounds. He greeted Loki cheerfully. Loki asked him if he had stolen Thor's hammer, and the giant admitted that he had. With a chilling laugh, he said that he had hidden it eight miles under the earth where no one would find it. The only way to get it back would be to send him Freya as his bride.

Even Loki was shocked at the thought of sending the fair goddess to this monster. Loki flew quickly back to ASGARD on his falcon wings and told Thor the news. Together they went to Freya and told her of the giant's request.

Freya was so furious and agitated that she broke the clasp of her golden necklace BRISINGA MEN. Never, never would she be the bride of Thrym, she vowed.

Then all the gods got together for a meeting. They knew that it was only a matter of time until all the giants found out that Thor no longer had his hammer and then would come marching on Asgard. The gods were worried.

Only HEIMDALL, the watchman who stood at BILROST, the RAINBOW BRIDGE, and could see far into the future, remained calm. He said that Thor must be dressed as a bride and go to meet Thrym.

The gods roared with laughter at the thought of the mighty, red-bearded Thor dressed as a woman, and Thor let out a shout of rage. But gradually he saw the wisdom of the plan and allowed the goddesses to fit his large frame into a long dress and drape a veil over his shaggy head. Freya's necklace was repaired and placed around his thick neck, a girdle hung with jingling keys encircled his waist, and his manly chest was covered with glittering jewels.

Loki was dressed as a bridesmaid. Together the peculiar pair climbed into Thor's chariot, and the two billy goats took off at great speed, making the wheels rumble like thunder.

Thrym was overjoyed when he heard that Freya was on her way. He ordered the halls to be swept, new straw laid down, and a gargantuan feast prepared.

Thor was well known for his great appetite, but Thrym was astonished to see what he thought was a maiden eating such huge helpings of fish and meat and downing large goblets of MEAD. Quick-witted Loki explained that the bride had not eaten or drunk for eight days, so anxious was she to meet her groom.

Delighted, Thrym reached over to lift the bride's veil and kiss her, but when he saw Thor's flashing, red-rimmed eyes glaring at him through the veil, he fell back in dismay. Once again sly Loki whispered an explanation. The bride had not had a wink of sleep for eight nights, so anxious was she for her wedding night.

At that, Thrym ordered that the hammer be brought to his bride and the wedding ceremony commence at once, as it was the custom of the Norse to invoke the blessing of Thor's hammer at their weddings. No sooner was Mjollnir placed upon his lap than Thor leapt up, tore off his veil, and started to kill every giant in sight.

Thor and the Giant Geirrod The tale of how the god Thor destroyed the formidable giant GEIR-ROD and his two fearsome daughters is a popular myth, told several times in Norse literature, including in the SKALDSKAPARMAL in the *Prose Edda* and in SNORRI STURLUSON's retelling of *THORSDRAPA*.

One day Loki put on a suit of falcon feathers and flew to the hall of the giant Geirrod, one of the meanest of the JOTUNS. Geirrod caught sight of the handsome falcon and ordered the bird to be brought to him.

It took several of the trolls to capture Loki, for he hopped about the wall, always just out of reach. When at last he tried to take flight, he found himself stuck fast to the wall by some evil spell.

He was set before Geirrod, who knew at once that this was not a real falcon. He locked Loki in a cage and kept him without food and water until at last Loki confessed who he was. The giant set Loki free on the condition that he would bring him the thunder god, Thor, without any of his weapons. Faint with hunger, Loki agreed to bring Thor to Geirrod. Off he flew, his trickster's mind already devising a plan.

Once safe in Asgard, Loki prattled on to anyone who would listen about the wonders of Geirrod's castle and how the giant was eager to meet the

A wooden reproduction of an Icelandic statue of Thor at the Swedish Army Museum *(Photo by Peter Isotalo/Used under a Creative Commons license)*

mighty Thor, to introduce him to his two beautiful daughters, GIALP and GREIP, and to entertain him royally. Of course, Thor heard the gossip and, being a simple soul, could not long resist the temptation to visit Geirrod, his new admirer.

At Loki's urging, Thor left his weapons behind, even the magic hammer, Mjollnir, and set forth, with Loki at his side to show the way. As the distance was long, they stayed overnight with the kindly GIANTESS GRID. She was friendly to the AESIR gods and liked Thor. When Loki had gone to sleep, she warned Thor about Geirrod and loaned him her belt of power, iron gloves, and magic staff.

The next day when Thor and Loki were crossing the rushing torrent of the VIMUR, the river began to rise higher and higher. Thor hung onto the magic staff, and Loki hung onto Thor, almost drowning in the blood-red river. Up ahead Thor saw the giantess Gialp. It was she who was making the waters rise. Thor threw a rock at her, and she ran off, howling. Then Thor pulled himself to shore with the help of the small ROWAN tree, or mountain ash.

When they arrived at Geirrod's hall, Thor was shown into a small room. He sat down wearily in the only chair and closed his eyes. Suddenly he felt himself rising toward the roof. Quickly he rammed Grid's staff against the roof beam and pushed. Then down he came, right on top of Gialp and Greip, who had been trying to raise the chair and crush Thor against the roof. The two ugly, evil creatures were themselves crushed to death by Thor's weight.

Thor went straight to Geirrod, who raised his hand in mock greeting and threw a red-hot lump of iron at Thor.

Thor caught it in Grid's iron gloves and threw it back at Geirrod, who leaped behind a pillar. The hot ball went right through the pillar, through Geirrod's head, and through the wall into the yard, where it bored deep into the earth.

Thor's Journey to Utgard This story is one of the best known of the Norse myths. It is also one of the longest and most richly told myths written by Snorri in the *Prose Edda*, its only source.

One day Thor decided to go to UTGARD, stronghold of the largest giants in Jotunheim. Because its chief, UTGARD-LOKI, was known to be a master of trickery, Thor brought along Asgard's own trickster god, Loki.

As it grew dark Thor's chariot, drawn by two billy goats, stopped at a small farmhouse. The farmer and his wife were very poor and had little to eat. With a wave of his magic hammer, Mjollnir, Thor killed Tanngniost and Tanngrisnir, his goats, and put them on the fire to cook.

Thor told the peasants to eat their fill when the meat was ready but to be sure not to break any of the bones. They should be placed carefully onto the goatskins that Thor had stretched on the floor. THJALFI, the farmer's son, disobeyed Thor and cracked a leg bone to suck out the delicious marrow.

Next morning, when Thor was ready to leave, he waved Mjollnir over the piles of bone and skin and up sprang the goats, as lively as ever, but one of them had a limp. Thor yelled in fury, for he knew that someone had disobeyed him. However, he accepted the terrified farmer's offer and took Thjalfi and his sister, ROSKVA, to be his servants. He left the goats for the farmer to take care of until his return.

Thor and Loki and the two youngsters journeyed all day. That night they came to a forest in Jotunheim where the trees were so tall that their tops were lost in the clouds. They saw a strangely shaped cabin that seemed to have no door. They crept inside to shelter from the cold and were soon asleep.

In the middle of the night they sprang awake as the Earth shook, and there was a frightful crashing sound, followed by a steady rumble and a whistling wind. Even Thor was frightened. He, Loki, and the youngsters crept into a narrow side room in the cavernous hall, Thor clutching his hammer to his chest.

At first light, Thor went outside and saw the cause of all the noise. At the foot of a tree lay the biggest giant Thor had ever seen. He was fast asleep and snoring mightily.

Thor put on the magic belt given to him by the giantess Grid to double his strength. He held his hammer even more firmly, though the giant was so big that Thor decided not to throw it hastily.

Soon the giant woke up. He picked up what the travelers had mistaken for a large cabin or cave. It was a giant glove. The side room was the thumb.

When the giant stood up, Thor and his companions had to crane their heads back to look at him. The giant introduced himself as SKRYMIR, sometimes called Big Fellow or Vasty.

After they had eaten breakfast—a poor one for Thor and his friends, a huge one for Skrymir—they set off again, this time with the giant crashing through the trees ahead to show them the way to Utgard. By nightfall they were exhausted and hungry. The giant flung down his huge food bag, telling the other travelers to help themselves.

Try as they might, Thor, Loki and the farmer's son and daughter could not untie the knots that secured the bag, so they lay down, hungry, and tried to shut out the sound of Skrymir's thunderous snores.

At last Thor could not stand it any longer. He hit Skrymir on the head with his hammer. Skrymir opened one eye and complained that a leaf had fallen on his head, then fell back to sleep.

Furious, Thor hit him again. Skrymir mumbled something about an acorn.

Beside himself, Thor took a running jump and hurled the hammer with all his might onto the giant's head. Skrymir finally sat up and rubbed his head. He decided that there must be some birds above his head. Skrymir got up and picked up his bag. He told the travelers to watch their step in Utgard, for the giants there were really big.

The four travelers breathed a sigh of relief as Skrymir lumbered off through the trees.

When they reached Utgard, the hall of the giant Utgard-Loki, who was their host, they found that the giants had assembled to meet them. Utgard-Loki told the visitors they must prove themselves worthy to stay by demonstrating a great skill.

Loki immediately announced that no one could beat him at eating. One of the giants placed a huge platter in front of Loki and sat down on the other side of it. The two began gobbling and in no time bumped heads as they met in the middle of the platter—or what was left of it. The giant had eaten his half of the wooden dish, along with all the bones, so he won the contest.

Next, young Thjalfi claimed that he was the fastest runner in the world. Utgard-Loki called forth a young giant named Hugi, and marked out a racecourse. Thjalfi was indeed as swift as the wind, but he was no match for Hugi. Thjalfi lost the race and retired to Loki's side, humiliated.

Thor strode forward, claiming that he was well known as a mighty drinker. The giants placed before him a long, curved horn. Confidently Thor took a huge drink, but when he looked at the horn, it was still brimming over with liquid. Once again he raised the horn to his lips. He opened his throat and let the liquid pour down until he was red in the face, but the horn was still almost full. After the third try, Thor put down the horn, mortified and angry.

Utgard-Loki shook his head sadly, remarking that the mighty Thor was not so mighty after all. Every one of his men could empty the horn at one draft. He suggested that Thor try his hand at something easier, like lifting a cat from the floor.

Grimly Thor put his hand under the cat's belly to lift it. It felt as heavy as lead. By using both his hands and all the strength of his mighty arms, he was able to raise the cat so that one paw was an inch off the floor. Then he fell back, exhausted.

Angry at the laughter of the giants, Thor shouted that he was the finest wrestler in all Asgard and would take on anyone.

The giant shook his head doubtfully. He could not think of a Jotun who would be bothered to fight such a weakling until he remembered his old nurse, Elli, and he summoned her to the hall.

Embarrassed, Thor put his hand out to grasp the arm of the skinny old crone, not meaning to hurt her. Suddenly he was flying through the air. He landed flat on his back. The wizened old woman cackled and the giants shouted with laughter. Then Thor wrestled Elli in earnest, but no matter what he did the hag outplayed him, until at last he gave up and slunk away.

The next morning Utgard-Loki led the crestfallen travelers to the gates of Utgard. There the giant admitted that he had practiced magic on them. First, he had disguised himself as Skrymir. He had used TROLL magic to tie the food bag with strands of iron. Then, when Thor thought he was hitting the giant's head with his hammer, he had been in fact hitting a hard rock. He told Thor that on his way home he would see the rock, a hillside with three very deep dents in it.

In the contests, too, he had used spells and trickery. Logi, the giant who had beaten Loki in gluttony, was in fact Fire, which consumes everything in its path. The runner, Hugi, was Thought, and no one can move as fast as thought. The drinking horn was anchored in the seas of the world. No one can drain the oceans, but from then on, said the giant, the tides would ebb and flow, just as they had when Thor drank so mightily. The cat was Jormungand, the Midgard Serpent, who is so big that he encircles the world. When Thor had made the "cat" lift its paw, the serpent's back had almost touched the sky. Finally, Elli was Old Age and no one had wrestled with her better than Thor.

Thor was so angry at the trickery that he raised his hammer to strike the giant, but Utgard-Loki vanished into the air. So did the castle and its walls and all the other giants.

Although in this myth Thor is upstaged by Utgard-Loki, he is not totally humiliated, for he did create dents in the hillside and the ebbing and flowing of the tides.

Thor and Hymir Go Fishing The myth of the fishing expedition of Thor and the giant Hymir and Thor's battle with Jormungand, the Midgard Serpent, was a favorite and was retold many times, not only in Scandinavia but in other areas settled by the Vikings. In Gosforth, England, carvings on two stone slabs clearly show Thor fishing with an ox's head and fighting with the serpent. The *Lay of Hymir* is in HYMISKVITHA, a poem of the *Poetic Edda*, and part of Snorri's *Prose Edda*.

The Aesir gods loved to eat and drink. No sooner was one feast over than they were making plans for the next. One evening they cast RUNES that told them that their next gathering should be at the abode of Aegir, the Jotun lord of the sea. Aegir lived under the waves with his wife, Ran.

Aegir complained that he did not have a cauldron big enough to brew ale for all the gods. TYR, the one-handed god, declared that he knew where he could find a cauldron a mile deep. With Thor as his companion, Tyr set off to find Hymir, who lived east of ELIVAGAR in Jotunheim, the land of giants.

When they came to Hymir's dwelling, an ogress with 900 heads blocked their path, but there was another Jotun, beautiful and kind, and she welcomed Tyr as her son, and she welcomed Thor. She said she would try to help them and advised them to hide underneath the biggest cauldron in the hall.

Hymir lumbered into the hall, icicles dangling from his bushy beard and his eyes sparkling dangerously. He sensed the presence of strangers.

The Jotun woman explained that Tyr had come to visit and had brought a friend and that they were hiding under the big cauldron, being a little nervous of Hymir. Hymir's eyes swept the hall. At his ferocious glance, pillars fell down and cauldrons shattered. But the biggest cauldron stayed whole, and Thor and Tyr crawled out unharmed.

Thor was an awesome sight, with his bristling red hair and beard. Hymir quickly ordered three oxen killed for their supper. Thor, who was famous for his huge appetite, ate two of the oxen. Hymir said that they would have to go hunting for the next meal. Thor suggested that they should fish for it instead.

For bait Thor took the head of a mighty black ox, HIMINBRJOTER (Skybellower). While Hymir rowed and caught a whale or two, Thor readied his tackle and cast his line into the water. Almost at once the terrible head of Jormungand, the Midgard Serpent, appeared above the waves, the ox's head in its mouth. Hymir's eyes bulged out in terror, but Thor coolly held the line and flung his hammer, Mjollnir, at the ghastly head. Again and again the hammer struck its mark and flew back to its master. Terrified, Hymir cut the line and the bloodied serpent sank beneath the waves.

Shaken, Hymir rowed back to the shore as fast as he could. Once safely on land, he decided to test Thor's strength. He asked him to either haul in the boat and tackle or carry the two whales up the cliff to the house. Without wasting a word, Thor took hold of the boat, dragged it out of the water and carried it, whales and all, to the house.

Tyr and the Jotun woman congratulated Thor on his feat of strength, but Hymir had yet another test for Thor. He handed him his goblet and asked Thor to try to break it. Thor hurled the goblet at the wall. Stone and rubble tumbled from the hole made in the wall, but the goblet remained intact.

Thor threw the goblet over and over again until the hall was in ruins. Then the giant's lovely wife whispered to him to throw the goblet at Hymir's head, which was the hardest object for miles around. Sure enough, when the goblet hit Hymir's stony head, it shattered into pieces, though the giant's head remained without a dent.

Then Hymir said that Thor could have the cauldron if he could carry it. Tyr tried to lift the cauldron but could not move it. Mighty Thor picked up the huge cauldron easily and wore it like a helmet. Then he and Tyr set off for home. On the way they were attacked by Hymir and many-headed giants, but Thor wielded his magic hammer and put an end to Hymir and his ugly followers.

The Aesir gods drank deeply from Hymir's cauldron in Aegir's halls for many a night to come.

Thor's Duel with Hrungnir This story is from Snorri's *Prose Edda*; Snorri based his telling of this legend partly on the poem *HAUSTLONG*. The story of the god Thor's duel with the mighty giant HRUNGNIR begins with a horse race between Odin and the giant. On one of his journeys, Odin, mounted on his eight-legged horse, SLEIPNIR, had met Hrungnir, the strongest of the giants. Hrungnir challenged Odin to a race on his splendid horse, GULLFAXI.

Odin agreed and was off in a flash, with Hrungnir close behind. Sleipnir knew the way home well and streaked through VALGRIND, the gate of VALHALLA, Odin's hall.

Gullfaxi was going too fast to stop until he and his master were well within Asgard, the realm of the gods. The laws of hospitality dictated that the gods could not hurt their guest, Hrungnir.

The goddess FREYA gave Hrungnir Thor's great drinking horn and filled it to the brim. (Thor was away that day, fighting trolls in JARNVID.) Freya had to keep refilling the horn, for Hrungnir emptied it in huge gulps and soon became noisy and quarrelsome. He boasted that he would take all of Valhalla under his arm and carry it back to Jotunheim for a plaything. He would take Freya and golden-haired SIF, Thor's wife, to be his own wives and servants.

At this the gods grew angry, and Odin had a hard time keeping them from attacking their unpleasant guest. Just then Thor burst into the hall, brandishing Mjollnir, his hammer. He, too, wanted to attack the giant. Instead, he agreed to meet the giant at Giotunagard, the Place of Stones, to fight a duel.

Hrungnir clambered onto Gullfaxi and rode back to Jotunheim with the news. The giants were uneasy, even though Hrungnir was the strongest of them all. They put their heads together and came up with a plan. They would frighten Thor by making a huge clay giant, nine leagues high. They named the clay giant Mokkurkalfi and put inside it the heart of a mare, which was the biggest heart they could find.

Hrungnir's heart was made of stone, sharp-edged and three-cornered. His head, too, was made of stone, and so were his shield and club. Together, Mokkurkalfi and Hrungnir made a fearful sight as Thor and his servant, Thjalfi, drew near

Thjalfi was quick-witted as well as fast. He ran up to the giant and advised him to hold his shield low rather than high, in case Thor attacked him from below. The stone-headed giant flung his shield to the ground and stood on it with his big feet. Then he threw his club at Thor.

Thor threw his thunderbolt hammer at the giant's head at the same time. Club and hammer met in midair with an awesome crack and a sizzling bolt of lightning.

The giant's stone club shattered into a thousand pieces and fell to the Earth, where to this day, it is said, the splinters may be found in quarries. But Thor's hammer zoomed on and struck the giant, who immediately fell dead. His outflung leg pinned Thor's head to the ground.

Thjalfi, who had already hacked Mokkurkalfi to pieces, tried to release Thor, but the giant's leg was so huge and heavy that even when Odin and the other gods came to help, they could not move it. Thor lay groaning, for a piece of Hrungnir's club (made of WHETSTONE) was stuck in his head.

Along came Magni, Thor's son, who was only three years old but already enormous. He lifted Hrungnir's leg easily, and Thor was at last able to roll free. Thor gave Magni Hrungnir's horse, Gullfaxi, as a reward.

Thor's head still hurt, so he sent for the clever witch, GROA. She cast some RUNESTONES, and whispered some magic words, and the pain went away. Thor was so relieved that he wanted to make Groa happy. He told her that he had rescued her lost husband, AURVANDIL. He had carried him across the poisonous stream Elivagar. Now Aurvandil was safe and waiting for Groa.

Groa was so happy at the news that she ran from the hall. In her excitement she forgot to cast a magic spell that would remove the stone from Thor's head.

Hrungnir was the strongest of Thor's adversaries, so the giants were uneasy about the outcome of the battle. With the defeat of Hrungnir, the war between the gods and the giants came to a turning point. Some mythologists believe that the giants now gave up hope of killing Thor and of storming Asgard.

THORSDRAPA (ÞORSDRAPA)   A late 10th-century poem by Eilif Guthrunarson. SNORRI STURLUSON included *Thorsdrapa* in his *PROSE EDDA* for an alternative version of the myth "Thor and the Giant Geirrod" (see under THOR).

THRALL (Slave)   The first son conceived by Rig, who was the god HEIMDALL as he journeyed through MIDGARD, the land of HUMANS, according to the poem *RIGSTHULA*, a part of the *POETIC EDDA*. In his first stop on this journey, RIG slept between the humans Ai and Edda (great-grandfather and great-grandmother). Thrall was born nine months later. He was an ugly baby with a twisted back, thick fingers, and dark hair. But he was strong and spent his days carrying home bundles of firewood. Thrall grew up to sire, with Thir, the human race of thralls, or slaves and servants. (See also KARL and JARL.)

THRIVALDI   Thrivaldi was a giant with nine heads, one of the many GIANTS and GIANTESSES killed by THOR, who was known for slaying many of the JOTUN. Little is known of Thrivaldi. His name survives in the *SKALDSKAPARMAL* by SNORRI STURLUSON, who quotes the work of an early poet, Bragi Broddason, one of the oldest SKALDS.

THRUD (Strength)   Most likely the daughter of the god THOR and his golden-haired wife, SIF. Little is known of Thrud, whose name survives in the KENNINGS, or metaphors, used by Old NORSE writers of SKALDIC POETRY. In one poem Thor is described as "father of Thrud." Scholars speculate from these kennings that the giant HRUNGNIR abducted Thrud, for he is referred to in one poem as the "thief of Thrud." As Thor's daughter, Thrud would be a half-sister of MAGNI and of MODI and a full sister of Lora. Some experts also believe she is the person described in the *POETIC EDDA* as the betrothed to the DWARF ALVIS.

THRUDHEIM (ÞRUÐHEIMR; Plains of Strength) Thor's realm in ASGARD, the realm of the gods, according to *GRIMNISMAL*. Traditionally, it lies near the edge of ASGARD and very close to the land of the ELVES. However, SNORRI STURLUSON says in *GYL-FAGINNING* and *Hymskringla* that the name of Thor's realm was Thrudvang.

THRYM (ÞRYMR) A HRIMTHURSSAR, or RIME-GIANT, sometimes called the king of the GIANTS. He stole THOR's hammer and demanded the goddess FREYA for his wife if he were to return the hammer. With the help of the trickster LOKI, Thor won back the hammer at a wedding ceremony in which the thunder god posed as the bride. Once MJOLLNIR was in his possession, Thor killed Thrym.

THRYMHEIM (Noisy Place) The mountain home of the giant THJAZZI and his daughter, SKADE. It was a cold and lonely place, noisy with the howling of wind and of WOLF. In the story of "Skade and Njord," the god NJORD hated the place. The god LOKI came here to rescue IDUNN after she had been kidnapped by Thjazzi.

THRYMSKVITHA (ÞRYMSKVIÐA; Lay of Thrym) A poem and the only source of the story "The Theft of Thor's Hammer" (see THOR). _Thrymskvitha_ is a part of the _CODEX REGIUS_ of the _POETIC EDDA_. Some scholars believe the poem was originally composed by a very talented poet and survived years of retelling with few changes until it took its final form in about 900 A.D. Others believe it was not composed or written down until the 13th century, when writing had become more common in ICELAND.

Thrymskvitha recounts Thor's efforts, disguised as the goddess FREYA, to rescue his stolen hammer, MJOLLNIR, from the giant THRYM. _Thrymskvitha's_ strong similarities to other works in the _Poetic Edda_, however, lead most scholars to accept it as a work of true NORSE mythology, rather than a poem written in imitation of the other great works in the _Poetic Edda_.

THULUR (ÞULUR) A list or catalog of NAMES, synonyms, or metaphors used in the poetry of NORSE mythology. Some of the surviving lists are very formal, such as the _Nafnathulur_, a portion of the works of SNORRI STURLUSON, which are available in manuscripts in their original language but which are rarely translated.

The _CODEX REGIUS_ manuscript contains an important section titled _Thulur_, which is simply a list of names and contains no prose or poetry. It is, in some instances, the only surviving use of some words associated with Norse mythology.

Snorri's primary work containing thulur is _SKALDSKAPARMAL_, a guide for SKALDS who began writing SKALDIC POETRY after the coming of Christianity to ICELAND and SCANDINAVIA. _Skaldskaparmal_ contains many of the alternative names and KENNINGS for ODIN and THOR, the AESIR and the ASYNJUR, the DWARFS, the heavens, and the SEAS. It is often included in translations with Snorri's most prominent work, _GYLFAGINNING_.

RIGSTHULA is perhaps the best-known example of a poem that is mainly a list of names. It is part of the _POETIC EDDA_. In this poem, the author relates the story of the god HEIMDALL's creation of the three races of man—slave, landowner, and ruler—and includes the names of many of the children of these races. Names for some of the slaves are: Fjosnir, "cattle man"; Drumb and Drumba, which mean "log"; Ambott, "servant." Examples of the names for the landowners are: Bui, "dwelling owner"; Boddi, "farm holder"; and Snot, "worthy woman." Names of the wealthy rulers are: Arfi, "heir"; Nith, "descendent"; and Kund, "kinsman." Each name represents an aspect of the lives of an individual of a particular race.

Some of the thulur are less formal and are simply presented, for example, in the poems that make up the _Poetic Edda_. The _VOLUSPA_ contains lists of names for DWARFS, VALKYRIES, and NORNS. _ALVISSMAL_, another poem in the _Poetic Edda_, contains a list of dwarf names and _GRIMNISMAL_ gives many of Odin's names.

In some cases, the name of a dwarf, hero, elf, HORSE, or the alternative name of a god is only mentioned in one of the thulur. These lists help scholars understand and decipher the meanings of the many kennings, or metaphoric phrases, that are so important to skaldic poetry.

THUND (ÞUND; Roaring) The torrent or great river that flows just outside VALHALLA.

THUNDER Thunder represented the power of nature and was an important part of many mythologies, including that of the Greeks. In NORSE myths, THOR was known as the god of thunder, as well as of many other aspects of nature and life. This connection to the roar of thunder gave Thor a strong, powerful image, much like the pounding of the hammer of a blacksmith and the strength a man needed to swing such a hammer.

THURSDAY In modern English, the fifth day of the week, or the fourth working day. Thursday takes its name from the NORSE thunder god THOR.

Some mythologists suggest that when VIKING settlers came to northern England, they appropriated the name of a local deity, Thunor, and thus an early version of the day's name was _Thunresdaeg_, or Day of Thunor. Others say that the local god's cult was

An illustration of the wolf Fenrir biting off Tyr's right hand. From the 18th-century Icelandic manuscript SÁM 66, in the care of the Árni Magnússon Institute in Iceland

too weak by the time the Vikings arrived in the late 800s A.D. to have been so influential and that people quickly began using Thor's name for places, objects, and even days of the week. In the VIKING AGE in GREAT BRITAIN, the fifth day of the week became known as *Thuresdaeg* and ultimately became Thursday as the English language continued to change.

TROLLS   Nature spirits, related more closely with the LANDVAETTIR, or land wights, and NORNS, than to the mighty gods of NORSE mythology.

Rarely mentioned in the *POETIC EDDA*, the *PROSE EDDA*, or the SKALDIC POETRY, trolls appear more often in the HEROIC LEGENDS, the family SAGAS, and the folklore of SCANDINAVIA than in the more formal stories of the mythology.

Some scholars suggest that trolls were originally the GIANTS of JOTUNHEIM or perhaps the DWARFS of the myths but that they evolved in more recent years into the earthy subhuman creatures that inhabit caves and woodlands. Giants, like trolls, were described in the mythology as living in mountains, forests, or the untamed areas surrounding homesteads and farms. Like dwarfs, trolls were said to go about at nighttime and to turn to stone when exposed to daylight.

That the people of the VIKING AGE would have recognized trolls as a part of the supernatural world is clear from the references in the manuscripts. Thor is referred to in *SKALDSAPARMAL* by SNORRI STURLUSON as "Adversary and slayer of Giants and Troll-women." Since Thor was known to slay GIANTESSES, some scholars use this phrase to support the suggestion that at one time the terms *giant* and *troll* referred to the same mythological beings.

TUESDAY   In modern English, the third day of the week, or the second working day. Tuesday is named after a GERMANIC god, Tiwaz, who in the mythology of SCANDINAVIA became the one-handed war god, TYR, and in England became the war god Tiw.

The names Tyr and Tiw translate simply as "god." Therefore, Tuesday means "god's day."

TYR   A god of war and the sky god, the bravest of all the gods. He was concerned with justice and with fair treaties. It is thought that at one time Tyr was even more important than ODIN and more ancient. By the time the NORSE myths were written down, Tyr's importance had diminished, and not much is known about him. In some stories, Tyr is the son of the giant HYMIR; in others he is the son of Odin.

Tyr was the only god brave enough and fair-minded enough to put his hand into the jaws of the terrible WOLF FENRIR. When the other gods broke their word to Fenrir and tied him up, Fenrir bit off Tyr's hand. That is why Tyr is always depicted as the one-handed god.

At RAGNAROK, the end of the world, Tyr and GARM, Hel's hound, killed each other.

TUESDAY was named after Tyr.

U

ULL (ULLER) The winter god of skiers and of hunting, snowshoes, the bow, and the shield. Son of the goddess SIF and stepson of THOR, Ull lived in YDALIR.

In NORSE poetry, a shield is often referred to as "Ull's ship." Scholars believe this reference means that Ull may have skied down hills on his shield much as one might use a modern-day snowboard.

SAXO GRAMMATICUS, the 13th-century Danish historian, refers to Ull as a cunning magician and says that Ull traveled over the sea on a magic bone. Archaeologists have found skates made of bones in ancient Scandinavian sites and suggest that it was to these that Saxo was referring.

Though the Norse authors, including 13th-century Icelandic writer SNORRI STURLUSON, wrote very little about Ull, he appears from other evidence to have been a very important god to the Norse people.

UPPSALA, OLD (GAMLA UPPSALA; UPSALA) A region in eastern SWEDEN, north of modern-day Stockholm, that was, in the VIKING AGE, a kingdom of its own. Old Uppsala was also the site of burial mounds built over the cremated remains of kings from the MIGRATION PERIOD and of gatherings of the local ruling assembly, known as a "thing."

According to SNORRI STURLUSON in the prologue to GYLFAGINNING, it was near Old Uppsala that the great warrior and leader ODIN made his final kingdom on the Scandinavian peninsula.

Archaeologists have excavated the royal burial mounds, finding artifacts that have helped them learn more about the times of these kings and that help tell the stories of NORSE mythology.

UPPSALA, TEMPLE AT A pagan temple to the NORSE gods, most likely a sacred grove of old-growth trees where a wooden temple to ODIN, FREY, and THOR was later built.

According to SAXO GRAMMATICUS, a Danish historian, and ADAM OF BREMEN, a German historian, the people of this kingdom offered human sacrifice in the temple grove. They hanged people and animals in the branches of the tree to honor Odin and his nine days of torment when hanging in the world tree, YGGDRASIL—a torment he put himself through to discover the secrets of the RUNES.

After the wood temple, worshippers built a gold building, according to Adam of Bremen. In the center stood an image of Thor, and on either side of him were

Runestone in Uppland, Sweden, depicting Ull on skis *(Photo by Berig/Used under a Creative Commons license)*

Royal burial mounds in Old Uppsala, Sweden *(Photo by C. J./Used under a Creative Commons license)*

statues of Odin and Frey. A golden chain girded the temple, and every nine years the people of Uppland, the region that included Uppsala, gathered at the temple for a festival that included human and animal sacrifices. Adam of Bremen explained that this temple, was built next to and on top of the sacred grove.

URD (WYRD; Past) One of the three NORNS, or Fates, who spun on their web the destiny of all living beings. Urd was the most powerful of the three. The sacred Well of Urd (URDARBRUNN) was named after her. She is the oldest of the three sisters and is usually pictured as looking backward. Her sisters are SKULD and VERDANDI.

URDARBRUNN (Well of Urd, Well of Fate) The well or spring at the center of ASGARD, which was the home of the AESIR gods.

Urdarbrunn was a powerful symbol in NORSE mythology. Its waters flowed out at the base of one of the three great roots of YGGDRASIL, the World Tree. The well was named after URD, one of the NORNS, or Fates, who determined the directions of people's lives. Based on the well's name, scholars argue that the Norse people believed the waters of this well contained great powers.

The gods rode their horses to this well each day and sat there in judgment over the world.

UTGARD (Outer Place) A castle in the land of the GIANTS, according to SNORRI STURLUSON. The stronghold was ruled by the giant king UTGARD-LOKI. The god THOR was humiliated and defeated in Utgard by the magic of the giant king.

UTGARD-LOKI (Loki of the Outer World) The strongest and most cunning of the GIANTS. Also known as SKRYMIR, he humiliated and outwitted the gods THOR and LOKI and their servant THJALFI in the story "Thor's Journey to Utgard."

VAFTHRUDNIR (VAFÞRUÐNIR) An old giant, the wisest of all GIANTS and famed for his talent of answering riddles. He lives in a hall some distance from ASGARD. In the poem *VAFTHRUDNISMAL*, from the *POETIC EDDA*, ODIN visits Vafthrudnir and challenges the giant to a riddle contest. Vafthrudnir is known only from this poem, though SNORRI STURLUSON does mention the giant in his recounting of the creation story in the *PROSE EDDA*.

VAFTHRUDNISMAL (VAFÞRUÐNISMAL; *Lay of Vafthrudnir*) A 10th-century poem from the *POETIC EDDA*. VAFTHRUDNIR, the central character, is described as a "wise giant and riddle master." ODIN, using the name Gagnrad, visits the giant to test his knowledge and to obtain some wisdom. The poem takes the form of a question-and-answer game between Odin and the giant.

First Odin answers Vafthrudnir's questions. The giant is impressed by his guest's knowledge and in turn answers Odin's questions about the Sun and the Moon, day and night, winter and summer, the first GIANTS, the VANIR gods, the hall of dead heroes, and the fate of the gods. Finally, Odin asks about the end of the world and the world thereafter. Odin in turn is impressed by the giant's knowledge and asks him how he acquired it. Vafthrudnir says that he has roamed far and wide, even to the home of the dead in NIFLHEIM, and can also read the RUNES.

The *Lay of Vafthrudnir* is a valuable source of information about the NORSE myths. All of it appears in the *CODEX REGIUS* and some of it in the *Arnamagnean Codex* of the *Poetic Edda*. SNORRI STURLUSON draws upon it extensively in the *PROSE EDDA*.

VALASKJALF (VALASKIALF; Shelf of the Slain) One of the many halls of the gods in ASGARD. Mythologists debate exactly who lived in this hall. In the poem *GRIMNISMAL*, part of the *POETIC EDDA*, Valaskjalf is described as a structure thatched in sliver and made by "the god" himself, but experts disagree over who this specific god might be.

In his work *GYLFAGINNING*, SNORRI STURLUSON wrote that the great god ODIN himself owned Valaskjalf, and that the gods made the great hall. In this hall is HLIDSKJALF, Odin's great high seat or throne.

VALGRIND (Carrion Gate, Death Gate) Either one of the gates of HEL (2) or one of the gates of VALHALLA, the hall of the slain. As a gate that guarded Hel, Valgrind stands with two others, Helgrind, which means "Hel Gate," and Nagrind, which means "corpse gate." The gates close so fast that they catch the heel of anyone trying to pass through them.

But in the poem *GRIMNISMAL*, Valgrind is portrayed as an old gate of Valhalla that guards holy doors that stand behind it. Some linguists also translate the name Valgrind as the "Grill of the Fallen."

VALHALLA (VALHOLL; Hall of the Slain) The hall built by the god ODIN in ASGARD to receive heroes slain in battle. The warriors, called EINHERJAR, fought all day and feasted all night. They were brought to Valhalla by the VALKYRIES, Odin's warrior maidens, led by the goddess FREYA. The heroes went to battle at Odin's side at RAGNAROK, the end of the world, in which all were slain once again.

In modern English the word *Valhalla* means a heavenly place where the deserving dead find eternal happiness, or an esteemed burial place on Earth.

Valhalla appears in the *POETIC EDDA* (especially in *GRIMNISMAL*) and SNORRI STURLUSON's *PROSE EDDA*.

The Hall of Dead Heroes Odin, the ALFODR and warrior god of the AESIR, built Valhalla, the Hall of the Slain. It was situated in GLADSHEIM, Odin's realm in Asgard. It was the most beautiful hall there. The roof was tiled with shining shields, the rafters were flashing spears, and on the benches were fine suits of armor, ready for the warriors to put on. There Odin planned to receive all the brave men who had died as heroes on Earth and give them everlasting life so they could help the gods fight the GIANTS at Ragnarok, the end of the world.

The Valkyries (some of whom were Odin's daughters) put on their gleaming armor and went down to MIDGARD, or Middle Earth, to choose which warriors were brave enough and strong enough to be rewarded with a new life in Valhalla. They returned with the heroes, or Einherjar, who had been slain in battle but were now miraculously alive, their wounds healed and their health robust.

The maidens donned white robes and poured MEAD from drinking horns into the warriors' goblets, the bony skulls of their stricken enemies. The supply of mead never ended, for it came from the enchanted GOAT HEIDRUN, who nibbled on the leaves of LAERAD, the tree around which the hall was built.

The food was abundant, too. It came from another magical creature, the BOAR SAEHRIMNIR. Each night Saehrimnir was killed, cooked, and eaten by the hungry heroes. Each morning the boar rose up again, ready to go through the whole ritual. The heroes never went hungry or thirsty, despite their enormous appetites, and Odin looked on with approval.

Odin directed the warriors to put on the shining new armor and find the horses in the courtyard. They could fight all day to their hearts' content. If they were wounded, they would be healed. If they were killed, they would come back to life again, ready to enjoy another night of feasting.

And so it was that Odin gradually built up a vast army of the world's best warriors, who would march out 800 each from the 540 doors of Valhalla and valiantly fight beside Odin and the Aesir gods at Ragnarok.

VALI (1)

A son of LOKI, the trickster god, and his wife SIGYN. Brother of NARFI.

The manuscripts containing the stories of NORSE mythology vary in the details they offer on Vali. The prose conclusion of *LOKASENNA*, a 10th-century poem found in the *POETIC EDDA*, says that the gods turned Narfi into a WOLF who killed Vali and used Vali's intestines to bind Loki to a boulder. SNORRI STURLUSON, who wrote his *PROSE EDDA* in the 13th century and likely used *Lokasenna* as a source, says that the gods turned Vali into a wolf, which then killed Narfi. The gods then used Narfi's intestines to bind Loki to the rock.

VALI (2)

The youngest son of the god ODIN. His mother was RINDA. Vali avenged BALDER's death by slaying the blind god HODUR with his arrow. He was one of the few gods to survive RAGNAROK, the end of the world.

Vali is a personification of the light of the days that grow longer as spring approaches. Because rays of light were often depicted as arrows, Vali was usually represented and worshipped as an archer.

Vali, the Avenger This myth tells of Vali's origins and of how he avenged the death of his half-brother, Balder. It is part of *BALDRS DRAUMAR* in the *POETIC EDDA*.

When Balder, Odin's beloved son, began having frightening dreams, Odin made a journey to the underworld to seek the knowledge of an ancient sybil. She told Odin that Balder would be killed and that his death would be avenged by another son of Odin's, Vali, as yet unborn. The child's mother would be Rinda. Vali would slay Hodur (Balder's killer) when he was but one night old, with his hands still unwashed and his hair uncombed.

Odin next sent HERMOD, the messenger of the gods, to the wicked but powerful wizard Rostioff, to find out more. Hermod took Odin's horse, SLEIPNIR, and runic spear, and set off. The journey was long and there were many perils, but at last Hermod reached the desolate country where the wizard dwelled. Rostioff was not welcoming. He took the form of a terrible giant and approached Hermod with a strong rope, but Hermod struck him with the magic staff, and the giant fell at once. Hermod bound Rostioff with his own rope.

The wizard promised to help Hermod if he could be freed from the rope. Hermod loosened the ties. Rostioff chanted spells until the sky grew dark; then the sky reddened into a vision of blood—the blood of Balder. Out of it rose a beautiful woman with a boy-child in her arms. The boy leaped to the ground and immediately started to grow into a man. He shot an arrow into the gloom and then the vision disappeared.

The wizard explained that the woman was Rinda, daughter of King Billing of the Ruthenians. She was to be the mother of Vali, who would slay Hodur with his bow and arrow. Hermod took the news back to Odin.

Then Odin disguised himself as an ordinary man and set off to find and win Rinda. He easily won favor with King Billing, but beautiful Rinda was strong-headed and resisted Odin through many of his cleverest disguises. He won her in the end by using magic RUNES, and she agreed to marry him.

Nine months later Vali, a newborn with hands as yet unwashed and hair uncombed, walked over BILROST into ASGARD. To everyone's amazement, he started to grow and grow until he was as big as a man. Odin realized that the boy was his son Vali. Vali drew an arrow from the quiver that he would always carry and shot it at Hodur, who died instantly, and Balder's death was avenged.

Vali became one of the youngest warrior gods, a god of light, and was one of the few to survive Ragnarok.

VALKYRIES (Choosers of the Slain) Warrior maidens of the god ODIN. They chose men doomed to die in battle and delivered them to Odin's VALHALLA (Hall of the Slain). There the resurrected heroes enjoyed a life of unending feasting and fighting, preparing for RAGNAROK, the end of the world.

The maidens went down to MIDGARD in full armor, their golden hair flying from underneath their winged helmets. They would hover over the chosen warriors in the thick of battle. When a hero fell dead or mortally wounded, a Valkyrie would sweep him up and carry him on horseback to ASGARD, where the gods lived.

The Valkyries had such names as Shrieker and Screamer, Storm Raiser, Axe Time, Spear Bearer, Shield Bearer, Mist, and others. The number of Valkyries varied between six, nine, and 13 at a time.

In some stories, FREYA herself was the goddess leader of the Valkyries. She was allowed to choose warriors to be entertained in her hall, SESSRUMNIR, in her realm, FOLKVANG, instead of sending them to Odin's Valhalla.

In Valhalla, the Valkyrie maidens would don graceful gowns and serve the EINHERJAR (slain heroes) with food and drink.

Most of the maidens were from Asgard, daughters of the gods and goddesses. Some were Odin's daughters. Odin allowed some of the maidens to take the form of beautiful white SWANS, but if a Valkyrie was seen by a human without her swan-like disguise, she would become an ordinary mortal and could never again return to Valhalla.

The German composer Richard Wagner wrote an opera *The Valkyries* (*Die Walküre*) as part of the *Ring des Nibelungen* cycle. In it Brunhilda is chief of the Valkyries. Wagner's "Ride of the Valkyries" is cited as one of the most stirring pieces of 19th-century orchestral music.

Statue of a Valkyrie in Copenhagen, Denmark, by Norwegian sculptor Stephan Sinding (1846–1922) *(Photo by Leonard G./Used under a Creative Commons license)*

VANAHEIM The realm or kingdom of the VANIR, the gods of the Earth, fertility, and plenty. This realm was neighbor to ASGARD, home of the AESIR gods. After the great AESIR/VANIR WAR, ODIN, the greatest of the Aesir, sent the gods HOENIR and MIMIR to Vanaheim, and the Vanir sent NJORD, FREY, and FREYA to Asgard.

Vanaheim also refers to the Tanais, an ancient NAME for the Don River in western Russia.

VANIR A race of gods and goddesses who lived in VANAHEIM. They were the original gods, more ancient than the AESIR. They were gods of fertility. Chief among them were the twin deities FREY and FREYA. After the war with the Aesir (see AESIR/VANIR WAR), Frey, Freya, and their father, NJORD, and possibly HEIMDALL went to live in ASGARD, home of the Aesir. After that war, all the gods were referred to as Aesir.

The Vanir gods brought peace and plenty to Asgard. They also brought their knowledge of SEID, magic and witchcraft, and instructed the Aesir in its practice. The Vanir were worshipped for centuries in northern lands.

VAR (Pledge) A goddess, one of the ASYNJUR, or females among the AESIR gods. Var's special responsibility was to hear the oaths and vows of faithfulness made between men and women and to punish those who broke those vows. THOR calls upon Var's power when he, dressed up as FREYA, pretends to marry the giant THRYM in the Old NORSE poem *THRYMSKVITHA.*

VE According to SNORRI STURLUSON in *GYLFAGIN-NING,* one of ODIN's brothers, along with VILI; son of BOR and the giantess BESTLA. Together the three sons of Bor created the Earth and the heavens from the body of the first giant, YMIR, and the first HUMANS from the trunks of two trees. In Snorri's version of the CREATION story of Norse mythology, it was Ve who gave the humans warmth and color.

In the *VOLUSPA,* the three sons of Bor are called Odin, HOENIR (VILI), and LOTHUR (Ve).

VEDRFOLNIR (VEÐRFOLNIR) The HAWK that sits between the eyes of the EAGLE that sits in the branches of YGGDRASIL, the World Tree. SNORRI STURLUSON gives the name *Vedrfolnir* to the hawk in *GYLFAGINNING.* Neither hawk nor eagle are named in *GRIMNISMAL,* which otherwise describes and names the creatures that live in the World Tree. Some scholars suggest that the verse naming the hawk and the eagle was lost as the manuscripts evolved.

VENOM Venom, like the word SERPENT, is a general term used in NORSE mythology; it often indicates poison, danger, and hardship. Venom represents the forces of nature that threaten gods and HUMANS alike. During the VIKING AGE, serpents represented graves, death, and the journey to the other world. Their venom was the threat of death.

As punishment for his mockery and all of the trouble he caused, the gods chained the god LOKI to a rock beneath a great serpent whose venom dripped upon the trickster god, slowly killing him. Only Loki's wife, SIGYN, faithfully holding a dish between the serpent and Loki, saved him from death.

A venomous, icy runoff from the well HVERGELMIR formed the ELIVAGAR, the collective name of the 11 rivers of the worlds connected by YGGDRASIL. The venom that rose in a mist from these rivers formed the RIME-GIANTS.

A harmful substance actually drips from the tips of the male DEER, EIKTHYIRNIR, that nibbles at the tree that stands next to VALHALLA, ODIN's hall.

In the realms of HEL (2), venom seeps through the walls and down the chimneys of the buildings as so many serpents live there. Even the MIDGARD SERPENT, JORMUNGAND, drools venom as THOR drags the giant snake into his boat and later spews venom to help destroy Thor and the gods at RAGNAROK.

VERDANDI (VERDANDE; Present) One of the three principle NORNS, or Fates, according to the poem *VOLUSPA* and SNORRI STURLUSON in *GYLFAGIN-NING.* Her sisters are URD (Past) and SKULD (Future).

Because her name is the present-tense form of the Old Norse verb *verda,* which means "to become," Verdande represents that which is happening now. She is usually pictured as young and beautiful and looking straight ahead.

VESTRI (WESTRI; west) One of the four DWARFS who represented the four main compass points. The others are AUSTRI (east), NORDI (north), and SUDRI (south). Though these dwarfs are mentioned in early NORSE poetry, only 13th-century Icelandic writer SNORRI STURLUSON assigned to them the job of holding up the four corners of the sky.

VIDAR (VIÞAR) Son of the god ODIN and the kindly GIANTESS GRID. His home was called LAND-VIDI, a place of tall grasses, wildflowers, and growing saplings, a silent and peaceful place. Vidar, too, was known for his silence, but it was he who would avenge his father's death at RAGNAROK, the end of the world. On that day, Vidar leaped from his horse and attacked the WOLF FENRIR, who had devoured Odin. Vidi placed one foot on the beast's lower jaw and pushed on the upper jaw with his hands until the monster was torn in two.

Legend has it that Vidar wore a special shoe or boot that had been made from the scraps that cobblers had saved over the years as they trimmed the leather they used for shoes. Another story says that his mother, Grid, made the shoe for Vidar.

Vidar was one of the few gods who survived Ragnarok and became one of the rulers of the new world.

A famous stone at Gosforth Church, in Cumbria, England, shows Vidar fighting with Fenrir.

VIDBLAIN The third and uppermost of all of the heavens, according to the author of the *PROSE EDDA,* SNORRI STURLUSON. In *GYLFAGINNING,* Har, one of the three gods who answer GYLFI's questions, explains that Vidblain lies above ANDLANG and above ASGARD, which lies at the top of the World Tree, YGGDRASIL. Har also tells Gylfi that, at the time of their meeting, only the LIGHT-ELVES dwell in Vidblain.

According to Snorri, in the poem *VOLUSPA*, the golden city of GIMLE stands within Vidblain. According to the *VOLUSPA*, Gimle is the city where the righteous and trustworthy will survive RAGNAROK, the battle between the gods and the GIANTS that ends the world.

VIDFINN (Wood-Finn) The human father of the children BIL AND HJUKI who were stolen to serve MANI, the man in the Moon. Vidfinn sent his children to the well BYRGIR for water. Along the journey Mani stole the children and put them to work on the Moon.

Only SNORRI STURLUSON mentions Vidfinn. Some scholars suggest that the name Vidfinn is Finnish and that Snorri or his sources wanted to connect this father and his children with a land they thought to be very distant from SCANDINAVIA.

VIGRID (VIGRIÐR, VIGRITH; Field of Battle) The immense plain on which the bloody battle of RAGNAROK will be fought, according to the *POETIC EDDA*. It stretches for a vast distance in every direction, but the boundaries of Vigrid form the boundaries of the battle. However, in the poem *Fafnismal*, the dragon FAFNIR tells SIGURD that this great plain is called Oskopnir.

VIKINGS (People of the Inlets) Scandinavian people, essentially from NORWAY, DENMARK, and SWEDEN, who raided the coasts and inlets of Europe and the British Isles from the ninth to the 12th centuries (the VIKING AGE). Their greatest achievements were in shipbuilding and navigation (see SHIPS AND SHIP BURIALS). The typical long ship was a graceful vessel with a high prow adorned with the figure of an animal, often a DRAGON, and a high curved stern. It had a square sail and was powered by oarsmen who hung their shields over the side of the ship. They ventured as far away as Greenland, ICELAND, North America, the Mediterranean Sea, and Russia. They founded colonies in the British Isles.

Their mythological and heroic legends form the content of Old NORSE literature. The Viking Age ended, however, in the 12th century with the coming of Christianity to SCANDINAVIA and the rise of European states, whose people were able to join together and protect themselves against further Viking invasions and raids. Many Vikings settled down in the lands that they had raided.

A Viking longhouse on the coast of Norway *(Shutterstock)*

In spite of their reputation for ferocity, not all Vikings were warriors. Most of them were farmers, hunters, and fishermen who led peaceful lives and had a stable social structure. Family and social bonds were vital, for many communities were small and isolated, especially in the middle of the dark, grim northern winters. The literature that has come down to us from the Vikings shows that they had a strong sense of humor, common sense, and fairness. They were a brave people, acknowledging that life can be hard and that death will come to all, but it is to be met bravely and without complaint. The poem *RIGSTHULA* gives a detailed picture of how people lived in the Viking Age.

VIKING AGE   The period in Scandinavian history from approximately 750 A.D. to the middle of the 11th century when military forces from DENMARK and NORWAY, known collectively as VIKINGS, sailed west in long ships to the British Isles and east to Russia, colonizing the land as they went. The Viking Age lasted until nation-states emerged in Norway, SWEDEN, and Denmark and leaders in this region were converted to Christianity.

The warriors who sailed the Viking long ships, raiding and destroying monasteries, villages, and settlements as they progressed, were followed by farmers and shipbuilders who made new homes in the conquered lands. During the Viking Age, Scandinavians had settlements along a route in the northern Atlantic Ocean that included northern England, Scotland, the Orkney and Shetland Islands, the Isle of Man, Ireland, the FAROE ISLANDS, and ICELAND.

The Viking Age is the time of the greatest RUNE-STONE carving activity in the Viking world. At the beginning of the period, symbols of the carvings were largely of NORSE gods and memorials to warriors who fought in Viking conquests. By the end of the age, the carvings contained crosses, other Christian iconography, and messages of conversion from the pagan religion to Christianity.

The Vikings spread the use of RUNES and Norse symbols as they ventured farther from home. Archaeologists have found evidence of the Viking Age in Western Europe, the Mediterranean Sea, and western Asia.

VILI   According to SNORRI STURLUSON in *GYLFAGINNING*, one of ODIN's brothers, along with VE; son of BOR and the GIANTESS BESTLA. Together the three sons of Bor created the Earth and the heavens from the body of the giant YMIR and the first HUMANS from

Detail of a Viking ship found in Vyborg, Russia *(Shutterstock)*

the trunks of two trees. In Snorri's version of the CREATION story of NORSE mythology, it was Vili who gave the humans their senses and the ability to move.

In the *VOLUSPA*, the three sons of Bor are named Odin, HOENIR (Vili), and LOTHUR (Ve).

VIMUR   A rushing river in JOTUNHEIM. The GIANTESS GIALP tried to raise the level of the torrent, some translations say by urinating in the river, to drown the god THOR, but Thor hit her with a well-aimed stone and she ran off, howling.

VINGOLF   (Friendly Floor, Friend Hall)   Possibly the mansion home of the goddess FRIGG and the other ASYNJUR. Vingolf stood in ASGARD, home of the AESIR, next to GLADSHEIM, the palace that contained the thrones of ODIN and the other 12 main gods.

SNORRI STURLUSON wrote in his *PROSE EDDA* that Vingolf is another name for VALHALLA, the palace that Odin built in Asgard as a dwelling for human heroes who died in battle.

VOLSUNGA SAGA   A late-13th-century prose epic, telling of the hero SIGURD (called Siegfried in

German), youngest son of Volsung. Volsung was a descendant of the god ODIN. The myth "Otr's Ransom" (see under OTR) and the legends of Sigurd are from the *Volsunga Saga*. Richard Wagner based his opera cycle *Der Ring des Nibelung* in part on the *Volsunga Saga*.

VOLUND The hero of the poem *Volundarkvida*, a part of the *POETIC EDDA*. This poem is preserved in fragments in the *CODEX REGIUS* and in the *ARNAMAG-NAEAN CODEX*. See HEROIC LEGENDS.

The son of a Finnish king, Volund marries a VAL-KYRIE who is disguised as a SWAN maiden. After she returns to her swan shape and flies away, Volund turns his skills as a blacksmith to work making treasures for his lost wife. Captured by a neighboring king, Volund is set to work at the smith's bellows making riches for the king until he is able to seek vengeance. He kills the king's sons and turns their eyes to gems, their teeth to brooches, and their skulls to silver charms, all of which he sends to the king and his family.

According to *Volundarkvida*, Volund himself was a prince of ELVES, called by his captor "The greatest of elves." But his skill as a smith aligns him more closely with the DWARFS, who were famous for their abilities to make metal treasures.

Volund, like the hero SIGURD in the *VOLSUNGA SAGA*, has strong connections with his GERMANIC counterpart, Weland the Smith.

VOLUSPA (The Sibyl's Prophecy) A NORSE poem from ICELAND, recorded in the late 10th or early 11th century. It is perhaps the most important poem in the *POETIC EDDA*. The poem takes the form of a monologue delivered by the VOLVA, or sibyl, in answer to ODIN's questions. The verses deal with the CREATION of the world, of the gods and of HUMANS; tell of the AESIR/VANIR WAR; and recount the death of BALDER and LOKI's punishment. They also tell of Loki's monstrous children, FENRIR, the WOLF, and JORMUNGAND, the MIDGARD SERPENT, and the part they played at RAGNAROK, the end of the world. At the end of the poem the new world begins, a kind of green paradise in GIMLE, marred only by the presence of the corpse-eating dragon NITHOG. Many scholars believe that the *Voluspa* is one of the greatest literary achievements in the Norse world.

VOLVA (VALA) A seeress or soothsayer; a kind of magician, usually female, able to see into the future and remember from the past, and capable of giving advice to the living who call her up from the grave for consultations.

In the myth of BALDER, ODIN goes to the underworld to consult a volva to try to learn the reason for his son Balder's frightening dreams. Odin learns from the volva that his son will die.

In the *SVIPDAGSMAL*, Svipdag calls up the spirit of his dead mother, GROA, a volva to ask her advice in the wooing of the fair MENGLOD.

The goddess FREYA is associated with the volvas, but no stories survive that describe her role as seeress.

VOR (Wary, Careful) One of the ASYNJUR, or goddesses of the AESIR, according to SNORRI STUR-LUSON in his *PROSE EDDA*. Other existing manuscripts also mention Vor but do not specify that she was a goddess. They do, however, say that she was very wise and searched out all things so that nothing was hidden from her. She had the gift of providence, of preparing well for the future.

WANES The English form of the Old Norse word VANIR. Used in early translations of the Icelandic manuscripts, particularly of the *POETIC EDDA*.

WATCHMAN OF THE GODS The title and task assigned to HEIMDALL, one of the AESIR gods. According to NORSE beliefs, the post of guardian was considered very important. As watchman, Heimdall sat at the edge of HEAVEN and protected the Aesir from the GIANTS. He also watched for events marking the beginning of the end of time, known as RAGNAROK, the battle between the gods and the giants. Heimdall warned the gods when the battle was about to begin.

WHETSTONE A stone used for sharpening tools. The stone is often quartz because of the hardness and sharpness of its broken grains. In NORSE mythology, whetstones were made from the pieces of the giant HRUNGNIR's club, which shattered when it was hit by THOR's hammer. In the story "Thor's Duel with Hrungnir," some pieces of whetstone lodged in Thor's head, giving him a headache whenever whetstones were carelessly moved or dropped near him.

In the story of how the great god ODIN obtained the MEAD of poetry, Odin uses a whetstone to sharpen the workers' tools. The workers are so eager to have the whetstone that they kill each other with their sharpened weapons in a wild scramble.

At the Sutton Hoo ship burial in England, an impressive whetstone, thought to be a scepter, was found in a seventh-century grave (see SHIPS AND SHIP BURIALS).

WOLF Wolves were both friends and enemies of the gods in NORSE mythology. They were companions of the great god ODIN, for example, who fed GERI and FREKI table scraps at VALHALLA. These wolves roamed throughout the great hall, walking among the souls of human warriors. HUMANS in battle, therefore, considered wolves to be signs of Odin's presence. A gray wolf on the battlefield was a positive sign to warriors, for they believed it would guide their spirits to Valhalla if they died in the battle.

More often, however, wolves were vicious enemies of the gods. Wolves chased the SUN AND MOON across the sky, threatening with growls and gnashing teeth to devour both, which they finally did at RAGNAROK, the ultimate conflict between the gods and the GIANTS. The gods turned VALI (1), a son of the trickster god, LOKI, into a wolf that then tore to pieces his brother NARFI. The gods then converted Narfi's entrails to iron and used them to bind Loki.

The most powerful wolf, the giant FENRIR, also a son of Loki, threatened the very existence of the gods. They eventually succeeded in chaining him as a captive, but at Ragnarok he broke free. Scholars see the binding of Fenrir as a symbolic attempt to protect humankind from this enemy of nature.

Y

YDALIR (Yew Dales)   The valley where YEW trees grow, according to the poem *GRIMNISMAL*. In this valley stood the hall of ULL, the winter god of skiers, snowshoes, and hunting. For many centuries people of northern Europe made bows from the wood of the yew tree.

YEW   An evergreen tree of the family Taxaceae. In ancient belief systems, the European yew (*Taxus baccata*) was thought to have magic properties. In NORSE mythology, YDALIR (Yew Dales), was the home of the winter god ULL.

YGGDRASIL   The ASH tree of NORSE mythology, called the World Tree because it forms a link between the NINE WORLDS.

At the uppermost level are ASGARD, home of the AESIR gods; VANAHEIM, home of the VANIR gods; and ALFHEIM, home of the LIGHT-ELVES.

On the next level lie MIDGARD (Earth), the home of HUMANS; JOTUNHEIM, home of the JOTUNS, or GIANTS; SVARTALFHEIM, home of the DARK-ELVES; and NIDAVELLIR, home of the DWARFS.

In the dark underworld, Yggdrasil's roots reach MUSPELLHEIM, land of fire, and NIFLHEIM, including HEL (2), the land of the dead.

Three wells water the roots of Yggdrasil. One is the Well of URD, URDARBRUNN, a sacred place tended by the three NORNS and where the gods sit in council.

The second is MIMIR'S WELL, near which is preserved the head of the wisest of all beings, MIMIR. ODIN himself consults Mimir when in need of knowledge.

The third spring is HVERGELMIR, in Niflheim, the land of the dead. The foul dragon NITHOG lives there, forever nibbling at the roots of Yggdrasil.

Writhing SERPENTS breathe clouds of VENOM onto the roots of Yggdrasil. Four male DEER and a GOAT eat the leaves and bark from the tree. Yggdrasil survives all these torments, helped by the NORNS who sprinkle Urd's water upon the roots. The tree will survive RAGNAROK, the end of the world, though it will tremble. LIF and LIFTHRASIR will hide in the depths of the tree, fed on its dew, and emerge afterward to repeople the Earth.

In the topmost branches of Yggdrasil sits a mighty EAGLE with a small hawk, VEDRFOLNIR, upon its brow, surveying the world. A squirrel, RATATOSK, scampers up and down the tree bearing tales from Nithog to the eagle and back again.

Once Odin hanged himself from the branches of Yggdrasil for nine nights to learn the secret of the RUNES. The Norse sometimes called the gallows a horse (*drasil*), and Odin, Ygg (Terrible One).

A tree is commonly used in myths to symbolize long life, fertility, regeneration, and knowledge.

YMIR (Confused Noise)   The first giant. He was formed from ice and fire at the beginning of time in the vast chasm of GINNUNGAGAP, which lay between icy NIFLHEIM and fiery MUSPELLHEIM. Ymir was nourished by the first cow, AUDHUMLA, and he grew to a huge size.

As Ymir slept, male and female GIANTS sprang from his armpits, and from his feet grew a six-headed TROLL. From these creatures began the HRIMTHURSSAR, the race of RIME-GIANTS, all huge and hideously ugly.

After the first gods, ODIN, VILI, and VE, were born from BOR and BESTLA, the gods quarreled constantly with the giants and at last killed Ymir.

From Ymir's body, the gods created MIDGARD, the Middle Earth. Ymir's blood formed the seas and all the lakes and rivers. His flesh became the hills and plains, his bones the mountains, and his teeth the rocks. His hair formed trees and all vegetation.

The gods placed Ymir's skull as a dome over the Earth, and his brains they cast to the winds to become clouds.

See also CREATION.

An ash tree in Burgwald, Hesse, Germany. The mythical tree Yggdrasil was of the same species. *(Photo by Willow/Used under a Creative Commons license)*

YNGVI Another name, or perhaps title, for the god FREY; also possibly a little-known son of ODIN.

This name is sometimes joined with Frey, as in Yngvi-Frey, in the poetry and legends of NORSE mythology. SNORRI STURLUSON, the author of the *PROSE EDDA*, explained that Yngvi was a term of respect used to refer to this particular god.

Yngvi, like ING, is used in Norse poetry to refer to kings and dynasties. Scholars suggest that Yngvi might refer to the Swedes and Norwegians, who are often called "Yngvi's people."

In the introduction to the *Prose Edda*, Snorri presents a version of history that says Odin was a powerful leader from Asia who traveled north into SCANDINAVIA and made many of his sons rulers in the lands he conquered. Yngvi was the son who became king of SWEDEN after Odin (see SAEMING).

SELECTED BIBLIOGRAPHY

GENERAL BOOKS ON MYTHOLOGY

Barber, Richard. *A Companion to World Mythology.* New York: Delacorte Press, 1979.

Bulfinch, Thomas. *Bulfinch's Mythology.* 1913. Reprint, New York: Modern Library, 1998.

Cotterell, Arthur. *A Dictionary of World Mythology.* New York: Oxford University Press, 1990.

Frazer, James G. *The Golden Bough.* 1890. New York: Wordsworth, 2001.

Gaster, Theodore H., ed. *The New Golden Bough: A New Abridgement of the Classic Work by Sir James George Frazer.* New York: Criterion Books, 1959.

Mercatante, Anthony S. *Facts On File Encyclopedia of World Mythology and Legend.* New York: Facts On File, 1989, 2003.

New Larousse Encyclopedia of Mythology. Trans. Richard Aldington and Delano Ames. New York: Hamlyn, 1968.

BOOKS ON NORSE MYTHOLOGY

Branston, Brian. *Gods and Heroes from Viking Mythology.* New York: Schocken Books, 1982.

———. *Gods of the North.* New York: Thames & Hudson, 1980.

Crossley-Holland, Kevin. *Axe-Age, Wolf-Age.* New York: E.P. Dutton, 1986.

———. *The Norse Myths.* New York: Random House, 1981.

D'Aulaire, Ingri, and Edgar Parin D'Aulaire. *D'Aulaire's Norse Gods and Giants.* 1967. New York: Delacorte, 1986.

Davidson, H.R. Ellis. *Gods and Myths of Northern Europe.* New York: Viking Press, 1990.

———. *Pagan Scandinavia.* New York: Frederick A. Praeger, 1967.

———. *Scandinavian Mythology.* New York: Peter Bedricks Books, 1986.

DuBois, Thomas. *Nordic Religions in the Viking Age.* Philadelphia: University of Pennsylvania Press, 1999.

Fitzhugh, William W., and Elisabeth I. Ward, eds. *Vikings: The North Atlantic Saga.* Washington, D.C.: Smithsonian Institution Press, 2000.

Gelling, Peter, and Hilda Roderick Ellis Davidson. *The Chariot of the Sun and Other Rites and Symbols of the Northern Bronze Age.* New York: Frederick A. Praeger, 1969.

Green, Roger Lancelyn. *Myths of the Norsemen.* 1960. New York: Viking Press, 1988.

Grimm, Jakob. *Teutonic Mythology.* Seventh ed. New York: Routledge, 2000.

Guerber, Helene A. *Myths of the Norsemen.* 1909. New York: Dover Publications, 1992.

Lindow, John. *Handbook of Norse Mythology.* Santa Barbara, Calif.: ABC-CLIO, 2001.

Lindow, John. *Scandinavian Mythology: An Annotated Bibliography.* New York: Garland Publishing, 1988.

McTurk, Rory, ed. *A Companion to Old Norse-Icelandic Literature and Culture*. Malden, Mass.: Blackwell Publishing, 2005.

Nordal, Guðrún. *Tools of Literacy: The Role of Skaldic Verse in Icelandic Textual Culture of the Twelfth and Thirteenth Centuries*. Toronto: University of Toronto Press, 2001.

O'Donoghue, Heather. *From Avgard to Valhalla: The Remarkable History of the Norse Myths*. London: Tauris, 2009.

Orchard, Andy. *Dictionary of Norse Myth and Legend*. London: Cassell, 1997.

Paige, R.I. *Norse Myths*. Austin: University of Texas Press, 1991.

Shetelig, Haakon, and Hjalmar Falk. *Scandinavian Archaeology*. Trans. F. V. Gordon. Oxford: Clarendon Press, 1937.

Snorri Sturluson. *The Prose Edda: Tales from Norse Mythology*. Trans. Jean I. Young. Berkeley: University of California, 2002.

Strayer, Joseph Reese, ed. *Dictionary of the Middle Ages*. New York: Scribner, 1989.

Turville-Petre, E.O.G. *Myth and Religion of the North*. Westport, Conn.: Greenwood Publishing, 1975.

ONLINE RESOURCES

Internet Sacred Text Archive
http://www.sacred-texts.com/neu/ice/index.htm
Translations of many of the primary sources of Norse mythology from Iceland

Northvegr Foundation. Northern European Studies Texts.
http://www.northvegr.org/lore/main.php
Highly regarded translations of most of the Icelandic manuscripts containing the stories of Norse mythology, including the *Poetic Edda*, *Prose Edda*, and *Flateyjarbok*

Project Gutenberg
http://www.gutenberg.org/wiki/Main_Page
Provider of online books, offering the English translations of the *Prose* and *Poetic Eddas* as well as many Icelandic works

INDEX